D0082183

Leadership and social movements

MANCHESTER
UNIVERSITY PRESS

Leadership and social movements

*edited by Colin Barker, Alan Johnson
and Michael Lavalette*

Manchester University Press
Manchester and New York

distributed exclusively in the USA by Palgrave

Copyright © Manchester University Press 2001

While copyright in the volume as a whole is vested in Manchester University Press, copyright in individual chapters belongs to their respective authors, and no chapter may be reproduced wholly or in part without the express permission in writing of both author and publisher.

Published by Manchester University Press
Oxford Road, Manchester M13 9NR, UK
and Room 400, 175 Fifth Avenue, New York, NY 10010, USA
http://www.manchesteruniversitypress.co.uk

Distributed exclusively in the USA by
Palgrave, 175 Fifth Avenue, New York,
NY 10010, USA

Distributed exclusively in Canada by
UBC Press, University of British Columbia, 2029 West Mall,
Vancouver, BC, Canada V6T 1Z2

British Library Cataloguing-in-Publication Data
A catalogue record for this book is available from the British Library

Library of Congress Cataloging-in-Publication Data applied for

ISBN 0 7190 5901 1 *hardback*
ISBN 0 7190 5902 X *paperback*

First published 2001

10 09 08 07 06 05 04 03 02 01   10 9 8 7 6 5 4 3 2 1

Printed in Great Britain
by Biddles Ltd, Guildford and King's Lynn

Contents

Notes on contributors

Colin Barker teaches in the Sociology Department of Manchester Metropolitan University. A long-time member of the Socialist Workers Party in Britain, he has authored and edited a number of books and articles, including *Festival of the Oppressed: Solidarity, Reform and Revolution in Poland 1980–81* (1986) and *Revolutionary Rehearsals* (1987). He has been active in the nuclear disarmament, anti-Nazi and asylum-seekers movements. He organises the annual conference on Alternative Futures and Popular Protest in Manchester.

Ian Birchall is an independent socialist historian. He is the author of *The Spectre of Babeuf* (1997) and translator/editor of Alfred Rosmer's *Lenin's Moscow* (1987) and Victor Serge's *Witness to the German Revolution* (2000). He is a member of the Socialist Workers Party in Britain.

John Drury is a lecturer in Social Psychology at the University of Sussex. His research interests include crowd behaviour and inter-group conflict, power and social influence. Recent publications include, with Steve Reicher, 'Collective action and psychological change: the emergence of new social identities', *British Journal of Social Psychology*, 39, 4 (2000). He has been active in the anti-poll tax movement and in claimants' rights campaigns.

Robert Gibb was a lecturer in European Studies at the University of Central Lancashire and is now an independent researcher based in Paris. His publications include 'Multiculturalism, integration and national identity: SOS-Racisme', *International Journal of Francophone Studies*, 1, 3 (1998), with Yasmin Ali.

Carol Hanisch has been a writer and activist in the women's liberation movement since 1968 when she became a founding member of New York Radical Women following nearly a year in the Mississippi civil rights movement. She was an editor of the Redstockings collection *Feminist*

Revolution (1975), and founding editor of the journal *Meeting Ground* (1977–91). Other work includes *Frankly Feminist* (1997), a collection of her columns in the *Hudson Valley Woman* newspaper, and a dramatic reading, *Promise and Betrayal: Voices from the Struggle for Women's Emancipation, 1776–1920* (1995). She may be reached at P.O. Box 1270, Port Ewen, NY 12466, USA or on-line at HanishCJ@aol.com

Nick Hopkins is a senior lecturer in the Department of Psychology at the University of Dundee. His research interests revolve around social and collective identities and action. With Steve Reicher he has published *Self and Nation* (2001).

Alan Johnson is a reader in Sociology and History at Edge Hill University College. An editor of the journals *Historical Materialism* and *New Politics*, he has published widely on social movements and Marxist thought. He is now writing a political biography of Hal Draper.

Michael Lavalette is a lecturer in Social Policy at the University of Liverpool. He has written widely on social movement activity, most recently as editor of *Class Struggle and Social Welfare* (2000). He is on the editorial board of the *International Socialism Journal* and is an active member of the Socialist Workers Party in Britain.

Ann Mische is an assistant professor of Sociology at Rutgers University. Her work combines cultural and social network approaches to social movement mobilisation. She is currently working on a book about Brazilian youth politics in the 1990s, as well as a longer-term theoretical project on how socio-cultural 'projections' of future possibilities influence social inter-action.

Jonathan Purkis is a lecturer in Media and Cultural Studies at Liverpool John Moores University. He is co-editor of *Twentyfirst Century Anarchism* (1997) and has written widely on, and been an activist in, contemporary environmental and anarchist movements.

Steve Reicher is a lecturer in Social Psychology at St Andrews University. He has written widely on social movements and social identities. His most recently published book, with Nick Hopkins, is *Self and Nation* (2001). He has been active in a range of social movements.

Louise Ryan is a senior lecturer in Sociology at the University of Central Lancashire. Her book *Gender, Identity and the Irish Press, 1920s–1930s: Embodying the Nation* will be published in 2001.

Alan Shandro is the author of a number of articles in Marxist political theory and is an editor of *Science and Society*. He teaches political science at Laurentian University in Sudbury, Ontario.

Clifford Stott is a lecturer in Social Psychology at the University of Liverpool. He has published in the areas of social identity, inter-group relations, power, crowd behaviour and football-related 'disorder'. He is currently developing research to examine the role of inter-group relations on stereotyping and group processes.

Acknowledgements

We would like to thank a number of people who helped us put this book together. First, thanks to the contributors for their patience and the good-natured way in which they dealt with our editorial queries. Second, the themes and debates produced here have been aired over the last few years at the annual conference 'Alternative Futures and Popular Protest' held at Manchester Metropolitan University, and we would like to thank all the participants for their contributions and involvement. Third, at Manchester University Press first Nicola Viinikka and more recently Tony Mason have been supportive of the project and we thank them for their advice and help. Finally, the time consumed by research often eats into other aspects of social and family life and we would like to thank Ewa, Debbie and Laura for their support, their insights and their shared involvement in a range of social movements.

Colin Barker
Alan Johnson
Michael Lavalette

1

Leadership matters: an introduction

Colin Barker, Alan Johnson and Michael Lavalette

Introduction

There is something of a black box in social movement studies, in that *leadership* has been under-theorised (Ratcliff 1984; Melucci 1996; Ganz 2000). Why has there been this relative inattention to what leaders do? Several reasons might be hazarded.

First, there is an understandable desire to avoid 'great man' theories of history and to give proper theoretical weight to both the circumstances in which movements develop and the part played by memberships. Yet there is a risk in this, of babies following bathwater down plug-holes.

Second, few academics want to revive conservative 'agitator' theories which imply that there would be no strikes, no militant movement activity, were it not for the malign trouble-makers who cause them. We must, it is argued, pay proper attention to the real grievances motivating movements, just as we must avoid treating movement members as nothing but mindless sheep. However, while grievances are real enough, *someone* still needs to articulate them and suggest practical remedies. Contrary to over-deterministic accounts (e.g. Plekhanov 1940), individuals do have significant effects on historical development. Nor is this just a matter of the role of famous individuals like V. I. Lenin or Martin Luther King. Immediate initiatives by unknown individuals can turn a moment of decision. Trotsky provides a famous example in his account of the February 1917 revolution in Russia, where a single revolver shot from an anonymous figure in a crowd of workers felled an army officer, opening the way to fraternisation between soldiers and people (Trotsky 1965: 139–41).

Third, academic theory is itself affected by activists' ideologies. Meyer and Tarrow suggest that thinking about movement leadership was once dominated by older movement forms like the 'traditional mass organisations of the European left', with their permanent presences, bureaucratic structures and centralised leaderships. However, these have now been supplanted by models of 'looser, more decentralised networks of activists and leaders without strong central offices' whose core participants 'are highly professional, even as they put forward ideologies of spontaneity and mobilise temporary coalitions of nonprofessional supporters around their campaigns' (1998: 16–17). Those 'ideologies of spontaneity' are themselves products of the hopes and disappointments aroused by movements of the 1960s. In response both to the bureaucratism of social-democratic and Stalinist organisations and to some of the lunatic 'Leninisms' which flourished in North America and Western Europe in that period, a loosely defined 'libertarianism' gained some predominance (Friedman 1984–85; Harman 1988; Epstein 1991). Into libertarianism were woven two parallel strands: a suspicion of 'leadership' and a celebration of 'spontaneity', both of which have themselves been partly imported into some academic theorising. The former, as Barker suggests in this volume, uncritically accepted the despondent conclusions of Michels's classic study of oligarchical tendencies in movements. The latter ignored Gramsci's observation (1971: 196) that pure spontaneity never exists, for there are always leaders and initiators, even if many remain nameless figures who leave few traces in historical records.

Fourth, leadership has often been identified with *particular* forms of organisation. Leadership has been identified, for example, with *monopolisation of decision-making* in groups, or with *domination* over a group (Weber's *Herrschaft*). In response, some activists reject the very notion of leadership entirely. Yet they leave unresolved paradoxes – to say 'we don't need leaders' is itself to offer a lead! The anti-leadership case can support domineering stances which themselves inhibit movement development (Freeman 1972–73; Hanisch in this volume). Rather undigested ideas of 'autonomy' can conjure real problems of leadership in movements out of existence, creating barriers to practical and theoretical advance.

Fifth, underlying patterns of social movement theorising have tended to divert attention from issues to do with leadership. The 'collective behaviour' tradition, stressing movement *irrationalism*, could never explore leadership questions satisfactorily. It was displaced by 'resource mobilisation' and 'political process' approaches. These, while they restored the dignity of movement rationality, also revealed a strong structuralist bias in explanation, paying less attention to actors' purposive agency and thus to direct questions about leadership.

Yet the *need* to study leadership has been a constant refrain. Back in 1966 Zald and Ash Garner wrote:

> Leadership phenomena are an even more crucial aspect of the study of an MO [movement organisation] than of other large-scale organisations. Because the situation of the MO is unstable, because the organisation has few material incentives under its control, and because of the non-routinised nature of its tasks, the success or failure of the MO can be highly dependent on the qualities and commitment of the leadership cadre and the tactics they use. (reprinted in Zald and McCarthy 1987: 135)

Thirty years later, however, Klandermans points out the lack of progress. Despite their obvious importance, 'Leadership and decision-making aspects of social movement organisations … are more often debated than studied empirically … systematic studies of the way in which movement leaders function are scarce' (1997: 333). However, recent efforts to integrate the concepts of political opportunity, mobilising structures and cultural framing (McAdam *et al.* 1996) seem to bring social movement scholars to the brink of more systematic theoretical study of leadership. 'Political opportunity structures' are now seen as dependent rather than independent variables, open to actors' creative agency (Tarrow 1996; Della Porta 1996). McCarthy suggests that without richer understanding of what activists do, taxonomies of mobilising structures by and large fail in 'bounding the forms empirically or conceptually' (1996: 142). New attention is proposed to 'framing' processes and especially to 'strategic framing' (McAdam 1996: 339). Indeed, McAdam, McCarthy and Zald see 'the central analytical focus of movement research shifting over [to] the life of the movement' (1996: 17). All these developments suggest the need for theoretical attention to leadership activities and relationships. Some scholars move in that direction. Tarrow, injecting historical imagination and a richer sense of agency, stresses the important role of 'organisers' who 'use contention to exploit political opportunities, create collective identities, bring people together in organisations and mobilise them against more powerful opponents' (1998: 3). Robnett (1997) extends our understanding of movement networks by exploring the vital role of intermediate leadership layers that link movement organisations and potential supporters; her work shows leadership as present *all the way down* a movement, with complex relations of antagonism and cooperation between local 'bridge leaders' and the formal leadership at the top.

By contrast, 'New Social Movement' theorists, focusing more on the relation between movements and their surrounding conditions than on questions about 'strategy', have contributed less to understanding movement leadership. Melucci seeks to rectify this in recent work, stressing leadership's *relational* nature. However, he models the relationship on an *exchange-transaction*, in which leaders supply scarce skills to assist their 'support base' in achieving desired advantages, and in return receive member involvement, loyalty, prestige and power. This exchange seems fair and equal as long as both parties deliver the needed goods (Melucci 1996: 332–8). There are disadvantages to this rather economistic model. It has a better 'fit' with some movement organisations – especially those whose members play rather *passive* roles, contributing little by way of creative input to movement development – than with others where membership commitment and pro-activity are higher. Melucci's conception seems rather undynamic, removed from the volatility of the practical conflicts involved in collective action (see also Mueller 1994). Melucci talks about 'the leader' in the singular, with little of Robnett's sense of movement leadership as something distributed among people at different levels, cooperating and conflicting with each other. Finally, Melucci does not inquire how far different *forms* of leadership activity and relationship promote self-activity and self-development among movement 'support bases', thus reducing 'skill shortages' by enabling *others* to lead effectively.

The contributors to this volume seek in various ways to re-open some questions about leadership. How might we understand leadership within social movements? Does it necessarily and automatically translate into 'oligarchy' and the weakening of movement democracy? If not, can we distinguish between *forms* of leadership, identifying those which are more and less compatible with aspirations to wider democratisation? This introduction proffers a small lead about some of these matters – with a due sense, in line with its argument, that readers will decide whether to follow.

The unavoidability of leadership

Human action, being purposive, involves strategising. Individuals and groups try to make sense of their situations and determine appropriate kinds of action. Just as we have learned to distinguish between individual and collective identities (Reicher 1996a; Melucci 1996), so we can also distinguish between individual and collective strategising. The former concerns what *I* can and should do in the light of *my* situation, the latter how *we* can and should act. It is with respect to collective identities, strategising and action that general questions of leadership are posed.

Social movements as entities are anything but homogeneous. They are not centralised organisations, but possess 'acephalous, segmented and reticulate' shapes (Gerlach and Hine 1970; Diani 1992), with unstable memberships and boundaries. Commonly they include numbers of distinct organisations, groupings and sub-networks, all of varying character. What gives movements a tendential unity is their relations with opponents. Like 'classes' in Marxist theory (Thompson 1963, 1965; Ste Croix 1981; Gubbay 1997), social movements are *relationally* defined by their place in a political, social or cultural conflict (Diani 1992). They are thus at once both differentiated and unstably unified, assembling diverse subjects around shared projects of social transformation.

As such, social movements face 'collective identity' problems (Offe and Wiesenthal 1985; Melucci 1989, 1995b, 1996). Their adherents must arrive at provisional but roughly matching answers to such questions as: Who are we? What sort of conflict are we involved in? What interests do we have and what kinds of claims can and should we make? Forming collective identities, however temporary, involves developing shared ideas, which define both participants and their allies and opponents; they also narrate how these identities and social situations have emerged. Collective identities thus embody theoretical and historical reflection.

Movements also face related 'collective action' problems. They are effective insofar as they can mobilise adherents into shared activity. Collective action demands some sense of 'collective obligation' which permits its sometimes heavy individual costs to be re-evaluated on a new calculus of mutuality and interdependence. Any such collective obligation depends on emergent shared evaluations: cognitively, of the character of the situation; morally, both of the problem requiring action and of the movement; and pragmatically, of the practicality of collective action itself.

However, movements cannot arrive at such shared evaluative complexes all together and at the same time. Because movements are networks composed from distinct strands and tendencies, they cannot, as entities, themselves formulate independent ideologies and strategies in the course of their struggles. They may move together (indeed, it is a condition of our identifying them as movements that they do so, in a certain sense), but they also move unevenly. It is only in mythological thinking that whole movements can be considered as thinking the same, or as acting as simple and undifferentiated entities. Rather, movements are arenas of discussion and argument, out of which there can emerge, at best, unstable and provisional forms of collective understanding, identity and action.[1]

For collective images and ideas, projects, forms of action and organisation to emerge, *someone* must propose them. It is here that the issue of leadership arises. Leadership in movements consists in proposing to these differentiated entities how they should and can identify themselves and act together. Without such proposals, and any assent they receive, movements do not exist, collective identity is not formed, collective action does not occur. The terms 'leadership' and 'social movement' are inseparably interconnected.

The nature of leadership

What, then, is leadership? It is, we propose, simultaneously a *purposive activity* and a *dialogical relationship*.

Leadership as activity

The heart of leadership is a set of doubly 'intellectual' and practical 'directive' or 'organising' activities. It consists essentially both in thinking about what movements can and should do, and in urging the conclusions of that thinking on others. Eyerman and Jamison (1991) discuss leaders as 'movement intellectuals', adapting Gramsci's (1971) idea of 'organic intellectuals'. What in part distinguishes such intellectuals from 'traditional' intellectuals is the inherent *practicality* of their activity: at some level their problem is always 'what is to be done?'. As a set of tasks, leadership operates at various levels of generality and concreteness. Eyerman and Jamison distinguish 'cosmological', 'technical' and 'organisational' problems and tasks.

'Cosmological' tasks include the enunciation of theoretical visions of the character of the social world and of the 'problems' affecting it, together with schemes for activity-patterns suitable to overcoming them. Ultimately, the adequacy of such theories sets limits to movements' development. Voss (1996) suggests that, in response to a series of defeats, the American Knights of Labor came to suffer from 'cognitive encumbrance', a sense that existing strategic formulations were insufficient. Something similar afflicted Polish Solidarity activists in spring 1981 after a planned general strike was suddenly cancelled: attendance at meetings dropped away and worker members became less willing to speak (Staniszkis 1984).

Eyerman and Jamison's movement intellectuals act as technicians, or artists, of protest. One crucial leadership function consists in proposing appropriate forms of action, from petitioning to barricade-building, from legal demonstrations to occupations of buildings, land or trees. This involves learning, often by trial and error, what works in given circumstances, as seen in the strategic evolution of the American civil rights movement from failure in Albany to success in Birmingham and Selma (McAdam 1982; Morris 1984; Garrow 1988). Additionally, a given element in a repertoire of contention (Tilly 1995) can be conducted in a whole variety of ways. Thus 'picketing' can vary from the maintenance of a small, symbolic presence outside a protest target to mass pickets, flying pickets and so on.

As for 'organisation', this is a practical activity – *organising* – central to leaders' task-lists. Organising, Ganz (1997) suggests, is a *craft*, a knowledge-based practice that includes elements of artfulness, prudence, knowledge of angles and wangles, creative adaptation. Such craft knowledge is transmissible, often by 'apprenticeship' rather than traditional academic means. Organising involves a host of particular skills, from persuading others of an idea or tactic to maintaining commitment and morale, from allocating resources to recognising opponents' weak points, from writing and speaking to taking initiatives in moments of decision, from forming (and breaking) alliances and conciliating opponents to issuing authoritative commands.

These three kinds of tasks are interrelated with each other. Ideological principles have to be translated into immediate strategies and tactics, in order to handle messy and uncertain daily realities. Different general principles, as Lavalette and Flanagan suggest in this volume, produce different strategies, tactics and methods of organisation. In their study of contested leadership in an industrial dispute, distinct 'ways of seeing and interpreting the world' shaped the 'strategic impulses', 'political logics' and self-conceptions of each group, along with their relations to rank-and-file members. Also in this volume, Mische traces the 'delicate balancing act' leaders must perform as they align their 'personal life projects and ambitions' with collective movement goals and projects. Here, those same 'ways of seeing and interpreting the world' are traced to the level of individual subjectivity. Employing Schutz's concept of 'projectivity', Mische rescues the humanity of

Brazilian youth leaders, reminding us that leaders seek to make their way in the same world they seek to transform.

Leaders must regularly grapple with competing leaderships' practices and ideas. Bernhard (1993: 205–7) documents how Polish oppositionists recaptured terms from the regime's political lexicon during the 1970s, preparing an oppositional culture that underpinned the rapid emergence of Solidarity in 1980. On occasion, a seemingly simple slogan can have an extraordinary resonance: witness the impact in 1960s America, and beyond, of 'Black Is Beautiful!'. Contesting the ideological terrain, though, is not always easy, for *opponents* may derail movements by adopting aspects of their language and converting it to anti-movement purposes. Collins (1996, 1999) offers examples of movements both succeeding and facing difficulties in this area. On the one hand, shop stewards' leaders at Upper Clyde Shipbuilders in Glasgow were able, in 1971, to seize key terms – e.g. 'cooperation' and 'negotiation' – from government propaganda and hurl them back, encouraging a mass mobilisation to save the yards from imminent closure. On the other hand, Collins's parallel study of a community campaign in Paisley reveals the authorities using a language of 'partnership' to draw leading activists into collaboration with them, conceding nothing of substance while dividing and confusing the campaigners. Here, no one achieved the needed clarity of ideas and counter-organisation in time to prevent the campaign's demoralisation and decline. What Volosinov (1986) terms the struggle over the 'tenancy of words' is a crucial leadership activity, with very material effects.

In this volume, Shandro defends the continued value of Lenin's model of political leadership because it confronts the brute fact that the oppressed and exploited not only resist but are also dominated, ideologically and practically, by their rulers. What Gramsci (1971) termed 'contradictory consciousness' means there is no automatic correspondence between social position and political action. Thus political intervention, which is 'sensitive to the struggles of the masses yet willing where necessary to counterpose its political analyses to their spontaneous movements', is needed to win the battle for hegemony against competing political leaderships and rival social forces.

If leadership has one predominant feature, it is that leaders *communicate*. Leadership is, above all, an activity of *persuasion*, reflecting its other aspect, leadership as a *relationship*.

Leadership as dialogical relationship
The major sociological tradition in which leadership relationships have been discussed stems from Weber and his three types of *Herrschaft* (Weber 1978). Weber's term, sometimes translated as 'authority', is better understood as 'domination'. Weber distinguished between traditional, charismatic and legal-rational domination, grounding his distinctions in people's reasons for obeying commands when no question of direct force applied. What is missing from his types – making the Weberian-conservative tradition less useful

for discussion of movement leadership – is any sense of people following others out of reasoned conviction in the correctness of their views. The very possibility of what might be termed 'democratic leadership' disappears from view (M. Barker 1980).

More promising is the theoretical school issuing from the post-revolutionary Russian thinkers sometimes called the 'dialogists'. Prominent names here are Bakhtin (e.g. 1981, 1986), Volosinov (1986) and Vygotsky (1986). These writers approached human thought, speech and action, and the relation between these and social structure, from a dialectical standpoint whose possibilities for illuminating the dynamics of social movement leadership are only beginning to be explored.[2]

Central to their account is their analysis of the 'utterance'. Every utterance is shaped by the situation in which speaker and listener find themselves, and by the focus of their immediate concern. The utterance has three elements – *speaker*, *topic* and *listener*. To begin with the *speaker*, each utterance embodies an intention and has both a plan and a form of composition. It is a form of action, an attempt to achieve something, and as such is an event in a developing social relationship between speaker and listener. The premise of every utterance is the expectation that the listener will respond. That expected response – agreement, sympathy, obedience, disagreement, an answer to a question, and so on – shapes the utterance's form. Second, every utterance has a *topic*, in that it is always about something, communicating meaning and intention. Utterances carry 'evaluative accents' towards topic, speaker and listener, expressing such stances as sympathy, tact, disrespect or humour, and achieved by such stylistic means as intonation and gesture. Third, Volosinov and Bakhtin place an unusual and original emphasis on the part of the *listener*. Their account assumes understanding as an *active* process, itself a creative form of action. The listener orients actively towards the utterance, grasping its plan and intention, its structure, the speaker's evaluative accent. In the process of understanding, the listener places the speaker socially, determining the kind of relationship the speaker seeks to activate. Understanding is itself evaluative: listeners incorporate the utterance into their own conceptual scheme in line with their own purposes and needs, giving it a new range of inflections and nuances. In the activity of understanding, listeners prepare their own responses.

Underlying the whole model of the utterance, at all its stages of elaboration, is a conception of language as pre-eminently 'dialogical'. Each utterance is but one link in an ongoing chain of social interactions, in which meaning, sense, and evaluative accent are all engaged in a developing process. The listener is as significant a participant as the speaker, indeed is preparing to switch places and formulate a 'counter-word', even if no more than a grunt of assent or dissent. Listeners become speakers, and speakers become listeners, in a transforming process of social dialogue. On both sides, we find agency and creativity.

The 'dialogical' approach, we suggest, offers a way of generating insights into the relation of leaders to movements. It points us to considering leadership in movements as part of a process of ongoing conversation, in which utterances and responses contribute to the development of practices and ideas. It demands that we consider not only the ways that people lead others by *persuasive speech and action*, but also how followers *respond*. Reicher and his colleagues in this volume, exploring the implications of social identity and categorisation theories, criticise widespread accounts of leadership rhetoric that treat it as simply *manipulative*. Such accounts focus only on the forms of speech, ignoring their content. Leaders are influential, they suggest, only insofar as their proposals speak to social identities and their audiences hear them as consonant with their own categories and purposes, as these develop in practical social interaction. The dialogical approach undermines all tendencies to elitism in the analysis of the transmission and reception of ideas, for all participants – including the 'quiet women' in Hanisch's chapter – are understood as active and engaged. It encourages us both to ask what motivates people to grant 'authority' to others' proposals, and also to explore to what degree and in what respects they agree and disagree, and how they respond.

It might seem, if we read Volosinov (1986) on language as class struggle, that dialogics are of use only for exploring discord. But a stress on the possibility of conflict over goals, strategies and tactics in movements by no means exhausts the area; we must also attend to the evolution of forms of mutual understanding and agreement within movements (see Bakhtin 1986: 121, 125). Strategic innovations are commonly the work of conversation among equals. Where people bring diverse perspectives and experiences to bear on a problem, they may, through dialogue, alight on a new solution. Ganz's history of the United Farm Workers of California provides a splendid example of activists discussing how to proceed in a struggle with the Schenley Company:

> As proposals flew around the room, someone suggested we follow the example of the New Mexico miners who had traveled to New York to set up a mining camp in front of the company headquarters on Wall Street. Farmworkers could travel to Schenley headquarters in New York, set up a labor camp out front, and maintain a vigil until Schenley signed. Someone else then suggested they go by bus so rallies could be held all over the country, local boycott committees organised, and publicity generated, building momentum for the arrival in New York. Then why not march instead of going by bus, someone else asked, as Dr. King had the previous year. But it's too far from Delano to New York, someone countered. On the other hand, the Schenley headquarters in San Francisco might not be too far – about 280 miles which an army veteran present calculated could be done at the rate of 15 miles a day or in about 20 days.... But what if Schenley doesn't respond, Chavez asked. Why not march to Sacramento instead and put the heat on Governor Brown to intervene and

get negotiations started. He's up for re-election, wants the votes of our supporters, so perhaps we can have more impact if we use him as 'leverage'. Yes,
someone else said, and on the way to Sacramento, the march could pass through
most of the farmworker towns. Taking a page from Mao's 'long march' we
could organise local committees and get pledges not to break the strike signed.
Yes, and we could also get them to feed us and house us. And just as Zapata
wrote his 'Plan de Ayala', Luis Valdez suggested, we can write a 'Plan de Delano',
read it in each town, ask local farmworkers to sign it and carry it to the next
town. Then, Chavez asked, why should it be a 'march' at all? It will be Lent
soon, a time for reflection, for penance, for asking forgiveness. Perhaps ours
should be a pilgrimage, a 'peregrinacion', which could arrive at Sacramento
on Easter Sunday. (Ganz 2000: 1038–9)

When finally the demonstration set off, its leading banner bore the words (in
Spanish) 'Pilgrimage, Penitence, Revolution!'. Here, we see a plan for action
emerging through dialogue, each participant drawing on their specific
knowledge about the overall situation, about other movements, about
potential supporters and their values, about tactical matters like march
distances, and so on. Through mutual dialogue, the activists produced an
innovative plan that, at the outset, had occurred to none of them.

Leadership purposiveness

Movement leadership, as simultaneously purposive activity and relationship, involves persuading others of ways of understanding, but also yoking
the wills of others to a common project. Leadership is an activity conducted
upon and in response to others: would-be leaders have to be aware of the
ideas, assumptions and moods of those with whom they seek to share a
collective purpose. They must monitor others' responses for fear and hope,
for readiness and reticence at the prospect of collective action, in order to
convince them.

Leadership is argumentative, *urgently* persuasive. To propose one idea is,
implicitly, to respond to *other* ideas, either expressed or threatening to be
expressed. Leaders not only propound a positive idea, but also combat
another, seeking to exclude an opposing socio-ideological influence. To offer
one lead involves trying to diminish another possibility. Alternative ideas
emanate of course from movement *opponents*, but also from *allies*: the complexities and uncertainties of collective action are such that rival conceptions
are almost bound to appear. Many of this volume's separate chapters explore
the contestable and negotiable qualities of leadership.

There is a permanent *tension* in leadership relations, a pressure to convince, arising from that very unevenness within movements which also
makes leadership – in some form – inescapable. Leadership involves both an
identification with and *projective distancing* from existing movement identities. To offer leadership is to express creative dissatisfaction with the situation as it is now and to deploy effort to activate movement energies in a

specific direction, in order to *transform* current identities and activities. Leadership involves, however dimly, a vision of a transformed movement, a judgement of the present in terms of an aspired-to future. Proposing an idea for common action, and defending it against others, even within very informal settings, involves investing oneself with a certain urgency in the effort to align others' wills and understandings with one's own.

One source of this tension is that offering leadership involves some element of 'outsidedness' with respect to current ways of thinking and acting. Of course, this is a relative matter. 'Pure outsiders' cannot lead, for they lack identification with the group, lack commitment to its future – never mind an audience willing to pay them serious attention. It is always some admixture of 'outsidedness' and 'insidedness', of partly distanced commitment, which marks leadership.

Resources of leadership

Exercising leadership functions depends on possessing *resources* of various kinds. In this volume, Johnson discusses the skills in which Martin Luther King was trained, while Purkis observes variations in 'cultural capital' affecting individuals' contributions in Earth First! As a preliminary orienting device, we can distinguish between resources which are the attributes of *persons* and those which are supplied by *structures*.

Personal resources

Performing leadership tasks involves a set of personal requirements, whose significance should not be underestimated. Goodwin and Jasper (1999) remark that 'Certain individuals are especially gifted at knowing what to do when, how to invent new tactics, how to time an action or response'.

Strategising for a collective group demands a passionate engagement of will and intellect, a focusing of energy and attention on the task in hand. Gramsci is pertinent here: 'strong passions are necessary to sharpen the intellect and help make intuition more penetrating.... Only the man [*sic*] who wills something strongly can identify the elements which are necessary to the realisation of his will' (1971: 171). But commitment alone is insufficient: capacities are also involved. Effective leaders must synthesise information, itself often partial, about the many contradictory elements in a given situation, in order to construct a persuasive case about the possibilities of action. They must also communicate ideas in ways likely to empower others to act. Such capacity to communicate is not simply a speaking power, but equally demands a capacity to listen – both to assimilate relevant information and to know how to speak. Persuasion is a dialogic achievement.

The self-confidence which is a pre-requisite of leadership, consisting of a pragmatic set of judgements about personal capacities and limits, is learned, and is itself situational. It requires an acquired familiarity with 'speech genres' (Bakhtin 1986) specific to given settings; embarrassment and fear of speaking is an impediment to leadership. Speech genres include local situational rules which have to be mastered: Fantasia (1988) describes how activists in a New Jersey foundry successfully organised two 'wildcat' strikes but – through inexperience with union procedures – failed in a challenge to the leadership of their union local.

In large part, such personal resources are 'trained' or 'learned'. Skills and capacities, with the confidence to use them, are honed by practice and testing. However, if leadership can be 'trained', there is a significant question about equality of access to such training. The matter is important for social movements. On the one hand, movements often question existing patterns of status and privilege within society, and would thus seem to undermine conventional notions about the social location of leadership. On the other hand, often the formally educated, the possessors of 'cultural capital' (Bourdieu 1990), do emerge to play some kinds of leadership roles in social movements, not least those involving writing and public speaking. Within the US civil rights movement, for instance, church ministers played prominent roles, as, later, did middle-class black students. Traditional cultural capital is, though, less useful in many movement contexts, where leadership attuned to local idioms is required. Here conventional cultural capital can be a positive hindrance, while other forms of knowledge and experience are at a premium.

One way of evaluating movements consists in asking how far they do train and empower participants. Purkis, in this volume, explores the efforts of an Earth First! group to realise an organisational philosophy based on consensus decision-making, cooperation and collective responsibility: a 'leaderless culture'. He traces how the group's 'prime movers', an 'accidental clique', sought to overcome power disparities within the group by a formal programme aimed at preventing their own emergence as an identifiable and permanent leadership. Using Foucault and Bookchin, Purkis theorises these efforts at 'leaderlessness' in a revealing study of anarchist theory and practice.

Of course, the question is not simply one about formal training programmes (though see Morris 1984 and Edwards and McCarthy 1992 on movement halfway houses and schools), for a good deal of real training happens through informal watching, listening, talking and participation, where 'learning' is as unplanned yet effective as the methods by which children acquire language. Movements encourage or discourage such training and development, not least through the repertoires of collective action they select. One instance must suffice: one feature of the 'May events' in France in 1968 was that communist union leaders sought to limit practical participation in the workplace occupations, restricting activity to their 'reliable' cadres and thus shutting down potential movement development (Cliff and Birchall 1968).

Structural resources

Personal qualities alone are insufficient. Leadership also has *structural* requirements. To lead is above all to communicate, and communication has 'means' of various kinds. The group with a loudhailer on a demonstration has an advantage over those without. Access to movement publications can be monopolised or relatively open. Movement cultures may regulate who is called on to write or speak, to chair meetings, to act as negotiators. Often such cultures are gendered, excluding some voices, as Ryan's chapter shows.

To lead it is not sufficient to have good ideas or confidence in expressing them. In the early 1930s, for example, Trotsky had far better ideas about combating the growth of the Nazis than did the German Communist Party's leaders. He argued powerfully that Communists should abandon 'ultra-left-ism' and work for a 'united front' with the Social Democrats – rather than condemn them as 'social-fascists'. But he argued from afar, with only 50 supporters in Berlin just before Hitler's accession to power, a puny force compared with Stalin's 50,000 followers (Trotsky 1969; Cliff 2000: 23). Effective leadership requires layers of people who share strategic ideas and can win over others.

Goodwyn (1991), in a fascinating reconstruction of the Poznan 'riots' of June 1956, draws similar conclusions. An organised group of activists at the Cegielski factory had developed a 'thick web of communication' across their own workplace such that they could shape a strategy for interacting with the Polish state authorities. When, however, they marched out of their factory into the city, the fact that their 'web' did not reach into *other* local workplaces meant they lost the capacity to control the situation. Other workers joined their march in large numbers, but with no cohesion or shared joint plan; these enthusiastic but uninformed allies precipitated a battle with state forces in which large numbers were killed. It took a number of years before such *inter-workplace* communications developed, to permit, in 1971 and especially in 1980, the interfactory strike committees and workplace occupation strategies that raised the Polish workers' movement to a whole new level.

In the Polish case, Solidarity's rapid expansion in the summer and autumn of 1980 retained a relative coherence of leadership, not least because a core group in Gdansk had already worked together and 'rehearsed' the leadership roles they assumed, developing informal networks between workplaces and industrial centres (C. Barker 1987; Goodwyn 1991; Laba 1991). But in some other cases of rapidly expanding movements, existing would-be leader-ship groups lose the capacity to steer a diversifying movement. In Germany, the November 1918 revolution found the far left disorganised. The ranks of the infant Communist Party, itself established only after the initial wave of mutinies and strikes and the Kaiser's fall, were suddenly swollen by waves of enthusiastic new revolutionaries. These new recruits were impatient and pressured a reluctant leadership, under Rosa Luxemburg and Karl

Liebknecht, into a premature attempt at an uprising in Berlin in January 1919. Luxemburg and Liebknecht were both killed, with damaging effects on the party's later development (Harman 1982; Gluckstein 1985).

In this volume Hanisch, in intriguing counter-point to Purkis, draws on her own insider's experience in the early women's liberation movement in the United States to explore leadership struggles. Ideologies of anti-leadership and hostility to clear structures of accountability, she argues, damaged the movement's ability to act strategically and fight back effectively when it found itself within its adversaries' sights. Hanisch poses important questions for contemporary arguments about the respective benefits of structured democratic leadership and 'leaderless cultures'.

Contexts of leadership

Movements and their constituent parts interact with other bodies and influences within a 'multiorganisational field', itself composed of 'conflict and alliance systems' (Klandermans 1992, 1997). Movement leadership can only be adequately grasped as a dynamic process, carried out in social contexts where others also strategise, opposing and aiding movement projects, and compelling movement re-thinking and re-organising (Ellingson 1995). The contexts of leadership appear as series of critical junctures, where new and creative responses are required.

In conflicts, opponents actively respond to movement strategies and tactics. Jasper and Poulsen (1993) show how the targets of an animal rights campaign learned over time new tactics for responding to demonstrations, effectively weakening the effects of protest. Movements have to respond to both practical and ideological innovations by their targets and opponents, to offers of compromise and partial concessions as well as to physical assaults and direct refusals.

Marx remarked of the 1848 revolutions that every revolutionary movement, at some stage in its development, has to face 'the whip of reaction'. Brutal opposition, however, may either cow a movement into submission, or raise it to new heights. What matters is the capacity of movements and their leaders to adapt strategies and tactics to the new situations created by violence. In the Iranian revolution of 1978–79, army shootings of demonstrators set off a cycle of mass funeral demonstrations which contributed enormously to the revolutionary movement against the Shah (Marshall 1988); similar effects were seen on a smaller scale in the major American strikes of 1934 in Toledo, Minneapolis and San Francisco (Preis 1972; Dobbs 1972; Quin 1979; Kimeldorf 1988). On the other hand, Solidarity leaders' uncertain and divided response to regime violence in Bydgoszcz in March 1981 produced demoralisation and demobilisation in their own ranks (C. Barker 1986; Bloom 1999).

Violence, of course, is but one element in opponents' repertoires of

contention. Cooptation, concession and partial reform pose their own problems. Movements don't just *have* targets, they *enter 'within the sights'* of
their adversaries, who seek to divide, subordinate and contain them
(Shandro 1995). As Offe and Wiesenthal (1985) suggest, employers and
states commonly seek to draw union leaders into varieties of collaborative
association, to convert them to 'monological' forms of liberal 'interest
group' representation, narrowing the potential range of claims unions
express and limiting members' militancy. US civil rights movement leaders,
similarly, were under constant pressure from government and sponsors to
moderate demands and contain more radical elements (McAdam 1982).

Actual and potential alliances also provide crucial problems for movements and their leaderships. For they determine a movement's structural
capacity to achieve its goals. Different social constituencies possess distinct
social weights, to the degree that they mobilise. One painful discovery of the
American new left movement in the 1960s was that students alone lacked
the power to change society, regardless of their commitment. Faced with
such problems, movements can either turn in on themselves, effectively trim-
ming their potential, or seek ways to reach out to more powerful social
forces – and thus transform their own sense of themselves and their goals.

Both from within and without, movement leaderships face shifting
demands and situations, which require innovative responses on any number
of fronts. Effective leadership thus involves a capacity to reassess, to change
tack, to explore unknown territory, to advance and to retreat, to learn creatively. New possibilities disclose themselves; old patterns of action prove to
be inefficacious. Immediate and long-term goals alter; existing means need
to be re-evaluated.

Who actually leads?

There is an empirical question, with varying answers in each case we examine: where, within movements, does leadership actually reside? Both movements' complex structures and their dynamic natures make such questions
rather open.

First, leadership is exercised at all manner of levels and locations within
movements, and not only by those obviously designated as 'leaders'. Sometimes people who never play publicly prominent roles undertake crucial
'backroom strategising' work. More important, movements depend on the
activities of sometimes hundreds and thousands of unsung local leaders.
Robnett shows that leadership within the US civil rights movement was not
limited to formal positions in organisational hierarchies, nor to the men who
were prominent there. Women, often marginalised at this level through
sexism, frequently led in informal settings, providing 'day-to-day lessons on
self-empowerment' (Robnett 1997: 23). Gibb, in this volume, examines the
dynamic interaction between formal leadership and activists in SOS-

Racisme in France, as they debated election policy. His narrative reveals both initiative and leadership as shifting, interactive and fluid all the way down the movement.

Leadership functions may be variously produced and organised. In the 'direct democracy' found within 'loosely organised collectives' and 'primary groups' (Rosenthal and Schwartz 1989), strategising is, in a sense, distributed among group members, and only close analysis can identify whose proposals are actually taken up as the group's common product. Fantasia's (1988) reconstruction of decision-making in a wildcat strike provides an example. In other settings, identifiable lay individuals and groups play leadership roles, endowed with titles such as 'steward', 'organiser', or 'chair'. In yet other settings, salaried officials play leadership parts. In any case, a movement's 'organisational plan' often provides only partial guidance to the actual practice of leadership.

As Ryan, in this volume, suggests, some literature has presented leadership in terms of a crude and unhelpful dichotomy between 'new' and 'old' social movements, with 'old' associated with formal, hierarchical and structured relations while 'new' means fluid, decentralised and flexible networks. Reconstructing leadership patterns in the early twentieth-century Irish suffrage movement, she shows the dangers of such manicheanism, offering insights into both the problematical nature of historical representations of past leaders and the significance of gender in movement leadership.

Second, the problem leadership addresses – 'What is to be done?' – can alter situationally from moment to moment. Fields of struggle are constantly shifting as the various parties strategise and counter-strategise in conditions of uncertainty, and the actual location of leadership is always liable to be mobile and contested. New strategic and tactical choices are posed all the time, and leadership in movements has to be won, and won again, as action contexts alter, sometimes with great rapidity. The 'elevation' of individuals and groups into leadership roles is always, in principle, provisional and situational; every leader is as good as her or his last effort. Leadership as a relationship engages the 'led' in constant evaluation, such that their agreement and even simple attention are conditional and inherently fragile.

Leaders are regularly challenged from within and without. Movements experience crises of growth as well as decline, sudden advances and reversals, in which adherents' perceptions of what is desirable and possible can change dramatically and in which potential new 'organic intellectuals' almost *self-produce* and offer new horizons of possibility, new repertoires of contention, new ways of thinking. The emergence of relative unity of direction in movements, with their network structures and their inherent unevennesses, is always an achievement, and an unstable one. Contests for hegemony, for the predominance of one directive idea rather than another, regularly mark the development of movement leaderships.

Development and transformation are inherent properties of the to-and-fro interchange of leadership, as an activity and relationship conducted across time. Reicher describes a London student demonstration where a minority of 'radicals' – whose ideas, at the outset, most participants rejected – *became* representative of majority opinion and took on the demonstration's leadership when police blocked and attacked the march (1996b; see also Reicher and his colleagues in this volume). Here, the persuasive power the radicals gained was due not simply to what *they* said and did, but equally to what *the police* said and did. The ensuing struggle translated fluidity of collective identity and collective action into a fluidity of leadership. In the midst of collective action – social movements' principal form of sanctioning activity – leadership can be immensely volatile. Dix (1999) describes one hectic afternoon during a Leeds civil servants' strike during which a national union official was semi-kidnapped by a section of his members, and led through the streets to address an unofficial meeting. Here leadership was almost tossed from hand to hand, taken up and then abandoned by particular individuals, contested at one moment, borrowed from others at another, as the action flowed from one site to another in a context of uncertainty and argument about what was going on and what to do.

This sense of volatility has implications for the ways we think about and study leadership. As Tarrow (1991) suggests, trying to capture movement realities requires not the still camera of the public opinion poll, but the movie camera. Melucci's 'exchange' model of leadership relations (see above) seems too constraining, with its assumption of stable 'partners' who come to a transaction already conscious of their interests. Models of consciousness that treat thinking and feeling as static and uni-dimensional are especially inappropriate for exploring the inner world of movement ideas (Billig 1996; Steinberg 1999a). *Narrative* and *dramatic* forms of description and analysis are required, enabling us to explore such issues as 'strategic dilemmas and impasses', 'trajectory shifts' and 'turning points' (e.g. Turner 1974; Friedman 1984–85; Abbott 1997; Bloom 1999).

Can leadership be democratic?

Two or more people conversing, taking turns in exploring some matter of mutual concern, may be said to be involved in leadership relations, except that the function of leadership passes back and forth between them. Here, leadership is not opposed to democracy or egalitarianism, rather each implies the other. Inter-communication – offering ideas for others to accept, reject, modify – is central to both leadership and democracy.

However, not all leadership is democratic in form and function. Some differentiation is needed. Purkis, in this volume, draws on Bakunin to suggest a distinction between the *authoritative* and the *authoritarian*. While this takes us in the right direction, the argument seems incomplete. Bakunin declared himself ready to follow 'special men' – his examples are architects and engineers – because to do so 'is imposed on me by my own reason'. However, his only examples are credentialled experts. Yet my own reason can persuade me to follow a formally unqualified child simply because he or she offers a good idea.

More promising as a starting point is Bakhtin's distinction between 'authoritative' and 'internally persuasive' words. The *authoritative word* – which may be religious, political, military, parental, etc. – demands obedience from us, regardless of any power it might have to persuade us:

> [We] encounter it with its authority already fused to it.... [It] permits no play with the context framing it, no play with its borders, no gradual and flexible transitions, no spontaneously creative stylising variants on it. It enters our verbal consciousness as a compact and indivisible mass; one must either totally affirm it, or totally reject it. It is indissolubly fused with its authority – with political power, an institution, a person – and it stands and falls with that authority. One cannot divide it up – agree with one part, accept but not completely another part, reject utterly a third part.

The alternative is the *internally persuasive word*. This is tightly interwoven with 'one's own word':

> [It is] half-ours and half-someone else's. Its creativity and productiveness consist precisely in the fact that such a word awakens new and independent words, that it organises masses of our words from within, and does not remain in an isolated and static condition. It is not so much interpreted by us as it is further, that is, freely, developed, applied to new material, new conditions, it enters into interanimating relationships with new contexts. More than that, it enters into an intense interaction, a *struggle* with other internally persuasive discourses ... The internally persuasive word is open in essence, has a capacity for further creative life in our ideological consciousness, our dialogical interaction with it is unfinished and inexhaustible. (Bakhtin 1981: 341–6)

Here Bakhtin distinguishes between words that allow us nothing but obedient acceptance (or total rejection), and those that can ferment with ideas we already possess, permitting our own further creative development. We can usefully map this distinction onto polar types of leadership in social movements and organisations. At one extreme stands authoritative or bureaucratic leadership, and at the other stands persuasive or democratic leadership.

The former involves issuing commands. It is 'monological', seeking to permit no other voice. Such leadership does not enable but disables development in its followers. Such leadership may act 'for' its recipients, like the schoolmaster beating the pupil 'for his own good', but does not promote their own self-activity. It is, in essence, domination (*Herrschaft*) in the Weberian sense.

The latter, by contrast, involves persuasive argument. Inherently 'dialogical' in function, it seeks understanding and agreement. It presumes that an initial proposal may be modified by the listener's response. It encourages the further critical self-development of the follower. As noted above, this form lacks any Weberian referent.

How *effective* are these two forms within social movements?

Democratic and inclusive leadership
Ganz (2000) provides a relevant case study, comparing two contemporaneous efforts to organise Californian farm-workers in the 1960s. The first was an unsuccessful unionisation drive by the AFL-CIO's Agricultural Workers Organising Committee (AWOC), the second a more successful campaign by the United Farm-Workers (UFW). AWOC was well funded, the UFW less so, suggesting 'material resources' alone cannot explain campaigns' relative successes and failures. Ganz argues that they were distinguished by differences in *resourcefulness* or 'strategic capacity', themselves resulting from distinct leadership styles.

'Strategic capacity' refers to leaders' ability to respond creatively to complex situations. Ganz relates the differences between AWOC failure and UFW success to two interrelated matters: the nature of their leaders, and the nature of their organisations. Movement leaders with high strategic capacity (UFW) have access to salient knowledge about their environment, including regular feedback about how other people's responses are changing. They use this knowledge to devise novel and imaginative answers to problems, and can 'play' with varieties of solutions. Their high motivation and commitment enhances their focus on their work, their persistence and their willingness to take risks. Lower strategic capacity (AWOC) marks leaders with less varied sources of knowledge, less space to break with routine solutions, and with more instrumental forms of motivation. Such differences are not accidental, but emerge from the nature of leadership teams and their organisational forms. Leadership teams with higher strategic capacity are more diversely networked, and conduct regular, open and authoritative deliberations with varied constituencies, in which they root their accountability. Less successful leaderships are more narrowly based, operate less democratically and are accountable upwards rather than downwards.

Ganz suggests that open and democratic organising forms, in creating conditions for variety of ideas, permit leaders to find richer solutions to strategic problems. There is an elective affinity between Bakhtin's internally persuasive word and such leadership forms. The effects on members and adherents are also important: their own commitment to movement projects is liable to be greater where their own voices are valued, i.e. where democratic leadership creates space for their own self-development.

Johnson, in this volume, explores those leadership forms that facilitate processes of popular self-emancipation. In a critical reading of Martin Luther King's leadership of the civil rights movement, he examines the skills, both of leadership and 'followership', which democratic leaders must possess. He stresses the conversational character of democratic leadership as part of the creative generalship needed to overcome adversaries, and the necessity for leaders to balance their 'leading' and 'led' selves, directing but also listening to the mass movement.

However, democratic leadership forms are by no means the only ones found within social movements. There are at least two ways in which leadership can be less democratic: by being bureaucratic, or by being exclusivist.

Bureaucratic leadership

Bureaucratic forms are common outside movement settings. As Weber (1978) suggested, modern state and capitalist organisations provide their key contemporary sites. But they also appear within movements, especially in 'mass membership' organisations (Piven and Cloward 1977).

Bureaucratic organisation involves a hierarchy of offices, with decision-making concentrated at the top, and commands flowing down. Members are either directly excluded from decision-making, or only indirectly consulted through intermittent elections to top offices, occasional conferences and ballots. Officials are commonly appointed rather than elected. Channels of communication are top-down and monopolised by the leadership. The other side of the bureaucratic coin is the relative passivity and low involvement of members. The classic sites of bureaucratic movement leadership are to be found within labour organisations, though other movements are anything but immune to the emergence of these forms, as even a casual scrutiny of the histories of nationalist, ecological, anti-racist, feminist and other movements suggests.

Barker (in this volume) suggests bureaucratisation is a by-product of leadership conservatism. In the classic case of trade unions and social-democratic parties, officialdom is drawn towards 'opportunism': that is, to elevating means over ends, organisational maintenance over collective action, and short-term gains over long-term goals, to using administrative means to isolate critics, and to narrowing the scope of member identities by promoting sectionalism. Officials seek to make the organisation's survival as independent as possible of members' motivation and willingness to act collectively: in Mills's (1948) phrase, they become 'managers of discontent'.

Such policies and leadership styles, we should note, are encouraged by movement *opponents and targets*: employers and states respond to the potential threat of working-class power not only by repression and legal limitation, but also by offering partial concessions – for example, by legitimising 'collective bargaining' while restricting the possible scope of negotiable issues ('recognition of management's right to manage'), and by admitting union leaders into various forms of 'corporative' arrangements. Unions, in return for a place in the 'corridors of power', are expected to police agreements and control members, thus diminishing unions' transformative potential and shifting them to merely one 'interest' group among others (Offe and Wiesenthal 1985).

Exclusivist leadership
If bureaucracy is a tendency in 'mass' organisations, movements also contain a whole variety of smaller bodies – sects, ginger-groups, factions and the like – which play significant parts in overall movement development. These bodies have different kinds of *internal* regimes, both centralised and decentralised, hierarchical and dialogical. However, they not only vary in their inward democracy but also in the degree of their 'dialogicality' with the movements around them. Some are more inclusive and some more exclusive in dealings with those outside themselves.

Some have a highly exclusivist orientation. They rely on committed action by an inner circle of activists, as distinct from wider movement circles. Any outer periphery of supporters is expected to accept core groups' decisions and to play more passive support roles as providers of material resources and/or admiration. Such groups seek to *lead* by the indirect method of *heroic example* rather than by the interactivity of persuasion. They *act for* society's interests, substituting their own dedicated activity for the potential disappointments of efforts at wider mobilisation. They rest on, and reproduce, the assumption of passivity within wider society. In a sense immunising themselves from wider contamination, they limit their own range of repertoires of contention.

One wing of nineteenth-century Russian populism adopted this form, engaging in terrorism not least from despair at the slowness of wider peasant opposition to tsarism. Their heirs in the twentieth century have been numerous, from Castro's movement to Black September, from the Italian Red Brigades to Shining Path in Peru. These practised exemplary violence as a means to achieve social and political change. However, this political form is not necessarily identified with the specific tactical use of violence, for some bodies committed to non-violence in pursuit of political objectives have also adopted forms of exclusivism, witness Greenpeace and Earth First! within the environmental movement.

Leadership forms and protest cycles
Despite their differences – apparent conservatism as against apparent radicalism – a common factor unites bureaucratic and exclusivist leadership forms. Both involve a relative devaluation of potential creativity in actors beyond their own ranks, closing off practical dialogue.

However, neither bureaucratic nor exclusivist leaderships have the social movement field to themselves. Other kinds of leadership practice are always liable to assert themselves, and to enter into practical contests for wider hegemony both across movements and within their various organisations. Movement leadership is a contested terrain. 'Discord' (Zirakzadeh 1997) is

a feature of the inner life of all significant movements, not least along lines
which regularly set 'radicalism' against 'moderation' and 'inclusivity'
against 'exclusivity'.

Within labour movements, for example, internal struggles recur over the
very meaning of trade unionism, with leadership conflicts that go well beyond mere contests for official positions to challenge bureaucratic principles
and policies. Nor is this peculiar to unions. The history of the US civil rights
movement includes processes of organisational splitting and competition,
fuelled by dissatisfaction with the limitations of earlier organisations. In
both the US and Europe, the women's movement from the early 1970s was
often wracked by arguments between 'liberal', 'radical' and in some settings
'socialist' feminisms. Solidarity in Poland was marked, especially after
March 1981, by acrimonious disputes between Walesa's group and various
'radical' oppositions. In Germany, the Green Party was famously divided in
the 1980s between 'realos' and 'fundos'.

Conflicts over leadership within mass organisations are especially significant during the upturn phase of 'protest cycles' (Tarrow 1998), when popular confidence in the possibilities of collective action rises, and new voices
challenge the normal routines not just of rulers but also of complacent movement leaders. New organisations spring up, while old ones are subjected to
new demands and enlarged aspirations from below. Militant factions within
movements, urging more combative policies, gain wider audiences. The
internal arguments and struggles that mark the inner life of movements take
on new potency, necessarily implicating issues of leadership personnel, style
and organisation.

The same 'wave' patterns also affect the appeal of 'exclusive' leadership
forms within movements. Small, relatively isolated militant groups relying
on 'guerrilla' actions and resources tend to be predominant in the downturn
phases of protest waves. They are in a sense the products of a politics of
angry despair, mixing radical aspirations with disappointment at the decline
of mass movements.

Birchall, in this volume, recovers the changing views on leadership of two
'reluctant Bolsheviks', Serge and Rosmer, who travelled from anarchism and
syndicalism to a 'libertarian Leninism' under the extraordinary impact of the
First World War and the 1917 Revolution. Historical context and leadership
style appear, in this chapter, as complexly interrelated. The degeneration of
the Leninist model into overtly bureaucratic and authoritarian forms is here
related to the ebb of a wave of protest, amid isolation, war and economic
crisis.

Leadership matters

Leadership is fateful for movement development at every stage and turning
point. Movement successes and failures – their growth and decline, their

heritages for the future and their mark on history – are all intimately tied up with their forms of leadership, the quality of ideas offered and accepted, the selections from repertoires of contention, organisation, strategy and ideology they make. We hope that the articles in this volume will convince readers, at the least, that it is worth poking about further in the black box of leadership.

Notes

1 McCann offers a brilliant journalistic account of the swirling character of movement ideas and feelings in his memoir of popular resistance in the Bogside area of Derry in Northern Ireland (1974: 27–116).
2 See for example Bakhtin 1986, 1993; Volosinov 1976, 1986; Vygotsky 1986. Valuable commentary includes M. Barker 1989; Bender 1998; Collins 1996, 1999, 2001; Gardiner 1992; Hall 1995; Shotter and Billig 1998; Steinberg 1998, 1999b.

2

Robert Michels and the 'cruel game'[1]

Colin Barker

> The democratic currents of history resemble successive waves. They break ever
> on the same shoal. They are ever renewed. This enduring spectacle is simulta-
> neously encouraging and depressing. When democracies have gained a certain
> stage of development, they undergo a gradual transformation, adopting the
> aristocratic spirit, and in many cases also the aristocratic forms, against which
> at the outset they struggled so fiercely. Now new accusers arise to denounce
> the traitors; after an era of glorious combats and of inglorious power, they end
> by fusing with the old dominant class; whereupon once more they are in turn
> attacked by fresh opponents who appeal to the name of democracy. It is probable
> that this cruel game will continue without end. (Michels 1959: 408)

Social movement activists regularly propose that social transformation is
both necessary and possible. Their opponents deny both propositions.

For most of the twentieth century, the left faced two powerful lines of
argument. The first sought to undermine them morally by linking them with
Stalinism's crimes, equating socialism with totalitarianism. That line of criticism weakened when the former 'communist' regimes fell. However, a second, older and more insidious case reflected the failures of social democracy
rather than communism. Socialism will always fail, went this argument,
because leaders always betray, the left is always sidelined, radicals grow out
of their youthful enthusiasms and those who believe them are easily bamboozled.

Within political science, one work above all symbolises this second argument: Robert Michels's *Political Parties* (Michels 1959). Subtitled *A Sociological Study of the Oligarchical Tendencies of Modern Democracy*, the
work is, as the covers of many editions announce, 'a classic of social science'.
Part of its significance is that, beside its appeal to the camp of reaction,
Michels's case has also affected wide layers of radicals and left-wingers.

The basic argument

Drawing most of his evidence from the German Social-Democratic Party (SPD) and its associated trade unions, Michels argued that movements for democratisation, though real and powerful, had hit against unexpected barriers. These barriers, which are insurmountable, are created not by these movements' enemies, but out of their own logic of development. To succeed, democratic movements must organise themselves, but that very fact of organisation itself breeds new forms of conservatism, in the shape of undemocratic structures and practices which stall movement progress. In particular, leadership, even in movements aiming at democracy, tends to become oligarchic, and thus a brake on the movement. It is 'a fundamental law of politics' that 'Who says organisation says oligarchy'. One chapter title refers to 'the iron law of oligarchy'. There is a twin inevitability: organisation engenders *both* oligarchy, the emergence of leaders who can prevent challenges to their rule, *and* conservatism, the diversion of democratic movements from their original goals.

Michels identifies three kinds of interrelated causes for this sad spectacle. Some are rooted in human nature, some in the character of the political struggle, and some in the nature of organisations.

First, human nature. Humanity falls into two types: members of the elite and members of the masses, each with their own characteristics. *Elites* share 'a natural greed for power'. In them 'The consciousness of power always produces vanity, an undue belief in personal greatness. The desire to dominate, for good or evil, is universal. These are elementary psychological facts ...' (1959: 205–6). By contrast, *the masses* are marked by apathy and incompetence. More interested in spectacles of the kind that attract a gaping crowd than in the details of political thought and action, and grateful to leaders whom they re-elect, they are incapable of genuinely practising full democracy. Michels refers many times to 'the incompetence of the masses [which] is almost universal throughout the domains of political life' (86). The masses have a 'psychological need' for leadership, and a pre-disposition to hero-worship. The masses' incapacity provides leaders with justification of their rule. It also facilitates their rule, for the masses' incompetence makes them easy to govern. They are swayed by demagogic oratory, especially in large crowds: they are 'enslaved by the phrases employed by the leaders' (25). Relying on accounts of crowd 'pathology' drawn directly from Le Bon (1947), Michels declares: 'The individual disappears in the multitude, and therewith disappears also personality and sense of responsibility' (24–5). While the masses may share *latent* opposition to their leaders, they cannot mobilise to change the existing state of affairs. True, they may erupt occasionally, when 'sudden blindness' strikes the dominant classes, but such eruptions are but 'transient' affairs which end with them being tricked again back to acquiescence.

Second, the nature of the political struggle itself shapes the players. Parties' participation in the parliamentary system produces an emerging cadre of professional politicians, who become a closed corporation, largely removed from members' control, and demanding permanent authority so as to protect the party's national reputation. Oligarchic tendencies are still more marked in the trade unions, whose leaders resist political strikes and determine wage bargaining, claiming that their expert understanding of the labour market enables them to protect members' interests against the claims of militant minorities. In both cases, the external institutional settings in which leaders move induce conservatism among them.

Third, and most important, struggles for socialism or democracy are self-defeating because of the organisational necessities they impose. Organisation, seemingly the weapon of the weak against the strong, is itself a source of oligarchy and conservatism. 'Organisation is, in fact, the source from which the conservative currents flow over the plain of democracy, occasioning there disastrous floods and rendering the plain unrecognisable' (22). Experts and leaders are technically indispensable, but they develop their own interests, along with the capacity to enforce these. They become a stratum distinct from and opposed to the rank and file.

Officials regard their offices as private property, resisting removal or control. To maintain their positions, they develop various means of control which Michels outlines with relish: for example, monopoly of party press and finances, demagogy, decision-making in small committees, threats of resignation, etc. The overall result is that the mechanism of organisation becomes an end in itself (187). Oligarchy is the result of a law of organisation, rather than of the policies that organisations pursue. 'Thus, from a means, organisation becomes an end' (373).

The outcome is that movement organisations give up the principles on which they were founded. Thus the SPD abandoned its commitment to such militant tactics as the general strike, supported the Kaiser's government in the First World War, and repressed its revolutionary wing. Though the party begins as a representative of workers' interests, it becomes petty-bourgeois. The leaders climb out of the working class, leaving their comrades behind, and demanding of workers now only that they continue to vote for them. They no longer need a social revolution, for they have had their own (305). The more the party develops, the more prudent and timid it becomes (369). The socialist party becomes just another party fishing for votes, willing to make unprincipled appeals to voters in order to win: thus it adopts the mantle of patriotism, support for imperialism, etc. 'The party no longer seeks to fight its opponents, but simply to outbid them' (374).

The consequence is that *socialism is impossible*. For socialism means more than simply an economic change; socialism involves at its heart the extension of democracy. However, all that happens in reality is that the movement generates a new stratum of rulers who fool their own supporters.

The masses are bamboozled: 'the modern proletariat, enduringly influenced by glib-tongued persons intellectually superior to the mass, ends by believing that by flocking to the poll and entrusting its social and economic cause to a delegate, its direct participation in power will be assured' (401–2). The whole process is a 'tragi-comedy'. In his final chapter, Michels allows that some qualification of his basic thesis must be allowed, in that democracy can make *some* progress. However, he insists, its movements will always smash on the same rocks. 'This cruel game will continue without end.'

The relevance of Michels

That Michels is discussing real phenomena seems indisputable. Indeed, the SPD went on, after his book appeared, to play a still more conservative role in German politics. At the end of the war, it assisted the army high command in creating a new and ferocious instrument of military control over workers, the Freikorps. In the early 1930s, in both Germany and Austria, it proved immensely ineffective even as a defender of liberal democracy against the assaults of fascism. For the remainder of the twentieth century, social-democratic parties and trade unions would continue to play the roles Michels predicted. Not only that, but within a few years of their foundation the communist parties, set up explicitly to challenge social-democratic conservatism, were themselves heading down the same road.

Michels's overall thesis, if correct, must affect what movements may reasonably hope for and how they set out to achieve it. That is, the sense we make of his arguments can reflect, and shape, larger political processes. Among later readers of Michels, three kinds of readings are, I suggest, particularly relevant.

Liberal-elitism and academic sociology

The first kind of reading I will term the 'liberal-elitist' response. Here, while Michels's thesis may require some modification and limitation, it presents no major problem. For, essentially, liberal-elitists lack commitment to the kinds of values whose attainment Michels declares impossible. For them, demands for democratisation wider than is compatible with liberal capitalism are quite utopian. The best and indeed the only form of democracy there can be is a limited one, consisting of elite competition for the votes of an electorate which is, mostly and fortunately, politically passive. One thing that makes 'democratic elitism' (Bachrach 1969) valuable is precisely that it helps keep the populace out of politics except at election time, for their active participation would be destabilising.

This is a view with a long heritage. Max Weber, for instance, argued that both the unions and the SPD in Germany constituted 'a very important counter-balance against the direct and irrational mob rule characteristic of purely plebiscitary peoples' (Weber 1978: 1460). Schumpeter and a host of lesser theorists sought to so de-limit the notion of democracy that any suggestion of positive participation would be outlawed as mere utopianism (Schumpeter 1965; Bachrach 1969; Pateman 1971). Although some writers (e.g. Bennett 1978) claim that Michels makes a positive contribution to democratic theory in challenging *naive* theories of pure equality and democracy, the literature of liberal elitism offers no significant critical response to Michels's main thesis: that is, to its claim that any movement for large-scale progressive social change will be derailed by its own organisational necessities.

The same limitation appears in some modern sociological assessments of Michels's *empirical* validity along various dimensions (e.g. Lipset *et al.* 1956; Zald and Ash 1966; Schwartz *et al.* 1981; Klandermans 1997; Rucht 1999). These authors suggest there are 'scope conditions' to Michels's thesis, in that organisations' developmental trajectories vary more widely than he allowed. Some organisations, rather than becoming oligarchic and conservative, become more radical or more democratic, or convert towards sect-like forms. We should thus ask which *kinds* of organisation are more and less subject to particular developmental tendencies. Although this literature has no answer to the *political* impact of Michels, some authors develop a significant general methodological point (e.g. Schwartz *et al.* 1981; McCarthy *et al.* 1991). Michels focuses his explanation of oligarchy and conservatism predominantly on factors 'internal' to organisations, while playing down the stance they adopt to their 'external' context. Yet the relationships into which organisational leaders enter, through parliamentarism in the case of parties, or collective bargaining in the case of trade unions, are surely vital in shaping organisational development.

Perhaps the academic critics who most effectively capture the political impact of Michels's work are those who explore the nature of his *rhetoric*. As Gordon Hands remarks (1971: 168): 'When one reads *Political Parties* for the first time, one is overwhelmed by the spate of plausible arguments and illustrative examples. It is more a matter of being taken by storm than of being persuaded by rational argument.' Alvin Gouldner (1955) cited Michels as a prime example of what he termed 'metaphysical pathos' in his case for the inevitability of bureaucracy. If we read him closely, we can see that Michels uses a whole bank of dubiously constructed arguments. He hardens potential tendencies into uni-directional laws, he over-extends empirical generalisations into universal statements, he uses proverbial statements uncritically, he ignores alternative explanations for various phenomena, he enunciates 'sociological laws' of doubtful provenance, he is frankly elitist in describing ordinary supporters of parties and unions, he relies on unexamined assumptions about 'human nature' and 'national character', and he runs together different meanings of the same word (e.g. 'democracy') and casually substitutes one term (e.g. 'organisation') for another (e.g.

'bureaucracy'). Max Weber, who otherwise largely agreed with his book's thrust, took Michels to task for some of these (Mommsen 1981; Scaff 1981).

Libertarian responses

Michels was never the sole critic of the SPD and the unions in pre-war Germany. His book emerged from a debate among syndicalists and Marxists about the same issues of conservatism and bureaucracy within the workers' movement. As Beetham (1977) remarks, what distinguished Michels was that he provided a right-wing answer to a left-wing question. In that same period, two predominant responses that have divided the left since then were shaped.

One of these, still apparent in the theory and practice of social movements to this day, is sometimes termed 'libertarianism'. This position is marked by its *acceptance* of Michels's basic premises. That is, conservative, bureaucratic and hierarchical forms of movement construction are indeed rooted in the sins of 'organisation' and 'leadership'. Libertarianism accepts what Hallas (1970) terms a secularised version of the myth of original sin. Organisation and leadership *corrupt*. Therefore, the only solution is to avoid them like the plague. The difficulty then is that – as Purkis's chapter suggests – they keep sneaking back in, sometimes in hidden guises. And movement dilemmas are not resolved.

By way of illustration, let us briefly consider two relatively influential works which enunciate versions of the libertarian case. The first is *Poor People's Movements: Why They Succeed, How They Fail*, by Frances Fox Piven and Richard Cloward (1977), and the second is Wini Breines's history of the American New Left, *Community and Organisation in the New Left, 1962–1968: The Great Refusal* (1982).

Piven and Cloward

Poor People's Movements offers a radical interpretation of the history of four social movements in twentieth-century America: unemployed movements in the early 1930s, the New Deal unionisation drives, the civil rights movement of the 1950s and 1960s, and the welfare rights movement of the 1960s. In each case, the authors' core argument is that mistaken efforts to build mass membership organisations diverted popular energies away from that activity which really gets results for movements of the poor, namely the generation of 'disruption' of the system. They thus counterpose 'organisation' to 'militancy' in a way any reader of Michels would recognise. Yet their case has significant problems.

First, their review of the history of the four 'poor people's movements' does not clearly differentiate between *forms* of organisation. They themselves appear to recognise at least three forms: first, 'mass membership organisations'; second, 'cadre organisations' or 'organisations of organisers';

and third, organisations and networks that people belong to before they ever join in protest activity, like the Southern black churches which played such important roles in the civil rights movement. Of the three types, it is solely the first of which they strongly disapprove. However, because they do not adequately explore the distinctions between these forms, Piven and Cloward give little indication as to how the different forms are and should be interrelated, either articulated or opposed. Yet each form implies distinct sets of actors, of relationships, and of purposes. If 'cadre organisations' are valuable, as they indicate (e.g. Cloward and Piven 1984), by what criteria should they be organised? Should they be constructed only in times of insurgency or also in periods of social quiet and reaction? What should be their roles and aims? Piven and Cloward give no answers to such questions, despite their correct insistence on a clear distinction between *social movements*, which are loosely constructed entities without clear aims of their own, and *social movement organisations,* which do have such aims. Were we to pursue the issue of distinctions of form we might begin to formulate significant questions about *the role of organisations within movements*, and about potential struggles between political tendencies over the *hegemony* of different strategic and tactical orientations. However, these matters, though implicit in Piven and Cloward's case, are never explicitly examined.

Second, it is not really clear from their analysis whether Piven and Cloward's objections to 'mass membership organisations' are to their organisational form or their purpose. Is the problem the simple fact of large-scale organisation, or is it that mass memberships are assembled in order to seek political representation and lobby officials inside the existing system? In reality, what they describe are not simply 'mass membership organisations' but *reformist* organisations whose orientations, not their membership size, are surely the real issue. As Piven and Cloward make clear, those leading such organisations come to depend on 'elites' for resources, and those resources are only provided on condition that the organisations work to reduce that power of disruption which Piven and Cloward see as the real power-resource of the poor.

Third, this ambiguity connects with a further feature of their argument. It is striking how very *modest* are their aspirations for poor people's movements and how *pessimistic* Piven and Cloward appear. The best they seem to hope for are some limited handouts or some small influence over decision-making. The poor are offered occasional moments, infrequent and temporary, when their own 'disruption' and 'turbulence' compels elites, for a while, to grant them small concessions. Such concessions are the best they can, seemingly, hope for. Piven and Cloward never discuss any possibility that the poor might transcend the limits of their current position and win, not temporary concessions from the table of the powerful, but permanent shifts in their own power-position – in effect, their own self-abolition as 'poor people'.

Fourth, Piven and Cloward seem to allow for no *strategic possibilities* for movements other than a choice between a rather inchoate 'turbulence' and 'disruption' and a deadening 'mass-based permanent organisation', as if popular organisation must always preclude effective militancy and the poor cannot control their own organisations (for a contrary case and argument see Johnson 2000b).

Fifth, part of the difficulty is embodied in their title: 'poor people's movements'. The same term 'poor' includes industrial workers, black people, the unemployed and welfare recipients – groups with very different organisational capacities or power-potentials. Some possible propositions about, say, the organisational capacities of industrial workers don't fit the 'poor'. Both can cause 'disruption', both indeed can 'riot', but industrial workers can (as in Poland in the winter of 1970–71) make a leap within days from fighting the authorities in the streets to organising factory occupations and building new mass organisations from below – thereby creating organisational frameworks which could pose issues about the complete transformation of society. It is difficult to see how, by themselves, either the unemployed or welfare recipients could possess such power.

Piven and Cloward acknowledge the direct influence of Michels. In a sense they offer their own version of the 'cruel game'. Popular movements appear trapped in an unhappy choice between on the one side 'disruption', with a powerful sense of its limits of possibility, and on the other side attempted entry into official politics with its own defining constraints. Disruption produces only short-term gains, before elites recover their position, while admission to official politics is a road to incorporation and conservatism. There appears no other choice.

Breines

Wini Breines reviews the experience of an American New Left movement of the 1960s, Students for a Democratic Society (SDS). The SDS, she suggests, undertook a conscious attempt to overcome the 'Michels problem' by pursuing 'prefigurative politics'. Breines writes about the very period in which Piven and Cloward formed their own views; indeed she aligns herself with their thinking – although without picking up their significant but underdeveloped discussion of 'cadre organisations'. In Breines's view, the SDS sought a form of participatory democracy and saw a 'power orientation' as something that would undermine this quest. Their approach to politics was thus characterised by a *refusal* to be 'strategic'. This, she suggests, amounted to a 'brave experiment'.

The difficulty with Breines is not her *description*, which is sympathetic and richly textured, but her evaluation of the SDS experience. SDS failed, and that needs explanation. The point about experiments, brave or otherwise, is that one is supposed to learn something from them. There was always an obvious risk in the SDS 'refusal to be strategic', based on its assumption that as leadership and hierarchy are the same and have similar consequences, they should therefore both be resisted. The effects were debilitating. The SDS in the later 1960s, faced with an impasse when it became clear to participants that further progress along its existing path was blocked, became highly factionalised, developing into what Friedman (1984–85) describes as a 'system of sects'. (Many, though not all, of those rival sects took up caricatured versions of 'Marxism-Leninism' marked by extremely hierarchical forms of organisation.) The reason for the change was that the former 'issue-oriented agenda' of SDS was not yielding the hoped-for results, for the movement's existing social bases (students and blacks) were proving insufficient to achieve movement goals (above all, stopping the Vietnam War). Participants were driven to a 'search for an ideology' in which different groupings seized on a variety of competing potential ways of organising, acting and theorising. The splintering of the movement was also a response to the existence of competing models of revolutionary practice (Friedman 1984–85: 11–13). What replaced the 'brave experiment' of the SDS was another experimental form, a 'system of sects' in which rival models were tested for their potential viability. An *ideal* result of that second 'experiment' might have been that one of these rival models proved widely acceptable, permitting a new growth of a reconstructed American left. That it didn't happen is another story.

The SDS's history, while it does reveal an empirical diversity of organisational developmental patterns which Michels does not discuss, hardly provides either a model of success or an adequate practical riposte to Michels's larger claims. Breines's rather celebratory tone seems inappropriate, in that this attempt to overcome the Michels problem by 'non-organisational' and 'non-strategic' means largely failed.

Overall, the problem with 'libertarian' responses to Michels is that they are too uncritical of his basic thesis. They *accept* the fundamental notion that 'organisation' and 'leadership' in and of themselves constitute the problem, and end up mired in defeatism or embracing failure. If the libertarian critique fails, can the socialist tradition offer an alternative? Can 'organisation' and 'leadership' be somehow *combined* with a struggle for radical democratisation, participatory democracy or socialism-from-below?

A socialist critique?

The major tendencies Michels identified within the SPD and the German trade unions were all too real. However, he falsely generalised his observations to 'organisation' in the abstract, without further discrimination. Rather than follow Michels down that path, we should, rather, see bureaucratism and conservatism as products of a particular kind of political practice, namely the politics of *social democracy*. The real problem, which Michels mis-identified, is *reformist politics*. Michels did not see that sufficiently, not least because he shared with the SPD's leaders some deep assumptions about parties and the struggle for socialism.

Within the SPD a particular account of the party's role had become hegemonic, and escape from its entangling assumptions would prove quite difficult – not least for the left. Karl Kautsky, the SPD's leading 'orthodox' theoretician, set out its assumptions very clearly in his programmatic work *The Road to Power* (Kautsky 1910). According to that account, the socialist party *represents* the working class, the party is the source and measure of the working class's consciousness, and the achievement of socialism rests squarely on the party's coming to power (Harman 1968–69; Hands 1971). The only relevant measure of working-class development is the degree to which it accepts and subordinates itself to the party's ideas and leadership. The task facing the working class is essentially to catch up with and accept an established doctrine, embodied in the party leadership.

This social-democratic conception of social transformation espouses what Draper (1992c) termed a 'socialism from above'. Social change is to be achieved *on behalf* of the working class and other oppressed layers within society. The matter was crisply expressed in the original 'Clause Four' of the British Labour Party's constitution, drafted by Sidney Webb. There the party's basic aim was stated: 'To secure for the workers by hand and by brain the full fruits of their labour', etc. The key word here is the third: *for*. What the Labour Party never set out to do was to encourage the workers by hand and by brain to *secure for themselves* the full fruits of their labour.

Social democracy adheres to a 'ballot box' notion of socialist transformation. Workers are expected to be politically active but in a limited fashion. They must first win the right to suffrage, then exercise that right by voting for the socialist party. Beyond the act of occasional voting, party supporters are not required to be self-active and self-organising. Party leaders do the thinking and decision-making, while the members get out the vote for them. The party is, fundamentally, a vote-chasing entity, whose aim is solely to transform the staffing of the state, not to enable the people to transform and emancipate themselves. The party is the crucial agent of transformation, carrying through, when in office, the legal changes the working class needs. The party's job is to grow in strength until it can replace the personnel of the existing bourgeois state. Socialism is, in essence, the socialist party in office. As for 'socialism' itself, it means essentially the enhancement of state power via the nationalisation of property and state planning. This is an inherently 'statist' vision of socialism, dependent on 'statist' means of attainment. Here, clearly, to the degree that the party is itself undemocratic in its methods of organisation, so too will socialism be.

Throughout *Political Parties*, Michels takes it for granted that the struggle for socialism will be conducted by means of such parties. No other possibilities are even slightly explored, although, as we shall see, by the time Michels was writing powerful new impulses were actually shaking up the former certainties.

What is clear, however, is that the SPD's conception of social transformation and the practices embodying it tend to produce the various empirical features which Michels described. The *effects*, in short, can be more satisfactorily attributed, not to 'organisation' in the abstract, but to social democracy's *politics*. We can trace this causal connection across a number of areas.

First, the separation of 'politics' and 'economics' into distinct spheres of parliamentary party work and trade unionism was an article of social-democratic faith. Trade unions should, largely, keep out of 'politics' and the socialist party should keep out of 'trade unionism'. 'Public affairs' are delimited, excluding many questions of practical concern to workers: wages, working conditions, the authority of employers in the workplace. Workers' concerns with these matters are not immediate issues for the social-democratic party. This very division of spheres, which Marx saw as characteristic of capitalism, is replicated within the workers' movement, contributing to what Michels mis-identifies as the inherent passivity of workers.

Second, the party's parliamentary focus requires its supporters to do little more than place their cross, once in a while, in the appropriate box on a ballot paper. The centrality of parliamentarism promotes the very division between 'leaders' and 'led', between parliamentary and council deputies and voters. In order to achieve its primary aim of winning votes, the party stands ready to subordinate and compromise its (theoretical) principles, playing for example nationalist and even racist cards if that promises to be vote-winning. Rosa Luxemburg (1966) was correct: those arguing for the road of peaceful, parliamentary reform were not simply arguing for a different path to an agreed goal, but for a different goal altogether.

Third, in the social-democratic conception, trade unionism *limits itself* to dealing with the effects rather than the causes of workers' problems. The key activity of trade unionism is what, in Britain, is known as 'collective bargaining', a process that takes for granted the continued existence of a class of employers. This form of trade unionism promotes a discontinuous commitment by members, and reliance on officials, whose role is to *mediate* between workers and employers – not to plan their dispossession. These limits to trade unionism, we might add, are actively encouraged by employers and states. Fantasia (1988: 57) cites Philip Taft's warning to employers against democratic unionism, and comments on the Taft–Hartley Act of 1948 that it 'sought to forge labor peace by outlawing traditionally successful forms of rank-and-file solidarity, while creating a stratum of labor bureaucrats to enforce the bureaucratic regime'. Here a movement's *opponents* contribute to its shaping.

Fourth, the strategy of parliamentary victory requires no basic alteration of everyday social relations and identities. Michels notes, in passing, the SPD's lack of concern with such matters as political education. In particular,

> Devoting all its energies to the imitation of the outward apparatus of power characteristic of the 'class-state', the socialist party allots no more than a secondary importance to psychological enfranchisement from the mentality which dominates this same class-state. This neglect of the psychical factor is disastrous to the democratic principle, especially in so far as it springs from psychological sources. (1959: 368)

However, 'psychological enfranchisement' – depending as it does on collective self-activity, thinking and organisation, the very things the party leadership actively discourages – is exceptionally unlikely as a by-product of a merely parliamentarist politics.

Fifth, social-democratic politics promotes a specific conception of 'leadership' as, at best, 'representation' – acting for the people, but outside, and when necessary against, their active control – rather than as encouragement to critical self-organisation and activity.

Sixth, as Miliband (1991: 68) argued, Michels places little stress on conflict *within* reformist parties between moderate leaders and left-wing activists. Such parties need these activists, who are attracted by the party's *myth* but are then liable to take it seriously, challenging the leaderships and thus *requiring to be controlled*. It is their existence especially, not some 'iron law of oligarchy', that creates the division of leaders and led, leaders and activists; and the conflict is not abstract but over concrete ideological differences.

Finally, as a century of experience with social-democratic *governments* has since demonstrated (and as Michels could only guess before the First World War), such parties, when in office, do not even live up to their *promises* of transformation from above. Rather, concerned to manage and defend existing social organisation and existing state systems, they are pulled towards the policies and practices of their more conservative political opponents (e.g. Miliband 1962; Birchall 1986).

In sum, Michels's analysis does have a kind of sense, if restricted to social-democratic and other reformist workers' bodies, but errs in the form of explanation it offers. Conservatism and oligarchy in these bodies are the product and corollary of their acceptance of the broad framework of capitalism, the state and its constitution and procedures, etc. Michels did not grasp this argument, for he did not distinguish between *forms of parties*, between those whose project is reformist and those which aim to raise working-class self-activity with a view to the system's overthrow. Michels was not peculiar in that, for the distinction was not properly grasped even by the left before 1914.

The left and the Michels problem before 1914

Michels was, as noted above, not the SPD's sole critic. Others in the same period also attacked the conservative and oligarchic tendencies within the SPD, struggling to find a way out of the bleak impasse Michels identified.

The most notable was Rosa Luxemburg. A major critic of 'revisionism' in the party at the end of the nineteenth century (Luxemburg 1966), Luxemburg attacked the institutional separation of trade unionism from the socialist party and the bureaucratised relationships existing in both wings. She sought an attempted solution in a brilliant pamphlet, *The Mass Strike, the Political Party and the Trade Union*, which drew on and generalised the experience of the Russian workers' movement before and during the 1905 revolution. The spontaneous energies released by such mass workers' movements, she suggested, offered both alternatives to and a cure for the ills of the German movement. Mass strike movements simultaneously overcame the artificial separation between political and economic movements and demands, and rapidly expanded movements beyond the constricting limits of existing organisation. They revealed the immense *creativity* of an insurgent working class and would, once under way, be unstoppable by conservative forces (Luxemburg 1964). In like manner, syndicalist movements and theorists across Europe and North America also sought solutions to the 'Michels problem', seeking answers in the development of militant non-party workers' movements.

Luxemburg was no syndicalist. She continued to argue for the necessity of socialist party organisation and activity. Indeed, she argued at one point that to break with the SPD would mean breaking with the working class itself (Dunayevskaya 1991: 60–1). Luxemburg's solution lay in somehow limiting party influence, and resisting its centralisation. The key mechanism for overcoming conservative tendencies appeared to lie *outside* the party, in spontaneous militancy. In an important sense, during the pre-war period Luxemburg (and others like the young Trotsky) agreed with Michels that 'organisation' itself was indeed a core part of the problem.

This perspective had its own difficulties. It left its holders at risk of doing little else but general propaganda for militant working-class socialism, while waiting fatalistically for a spontaneous upsurge to begin realising their hopes. It also affected the way that they made sense of organisational disputes in other settings than the German. Both Luxemburg and Trotsky responded with hostility to Lenin's proposals for Russian party centralism, maintaining friendly relations with the Mensheviks, despite the fact that they were, of the two wings of Russian Social-Democracy, by far the less friendly to workers' spontaneous activity and organisation (Harman 1968–69).

Almost the entire left before 1914 shared one characteristic: they did not set out to build effective revolutionary organisations in opposition to the reformist parties of the Second International (Gluckstein 1984). Socialism was not yet irrevocably divided – as it would be, first by the First World War and then by the Russian and German revolutions of 1917 and 1918. The implications of that division were far-reaching, involving a whole series of challenging breaches with previous assumptions, not least with Kautsky's hegemonic model of socialist transformation. Transcending that model meant far more than a critique of organisational practice, but entailed the very meaning both of socialism and of the potential power of workers' and other popular movements.

The emerging new revolutionary model required socialists to develop parties that related directly to all popular movements, taking measure of working people's real consciousness and the forms of collective organisation they developed. For within actual forms of popular self-activity were embodied the very possibility of socialist transformation, even if in partially concealed and contradictory shapes. Here might be found the key to linking day-to-day conflicts within capitalism with the struggle for a new society. Socialists must learn to intervene in ways that would both develop an effective revolutionary leadership with deep roots in those movements and amplify popular militancy to the point where it could challenge state power from below.

In Michels's framework, where workers formed a passive 'mass' defined by incompetence and inactivity, such notions were meaningless. But for the left, their development entailed major theoretical and practical consequences. The argument about 'socialism' would shift away from classic social-democratic theses about the rationality of state control and planning, towards propositions centred on radical extensions of popular democracy, including the workplace. Existing state machineries would now appear, not as things to be 'captured' electorally and used for socialistic purposes, but as direct impediments to socialism which must themselves be overthrown. The significance of electoral politics would be greatly diminished, by comparison with direct struggles and organising 'from below'. As the opposition between two alternative conceptions of socialism, 'from above' and 'from below', was clarified, a sharpened political conflict between these two opposed trends would follow, with obvious consequences for questions of organisation.

However, for such developments on the left to come to full fruition, a complex mixture of experience and theorisation was needed. That process proved highly uneven, generating enormous theoretical and practical leaps but also radical incompleteness and disjointedness. Underlying the new experiences and ideas was a huge increase in the scale of capitalist accumulation, producing new concentrations of workers far beyond anything Marx and Engels had known. Major shifts in the nature of workplaces and the labour process prepared the way for convulsive new connections to be drawn between politics and economics. When, in 1871, Marx attempted to sum up the experience of revolutionary struggle in the Paris Commune, the average workplace employed less than ten workers – fewer than are found in a modern primary school, let alone the great factory and office complexes of the twentieth century. Strikes played no significant part in the development of the Commune, nor did workplace organisation or economic demands other than the abolition of night-work in bakeries. By comparison, the social world of the early twentieth century was already markedly different.

The differences were not, however, immediately registered in changing levels and forms of popular struggle. Working-class militancy did not immediately increase with the scale of capitalist production: union organisation certainly expanded across Western Europe in the last part of the nineteenth century and the early years of the twentieth, as did reformist party building in working-class districts, but the strike level in Germany, Britain and elsewhere remained quite low. The first significant alteration came, not in the heartlands of advanced capitalism, but in Russia, where working-class revolution exploded in 1905. Michels, significantly, makes nothing of Russian developments, but for the left 1905 provided the occasion for a number of major theoretical and practical developments.[2] As well as Luxemburg's *The Mass Strike*, 1905 provoked Trotsky's first formulation of his theory of permanent revolution: both writers sketched out important new developments in the likely pattern of future working-class revolutions (C. Barker 1996, 1999). Luxemburg argued, in particular, that the Russian movement was more *advanced* than anything yet seen in Germany, offering the patterns revealed in the Russian mass strikes as a pointer to the future. Yet she did not arrive, at one bound, at a completely new conception of working-class politics and its implications for socialists. She exaggerated the power of 'spontaneity' as an effective counter to union and party bureaucracies; she did not begin to argue for a political and organisational *break* with the SPD; and she argued that socialist organisations need not involve themselves in 'technical' matters to do with the conduct of strikes and the like – a notion that subsequent generations of socialists and communists would find extraordinary, and quite counter to their everyday experience of workplace and community activism. At the tragic end of her life, Luxemburg's previous underestimation of the practical power of conservative forces within the workers' movement would be revealed just when the German revolution broke out on a scale that made the 1905 events in Russia look like small beer (Harman 1982; Gluckstein 1985; Bessel 1993).

If, in Western Europe, the left was still only stumbling towards an alternative conception of socialist politics, things were not that much clearer elsewhere. To be sure, by comparison with left groupings in Western Europe and the USA, the Russian Bolsheviks did build a party with deeper roots among worker militants; they did polemicise more fiercely against reformist and syndicalist rivals and organise themselves separately; they did occupy themselves more with the everyday details of working-class struggle; they did continually insist on the need for revolution; and (certainly in Lenin's case) they had a more fully formed conception of the contradictory development of popular consciousness. Yet Lenin did not break with social democracy until 1914, nor did he, any more than Luxemburg or Trotsky, grasp the significance of the formation of *workers' councils (soviets)* in the 1905 revolution. For none of the left before 1917 did the Russian workers' organisational innovation re-orient either their theories of the state or their daily practice. Only in 1917 and 1918 did the issue of workers' councils become a defining matter for them. Only then did it become completely clear that two incompatible, indeed utterly opposed, trends existed in working-class politics: one focused, like the SPD, on parliamentarism, the other on workers' revolutionary self-activity; one on reform, the other on revolution; one 'from above' and the other 'from below'.

An alternative conception

Between 1917 and the early 1920s, a conception of working-class socialist politics took shape that was sharply distinguished from the social-democratic model. It implied a distinct view not only of the state and the struggle for a new society, but also of questions to do with organisation. Embodied in the experiences of the new communist parties of the period, and the debates of the early congresses of the Third International, its fate was to flower briefly and then to be distorted and finally destroyed as those parties and their International succumbed to Stalin's deadening control. A proper account is impossible in a few lines, but we can at least attempt some general points.

To begin, no adequate account of working-class politics can start with the principle Michels took over from elite theory: the assumption of a passive, undifferentiated 'mass'. As Beetham (1981) notes, this will not do as an account of the internal workings even of parties, whose officers, members and supporters comprise complex webs of association and different levels of commitment and activity. *Even less* can the 'mass' assumption make sense of working-class life. The position is fundamentally ignorant and prejudiced. Michels reveals no understanding of the rich associational life of the German working class of his period, nor of its actual forms of organisation and struggle and thus its potentials for further development. One simply could not begin to guess, from Michels's account, that his caricatured workers' movement would, within a decade, overthrow the Kaiser's imperial regime, force an end to the war, engage in an explosion of mass strikes and armed battles with state forces, expand trade union membership five-fold, develop insurgent workers' and soldiers' councils, and split its political forces between the SPD and a new Communist Party (Harman 1982; Gluckstein 1985; Bessel 1993).

No account of the working class that presents its forms of life and consciousness either as passively integrated or as homogeneous can suffice. That a variety of such accounts have been offered reflects more the isolation of middle-class intellectuals from everyday working-class life than it does any reality.

Workers' experience within capitalism promotes tendencies to resistance and revolt, and in that sense generates an 'elective affinity' between

working-class life and the idea of socialism. But this is anything but automatic. The very openness of working-class life to a whole variety of other
influences means that all 'socialist' tendencies are counteracted and contra-
dicted, not least by material and ideological pressures towards passivity and
accommodation with the existing order, and towards division rather than
unity in working-class ranks. Working-class culture is thus a field of oppositions, embodying an immensely complex series of associational forms and
networks, ways of coping and lifestyles, rituals and routines of both resistance and accommodation, solidarities and antagonisms, contradictory ideas
and tendencies which only very 'thick' ethnographic descriptions and social
histories can hope to capture (e.g. Thompson 1963). Far from being fixed
and simple, working-class consciousness and organisation are always
uneven, prone to leaps, reversals, and transformations in form and content,
as they are shaped by the ongoing interactions among workers and with
their various allies and antagonists. Working-class movements construct
themselves out of this rich brew and add to it their own distinguishing
characteristics.

Movements are not reducible to formal organisations – indeed, one merit
of modern social movement theory is its conceptual distinction between
'social movements' and 'social movement organisations'. Movements have
their own shape, being multi-centric networks without one single focus of
authority (Gerlach and Hine 1970; Diani 1992). What distinguishes them
within the broader cultures of which they are an expression is that they are
joined together, in complex webs of filiation, by all manner of activists.
These activists, in turn, belong both to informal networks and to an
immense variety of formal organisations – parties, unions, cooperative bodies, clubs, associations, churches, etc. The term *working-class movement*
refers to those forms of resistance to capitalist domination and exploitation
which are both collective and explicit. Such movements include both formal
institutions with codified organisational structures and also such 'quasi-
institutions' – with more informal rules and procedures – as shop steward
committees, tenants' bodies and simple friendship and other networks
(Wickham 1979). Such networks possess complex internal configurations
and external linkages, and are interwoven with all manner of other forms of
associational life, from families and local communities, charities, cross-class
movements, racist and anti-racist groupings, ethnic- and gender-based forms
of social organisation, to a host of special interest groups from sports groups
to Alcoholics Anonymous. It is through such a multiplicity of inter-relations
that a working-class movement is 'made' and 'makes itself', sometimes in
highly fragmented and serial forms, and sometimes in wider linkages and
solidarities. Modern workers' movements have, in Thompson's phrase
(1965), 'warrened society' through and through.

As with working-class culture, so with workers' movements: they contain
different tendencies pulling in opposing directions, composed of varieties of

shifting layers, 'advanced' and 'backward', combining leading and 'vanguard' groups with reactionary and accommodating forces. They are fields of argument as much as of unity, in which tendencies to combativity and to subordination are in constant tension. In the course of the actual *events* that constitute the everyday class struggle there run powerful impulses and swings of mood and opinion that give working-class movements renewed life and a renewed sense of their own inter-linkages, but also defeatism and depression. Within them, a variety of more or less organised voices propose and debate all manner of concrete projects for both resistance and accommodation with the forces of capital and the state. There is never a single 'class consciousness', but only majorities and minorities.[3]

It is into that complex web of activity and association, in reality, that real questions about 'organisation' insert themselves. What distinguishes socialist theory is the argument that such movements, despite their inner contradictions, possess huge power-potentials. They have the capacity to reconstitute their own forces, both to defeat the power of capital and the state and to become centres of a new and more democratic popular power. This vision of working-class self-emancipation powered Marx's account of the Paris Commune; Luxemburg rediscovered and celebrated it in the mass strikes of 1905; it flourished briefly in the *soviets* of 1917 and animated the demands of communist parties until the early 1920s; and it would surface again through the twentieth century in some of the largest revolutionary and near-revolutionary workers' movements – in Spain in 1936–37 right up to Solidarity in Poland in 1980. Here, at least in aspiration, the fullest democracy in the state would combine with forms of 'participative democracy' in workplace and community. That vision was distinct from, and opposed to, a mere *parliamentary* socialism. It argued, not that this or that *party* should take power, but that new directly democratic institutions rooted in and expressing *movements* should do so.

Leadership and self-emancipation

Pursuit of such a vision certainly implies party organisation, but of a kind very different from the social-democratic bodies Michels anatomised. Far from being, in fact or aspiration, the kind of 'catch-all' parties implied in the social-democratic model, such parties aim to provide a shared framework of activity for socialist militants. Piven and Cloward's term 'organisation of organisers' catches an aspect of this form, for it brings together those activists who share, and collectively promulgate, a socialist vision of transformation. Such activists most certainly seek to 'lead' others, though not essentially by 'representing' them within existing political institutions but by seeking to *mobilise* their fellow-workers in collective action, and to win fellow-militants to a common framework of understanding and intervention. Far from promoting passivity, they encourage activism; instead of neglecting education and 'psychological enfranchisement', these are their very *métier*, their be-all-and-end-all. What counts for them is the development of rank-and-file confidence, consciousness and self-organisation. Characteristically (as Lavalette and Flanagan suggest in this volume), they come into conflict with the bureaucratic apparatuses of social democracy and the trade unions, and their attempted leadership consists in good measure in *challenging the leadership* of more conservative forces within the same movement. They are the aspirant leaders of the 'worker opposition movements' discussed by Friedman (1985).

Such parties and proto-parties share an intense internal ideological life of education and debate. Performing their function requires a high level of commitment from their members, and the development in all of them of a capacity to offer leadership within their own milieu. Part of their task is to assist their members to act confidently, to make independent judgements, and to evaluate their experiences along with others. Typically, social relations among members, and between members and leaders, are far less hierarchical and distant than those which characterise social-democratic organisations.

There is, as Harman (1968–69) concedes, a kind of 'elitism' associated with the formation and membership of such bodies They (necessarily) regard their own ideas as superior, and draw more or less firm boundaries between themselves and their milieux, both to contain their internal discussions to fellow-thinkers and to sharpen the quality of their interventions into those milieux. Adherents of certain positions are *excluded* on principle: racists and nationalists, for example. On the other hand, the 'elitism' involved is very different from that underpinning Michels's analysis, for its presupposition is not some permanent quality of apathy or gormlessness in the mass of workers, but a simple recognition of the fact of immediate unevenness in consciousness and commitment. Indeed, their primary theoretical assumption – that popular empowerment and transformation in struggle are both possible and desirable – is quite the opposite of elite theory.

A temptation facing such parties or would-be parties is not so much bureaucratism and conservatism as *sectarianism*. Inherently concerned with *ideas* and *principles*, distinguishing themselves from those they seek to persuade, and anxious to avoid social-democratic *opportunism*, they risk fetishising some particular point of difference. Drawing an exaggerated line of division that makes dialogue and the search for unity with others impossible, they can lose the capacity to 'point the way forward' (in the phrasing of the *Communist Manifesto*). In different ways, the sectarian path has snared a variety of movements in the later twentieth century, from the far left to the anti-racist and feminist movements. However, while the sectarian danger is real, it is not a necessary fate. Its avoidance requires practical and theoretical *modesty*, above all a sense that 'the party' is never the repository of all socialist wisdom. The real development of socialist theory and practice is achieved in dialogue with larger movements, from which there spring most of the creative impulses that impel it forward – both the invention of workers' councils on the large scale and a multitude of tactical innovations in everyday struggle, plus indeed the formulation of new demands and ideas that enrich the very conception of human emancipation itself. A living theoretical tradition is always incomplete, always seeking to catch up with changing reality.

Conclusion

This kind of organisation, when combined with the organisational forms which movements themselves develop, offers a way of overcoming the sterile opposition of 'spontaneity' and 'organisation' that the libertarian tradition identified as the sole alternative to Michelsian pessimism. What appears 'spontaneous' is always, in some form, the work of leaders and of organisation. Often calling something 'spontaneous' amounts to an admission that one doesn't know who made it happen, and how (Goodwyn 1991).

The adherents of the revolutionary socialist conception of organisation are – at least ideally – always on the look-out for forms of popular struggle emerging from below. Here, people challenging existing power set-ups and ruling-class decisions generate creative new social impulses, organise themselves into new networks and in that very process transform themselves and their capacities. Such processes are constantly occurring, across the face of society, not only in workplaces (e.g. Fantasia 1988) but also on the difficult terrain of community struggles (e.g. Naples 1998).

The real counter to Michels lies not in denying any role to leadership and organisation, but rather in seeking combinations of forms of organisation and leadership which are practically compatible with larger struggles for popular self-emancipation.

Notes

1   My thanks to my fellow-editors for critical comments on an earlier draft of this chapter.
2   Shanin (1986) suggests the 1905 revolution was a watershed in thought and practice. He distinguishes, on both left and right, between those who learned *something new* from these events (among them Lenin and Luxemburg, but also Stolypin) and those who learned nothing (the Mensheviks and the tsarist autocracy).
3   Nor, it should be added, can there ever be. It is non-Marxists who wish onto socialist theory the idea that 'one day' there will be a unified consciousness, in a glorious 'proletarian end-shift' (Lockwood 1992) when all contradiction will be resolved and simple unity will prevail.

3

The 'reluctant Bolsheviks': Victor Serge's and Alfred Rosmer's encounter with Leninism

Ian Birchall

Introduction

The decade between the outbreak of war in 1914 and the death of Lenin in 1924 was a time of profound upheaval for the European left, when all accepted ideas had to be questioned and rethought. A number of fundamental questions – reform or revolution? soviets or parliament? – were the subject of heated debate. Among these the question of revolutionary leadership was far from the least important.

The collapse of organised working-class internationalism in August 1914 posed the issue of leadership in dramatic form. Right across the spectrum of the left, leaders (using the term in its broadest sense) had failed to oppose the war – not only Kautsky and Jouhaux, but Kropotkin had abandoned internationalism. This was not *simply* a betrayal of leadership – there was substantial popular support for the war, though far less unanimous than is often claimed – but it showed that a wholesale renewal of leadership, not just in personnel but in organisational structures, was on the agenda.

In 1917 the Bolshevik Revolution, widely welcomed by a war-weary proletariat, threw a new element into the debate. Leninism had been a marginal current in the Second International, but October brought it to the centre of the stage. The creation of the Communist International produced heated controversy throughout the European labour movement about the validity of the Bolshevik model of organisation and the concept of leadership it incarnated. (There was no single model of the 'Leninist' party; Lenin's organisational views varied sharply with the changing conjunctures between 1902 and 1917. But the Bolsheviks always insisted that spontaneity was not enough, and that the most consciously revolutionary elements in the working class must be drawn into a structured and disciplined party organisation.)

Subsequent events meant that the creative ferment of this decade became obscured, and its complexities and contradictions were lost to view. Russian Stalinism claimed that its monolithic authoritarianism was the legitimate inheritance of Leninism, a claim enthusiastically endorsed by anti-communist orthodoxy. Only a relatively small anti-Stalinist left resisted the Lenin = Stalin equation, and it did so largely at the price of taking a defensive and uncritical approach to the Leninist experience.

In attempting to recover what Bolshevik leadership meant in practice in the 1917–24 period, we have the valuable but often neglected testimony of two significant witnesses from the francophone left, Alfred Rosmer[1] and Victor Serge.[2] Both came from the anti-authoritarian left: Serge was an individualist anarchist, Rosmer a revolutionary syndicalist. Both wrote a considerable amount of journalism[3] revealing their positions at the time; both gave us important retrospective accounts of the revolutionary period (Serge 1967; Rosmer 1987). Both were enthusiastic partisans of the Revolution, and yet, because of the traditions they emerged from, both were reluctant Bolsheviks. It is that very reluctance which gives their testimony value, in their recognition both of the power of the Bolshevik model of leadership and of the problems and ambiguities it contained.

Before 1914

The French anti-authoritarian left before 1914 was diverse and riddled with opposing political currents (Maitron 1975). The term 'anti-authoritarian' (deriving from the antagonisms of the First International) is appropriate because what united anarchists and syndicalists of all varieties is that they saw the central opposition in society as being the principle of authority rather than the exploitation analysed by Marx. As Victor Serge was to write in a pamphlet of 1921, 'I can state it as axiomatic that *the exercise of authority is one of the most pernicious forms of the exploitation of man by man.* For whoever carries out the will of another is exploited by another. And in such a matter, use is inseparable from abuse' (Serge 1997a: 115).

This anti-authoritarianism had profound implications for political leadership. The primary target was the authority of state, capital and church, but there was great wariness of any exercise of authority within the movements of the oppressed – intellectuals and parliamentarians were regarded with especial suspicion. Moreover, since the anti-authoritarians rejected the Marxist view that linked social transformation to economic development, their view of revolutionary action was voluntaristic, and such leadership functions as were recognised were conceived in moralistic terms.

The writings of the young Victor Serge cast the anti-authoritarian position in its starkest form. All revolutionaries were the same – their slogan amounted to 'Get out of that position – so that I can take it over' (Serge 1989: 71). For Serge the leaders of the Socialist Party and of the CGT trade-union confederation, whether reformists or revolutionaries, were all lumped together as undeserving of trust (Serge 1989: 58–9, 182).

This distrust of all leaders and organisations led Serge to a strange abstentionism. At the time of the 1910 railway strike, he argued that anarchists should be indifferent to the outcome of the conflict: victory would merely confirm the 'working-class mentality' in its errors and dogmatism, while defeat would strengthen the state. Admittedly he went on to argue that anarchists should not stand aside but intervene with propaganda in words and deeds (Serge 1989: 117–19), though understandably he did not specify what such propaganda would be *about*. Indeed, Serge's wilder utterances from this period would undoubtedly have led most Marxists to write him off as a hopeless case.

Serge's rejection of leadership meant that he had little interest in the process of social change. He summarised the teachings of his hero, Albert Libertad: 'Don't wait for the revolution. Those who promise revolution are frauds just like the others. Make your own revolution, by being free men and living in comradeship' (Serge 1967: 19). Hence the anarchist creed became in essence a question of personal moral transformation: 'But if you want to be, not a leader, not an agitator, but simply a man; if you think that to command is as insane as bowing down to a master; if you take pride in asserting your individuality, don't ask the crowd to listen to you, and hope for nothing from it. Count on yourself, free Man, and perhaps on your fellows' (Serge 1989: 47).

Serge's thought at this stage was not authoritarian, but it was profoundly elitist. Anarchists did not give orders, but by their contemptuous rejection of the constraints of authority they proved their moral superiority and thus exercised a leadership role by setting an example to the rest of humanity. 'Let us go among the common people, sowing at random the seed of good revolts' (Serge 1989: 106). This elitist strand in Serge's thought has frequently been noted (Sedgwick 1984; Haberkern 1998a[4]). Despite the profound effects of changing circumstances, it never completely disappeared from his thought, and the insistence that political leadership must have a significant moral component was to remain a constant theme.

Although many syndicalists, like Rosmer, had emerged from the anarchist tradition, they did not share the fetishism of anti-authoritarianism. They worked within the CGT and saw the trade union as the organisation which, by means of the general strike, would abolish capitalism and establish an anti-authoritarian society.

The CGT was a structured organisation with leading committees and elected officials; these were far more acceptable than parliamentary representatives. While syndicalists rejected any kind of party organisation, the union itself was seen as a leadership for the class, since it contained only a minority of wage-earners. Pre-war membership of the CGT was around 300,000, and union militants were perceived as an 'active minority' (*minorité agissante*). In this way the syndicalists confronted one of the most potent arguments in favour of the need for revolutionary leadership, namely the unevenness of working-class consciousness, the fact that in most circumstances only a small minority of workers would hold revolutionary ideas, while the majority were steeped in reformism and liable to be swayed by openly reactionary ways of thought.

In 1909 two leading syndicalists, Emile Pataud and Emile Pouget, set out an imaginary account of the overthrow of capitalism in *How We Shall Bring About the Revolution* (Pataud and Pouget 1990). An army attack on workers led to a general strike, the dissolution of parliament and the taking over of all economic and social functions by the trade unions. A counter-revolutionary invasion was repulsed and all lived happily ever after.

The syndicalist approach to leadership was clearly revealed in this narrative. Although it was ostensibly a novel, with many references to real geographical locations, no named person appeared at any point of the narrative. The CGT played the leading role throughout, entirely through its existing structures; in other words, leadership was entirely unproblematic – the question of bureaucracy simply did not exist. Union members were shown as a minority, offering leadership to the rest of the class, and while there was a healthy ferment of argument, revolutionary ideas always came out on top. Government repression was in vain, because however many activists were arrested, there were always more to replace them.

Rosmer and the grouping around *La Vie ouvrière* did not go all the way with such naivety. While they had no intention of forming a party or a faction, they regarded the near-2,000 subscribers to the journal as a minority within a minority – a nucleus (*noyau*) which could raise the political and cultural level of union activists and develop a leadership cadre in the class (Rosmer 1951). Necessarily such a strategy had a strong moral component. It was in the pages of *La Vie ouvrière* that Albert Thierry had launched the concept of 'the refusal to make a career' (*le refus de parvenir*) (Gras 1971: 20). The leaders needed by the working class must reject the lure of authority and the trappings of leadership.

Rosmer was aware of the dangers of bureaucracy within the labour movement. In April 1913 he went to Belgium to report on the general strike called by the Belgian Workers' Party, affiliate of the Second International. He observed a situation in which the action caused more suffering to the striking workers than it did to the employers, whose vital interests were not hurt because of the conciliatory tactics of the labour leaders. His articles show an awareness that working-class leadership was far more problematic than Pataud and Pouget had imagined (Gras 1971: 47–8). Just how problematic was to be revealed the following year.

The First World War

The collapse of the international labour movement, and especially of French syndicalism in which he had such high hopes, was a traumatic turning-point in Rosmer's life. He has given us a powerful account of the terrible isolation in which the tiny handful of internationalists found themselves, as socialists and syndicalists flocked to support the war (Rosmer 1936: 96, 209–16).

In his efforts to respond to the new situation, Rosmer found himself faced with a major reconsideration of working-class leadership. Initially, as an internationalist, he felt profound disgust with the leaders who had betrayed their principles and identified 'the aims of socialism with the aims of the war' (Rosmer 1936: 8). But in going beyond revulsion to organisation, Rosmer encountered other aspects of the problem. In 1915 he circulated a statement to former subscribers to *La Vie ouvrière*, setting out the bases for opposition to the war. Here he denounced those French socialists who 'make all German workers unanimously responsible for the treachery of some of their leaders' (Rosmer 1936: 548). Only by establishing a clear distinction between the treacherous leadership (with the exception of a small minority such as Liebknecht) on the one hand, and the rank and file on the other, was it possible to argue for proletarian internationalism.

The war opened up Rosmer's knowledge of the European working-class movement. As a syndicalist he had been deeply sceptical of the socialists in the Second International, but the war brought together the minority of oppositionists from both camps. He worked closely with a group of Russians who produced a daily paper, *Nashe Slovo*, in Paris – not only Trotsky, but Lunacharsky, Lozovsky, Radek, Rakovsky and others, who were to become leading Bolsheviks and play an important role in Russia during and after the Revolution (Rosmer 1936: 244–9). In his agitation in support of Zimmerwald,[5] Rosmer became aware of the positions of Lenin, hitherto an unknown figure in syndicalist circles (Gras 1971: 160). From such encounters emerged the perspective of struggle for a new leadership in the international working-class movement.

Twenty years later Rosmer set out his considered analysis of the crisis of leadership in 1914. He demarcated himself clearly from those who saw events in simplistic terms of betrayal – what he called the 'pedants' who saw the 'masses' as 'troops impatient to go into action'; he reminded them that at the beginning of the war it had been the masses who were chanting 'Up With War! To Berlin!'. The rank and file were susceptible to the pressures of press and government because they had been 'abandoned by their leaders'; but at the same time those leaders were able to use the elements of spontaneous chauvinism among the masses to justify their own refusal to stand up against the war (Rosmer 1936: 475–6). This awareness of the interaction between leadership and masses, which must have germinated in Rosmer's mind during the early days of the war, was to be crucial in preparing his response to the Russian Revolution.

Serge, in jail until 1917, did not feel the impact of the war so directly. Prison afforded him time to think; and during his five years of incarceration he began to reconsider his political stance. In a letter written just after leaving jail he expressed some scepticism as to the 'anarchist ideal' (Maitron

1964: 57). But it was his experiences in Spain that drew Serge towards an understanding of working-class leadership. As he recounts in his novel *Birth of Our Power*, he saw how the 'active minority' of syndicalists could mobilise their fellows: 'at the call of a union of about a hundred comrades, thousands, perhaps tens of thousands of workers would be there, in the street, at our side' (Serge 1970: 64).

In this new view there were still traces of the anarchist view of the moral elite, but now that elite aimed to have a direct impact on the masses, rather than rising disdainfully above them. In words he attributed to a Spanish comrade: '*Our* job is to give a good shove to that first big stone that will perhaps bring on the avalanche' (Serge 1970: 94). Later, in a French concentration camp, Serge had his first encounter with a Bolshevik, arguing vehemently in favour of 'libertarian' as against 'authoritarian' revolution (Serge 1967: 63–4). His ideas were still very much in a process of change when he finally made his way to Russia.

The Comintern

Serge was the first of the two to arrive in Russia, in February 1919. The realities of civil war and the dictatorship of the proletariat contrasted sharply with his preconceived images of revolution. In *Birth of Our Power* he evoked the sense of surprise:

> In a few hours, we had learned more about the revolution than in many long meditations. And it had appeared to us under aspects very different from those suggested by our imagination, shaped by legend and by history, which is very close to legend. We had been thinking of the squares transformed into tumultuous forums, of the excited clubs of '92; of the blossoming of many little journals, each crying out its own solution, its system, its fantasy; of the great 'days' of the Soviets, like Conventions. In the language, in the slogans posted everywhere, in the only two newspapers published, among the men, we discovered one enormous uniformity of a single way of thinking, imperious, almost despotic, but supreme, terribly true, made flesh and blood at each moment through action. We found not the passionate mobs going forward under new flags to struggles begun anew each day in tragic and fruitful confusions, but a sort of vast administration, an army, a machine in which the most burning energies and the clearest intelligences were coldly integrated and which performed its task inexorably. (Serge 1970: 230)

Clearly all ideas about the nature of revolutionary leadership would have to be reconsidered radically.

Serge arrived in Russia at the height of the civil war. Twice in 1919 Petrograd was under attack from the counter-revolutionary armies of Yudenich. Serge described these events in two short pamphlets he wrote for French readers, *During the Civil War* and *The Endangered City* (Serge 1997a). Here he showed how the need for revolutionary terror had grown out of the necessities of the situation, rather than from the leadership's desire for power.

In his accounts of the early phase of the Revolution, Serge revealed just how far he had moved from his youthful anarchism. The leading role of the Bolshevik Party was shown as essential; indeed, the party was perceived as an organic part of the class's development: 'The party is the nervous system of the working class, its brain'. And he also stressed the importance of leadership within the party's own structure: 'The leaders and the key members perform the role of brain and nervous system within the organism of the party also'. For the rank and file of the party were unable to see the situation as a whole, and must therefore depend on the 'core of party members who have been selected and tried by long years of struggle and work, enjoy the goodwill of the movement as a whole, have access to the apparatus of the party, and are accustomed to thinking and working collectively' (Serge 1992: 57–8).

In his 1925 pamphlet on Lenin, Serge applied the same approach. Lenin was the 'organiser and the brains' of the October Revolution, but Serge insisted on the qualities that made Lenin able to play this role: first of all, 'a remarkable insight into the masses' state of mind', what Serge termed his 'clear-sighted Jacobinism' (Serge 1994: 18, 40). Hence Lenin was able to operate, not by authority, but by persuasion: 'the good faith of the masses is obvious; and it is by persuasion that they can be won' (Serge 1994: 10).

This interaction of leadership and class is a recurrent theme in Serge's writings on this period: 'The role of the proletariat's true leaders is crucial precisely because they cannot be replaced. Personal merit, authority, influence, all are historical products formed by the working class with the assistance of time and of the events for which nothing can substitute.' And just as the class produced the party, so the party produced Lenin: 'it is the party that makes the leader, for without the party there can be no leader' (Serge 1992: 287, 61).

In Serge's account of Lenin and the Bolsheviks, the party is the brain of the class, and a brain without body is as useless as a body without brain. The organic metaphor has deep roots in conservative thought, yet Serge showed that the relation of party and class was not some mystical bond, but was mediated through the institutions of the Soviet state:

> The dictatorship of the proletariat is not the dictatorship of a party, or of a central committee, or of certain individuals. Its mechanism is complex. Each Soviet, each revolutionary committee, each committee of the Bolshevik Party or the Left SR party holds a portion of it and operates it after its own fashion. Lenin himself is obliged to follow strict rules. He has to convince a majority in the central committee of his party, then discuss with the Communist fraction in the *Vee-Tsik* [All-Russian Executive Committee of Soviets] and then, in the *Vee-Tsik* itself, brave the fire of the Left SRs, anarchists and International Social Democrats, all doubtful allies, and of the Right SRs and Mensheviks, irreduc-

ible enemies. All the decrees are debated during sessions which are often of tremendous interest. Here the enemies of the regime enjoy free speech with a more than parliamentary latitude. (Serge 1992: 245)

This was a somewhat rosy portrayal of a state of affairs not destined to last for long. But it revealed Serge's positive evaluation of the Bolshevik experience, a leadership which could be both vigorous and stern, but was deeply rooted in the masses, what has been described as 'libertarian Leninism' (Spencer 1997).

Serge had not, however, completely broken with the ideas of his youth. An important aspect of the Bolsheviks' leading role lay in their moral qualities; time and again he referred to the moral superiority of the Bolshevik forces at the time of the civil war: 'at certain moments one is profoundly aware that in the whole vast expanse of Russia, these men are the only ones in whom moral force resides' (Serge, 1997a: 58). The relation of trust and understanding between the Leninist leadership and the rank and file could be understood only in terms of the moral integrity of that leadership. This moral superiority enabled Lenin and his comrades to withstand the constant lies and slanders thrown against them. Serge reported the response of one of his Spanish comrades when accusations were made that the Bolsheviks were being financed by the Germans. '"Taking money," says Dario, "being incorruptible ... What is the point of being incorruptible if you don't take the money?"' (Serge 1970: 90).[6]

In stressing the moral dimension of leadership Serge was using a language which would have been foreign to the Bolsheviks themselves. Yet it enabled him to identify one of the great weaknesses of Bolshevism. Paradoxically, Serge, the former anarchist, pointed out that one of the major problems for the Russian Revolution, and even more so for the Communist International, was a shortage of leaders. Tsarist repression had meant that the Bolsheviks were relatively few in numbers, and of these all too many, the best and the bravest, perished in the civil war. In the rest of Europe, where the task of building communist parties had to begin from scratch after the betrayals of the established leadership in 1914, the problem was even more acute.[7]

Serge saw in this shortage of leadership the roots of the abuses of power that grew up from the earliest days of the Revolution:

Following the seizure of power, the proletariat, called to tasks without number, firstly resolves the more important: food supplies, city organisation, external and internal defence, the inventory of expropriated goods, the seizure of wealth. It devotes its best forces to them. Revolutionary repression – and this is a cause of mistakes and abuses – is left only with second-rate personnel ... (Serge 1979: 75)

Even though the party had taken care that the Cheka (Special Commission for the Repression of Counter-Revolution, Speculation, Espionage and

Desertion) should be headed by 'incorruptible men' like Dzerzhinsky, 'a sincere idealist', the shortage of leaders was felt here with disastrous results:

> The Party had few men of this stamp and many Chekas: these gradually came to select their personnel by virtue of their psychological inclinations. The only temperaments that devoted themselves willingly and tenaciously to this task of 'internal defence' were those characterized by suspicion, embitterment, harshness, and sadism. (Serge 1967: 80)

Serge was dealing with only one aspect of the complex question of revolutionary terror and its degeneration, but it is an important insight.

When it came to the Communist International, the sole hope for spreading the revolution before it perished, Serge was even more scathing in his judgements. 'To tell the truth, outside Russia and perhaps Bulgaria, there were no real communists anywhere in the world.' When he arrived in Germany in 1922, he observed that 'the editorial staff of *Inprekorr*, the intellectual and political mentor of the world Communist movement, was of an outstanding mediocrity' (Serge 1967: 104, 162).

Rosmer came to Russia later than Serge, and in very different circumstances. Serge had been an unknown individual who joined the party and was given numerous responsibilities when his talents were recognised. Rosmer had long been a supporter of the Bolshevik Revolution; he arrived in Moscow in the summer of 1920 as part of the French delegation to the Second Congress of the Communist International. Though he had no personal ambitions, he was being groomed for leadership in the French Communist Party, and for an international role in helping to draw the revolutionary syndicalists towards communism.

Nonetheless, the discovery of revolutionary Russia held some surprises for Rosmer. The actual problems of the transition to socialism revealed the inadequacies of previous theoretical speculation on the question. Recalling Pataud and Pouget's scenario, he noted: 'this was the realm of fairy-tales. In Moscow, in 1920, we were facing reality' (Rosmer 1987: 71).

Rosmer's thoughts on leadership in post-revolutionary Russia coincided to a considerable extent with those of Serge. He too saw the essence of revolutionary leadership in the interaction between leaders and the revolutionary process. Lenin and Trotsky were not simply outstanding individuals; 'the revolution had made them greater as it had made all the militants greater'. He went on to observe that when he met some of the *Nashe Slovo* group he had already known in Paris, he could see how *émigré* politicians had been transformed by the experience of revolution:

> The most typical case in this respect was Dridzo-Lozovsky. I had seen a lot of him in Paris; he had always been a good comrade, devoted and serious. That he was not of the greatest stature or of a steady character was to be shown by events after 1924. But in Moscow in 1920 I observed in him an air of assur-

ance, of self-confidence, decisiveness and certainty which were new features as far as he was concerned. (Rosmer 1987: 70)

His account of his first meeting with Lenin presents a man quite unrecognisable in terms of the caricatures of Stalinism and Cold War anti-communism. Here was a leader who exercised his authority, not through orders, but by listening, learning, and correcting his own mistakes:

> One remark he made suddenly revealed to me the secret of the exceptional position he held in his party, and of the predominant influence he had got there. As we were talking about the Zimmerwaldian minority in the French Socialist Party, he said to me: 'It's time for them to leave the Party now to form the French Communist Party; they've waited too long already.' I replied that this was not the view of the leaders of the minority. Previously they had sometimes been impatient to leave the Party *en bloc*, but the recent Strassburg conference had been so favourable that they were now opposed to the idea of leaving. They had hopes of becoming the majority quite soon. 'If that's the case,' he said, 'I must have written something stupid in my theses. Ask for a copy of them at the secretariat of the Communist International and send me the corrections you are proposing.' (Rosmer 1987: 53)

Rosmer, who before 1914 had been vehemently opposed to all party organisation, had made a major reconsideration of his position by accepting a leading role in the Communist International. Yet his role there was precisely to facilitate dialogue between the Bolsheviks and the revolutionary syndicalists, especially those from Britain, Spain and France, where syndicalism had attracted many of the best working-class militants. The tone of the debates at the Second Congress was conciliatory; Lenin and Trotsky in particular stressed what Bolshevism and syndicalism had in common. Lenin, replying to the British syndicalist shop steward Jack Tanner, argued that the difference was largely verbal; what the syndicalists called the 'active minority', the Bolsheviks called the party. Trotsky insisted that he had more in common with syndicalists who rejected party organisation but sincerely wanted to destroy the bourgeoisie, than he had with treacherous social democrats like Scheidemann, who defended party organisation (Rosmer 1987: 80–4).

Like Serge, Rosmer noted that competent leaders were in short supply: 'the overriding fact is that there was a shortage of men.[8] The war had wrought havoc among the best, and those who remained could not do everything, despite the long exhausting days they worked' (Rosmer 1987: 109).

Leadership in practice

Rosmer and Serge held Lenin and Trotsky in the highest esteem; but they recognised that revolutionary leadership was not a question of great individuals, but rather of a whole social category, the activists who took the initiative in any struggle or organisation. In his 1930 pamphlet *The Life of Revolutionaries* Serge gave a series of brief sketches of some of the unknown figures who had made the Russian Revolution – workers, intellectuals, women, youth, etc. – in order to demonstrate that the Revolution had not been made by a handful of Bolshevik conspirators, but rather by thousands of dedicated individuals who had taken the lead on the various fronts of the Revolution, in many cases sacrificing their lives (Serge 1961).

The same emphasis came through Serge's articles from Germany in 1922–23. Amid a potential revolutionary situation, Serge wrote regularly for the Comintern press under the pseudonym of R. Albert (Serge 1990[9]). Much of what has been written on the lost German revolution of 1923 has focused on the leadership of the German Communist Party and its relations with Moscow (Broué 1997: 293–330). Serge, writing for the public press, had nothing to say of behind-the-scenes manoeuvres, but concentrated on how leadership operated at the base of the party. He described a group of comrades discussing matters in the autumn of 1923. After some intellectuals had expressed doubts as to the outcome of the situation, a district organiser spoke up saying: 'I believe in the revolution, because I want it; because I live among people who want it' (Serge 1990: 188). As in Russia, it was these anonymous activists who made up the party, and whose strengths and weaknesses determined the outcome of events at least as much as telegrams from Moscow.

Beyond this there was the battle for leadership on the streets. Unemployment and unheated homes drove workers onto the streets; often they congregated outside newsagents' shops where they read the papers they could not afford to buy. Here was a ferment of political debate. 'The cold, unlit house with no bread is uninhabitable. They go out onto the street, gather in groups, wander aimlessly, listen to the nationalist agitator, read the anti-Semitic leaflet that is being given out ...' (Albert 1923: 460).

This was the struggle for leadership in concrete terms. As Serge reported, where there was effective intervention, the Communists could win: 'All day, until midnight, at busy cross-roads, groups of men are discussing. The unemployed. I've often listened to their discussions: the Communist, the Social Democrat and the National Socialist are usually all there; and the Communist has the best of the argument' (Serge 1990: 126).

For Rosmer the question of rank-and-file leadership was posed above all in relation to work in the trade unions. In preparing the foundation of the Red International of Labour Unions (RILU), Rosmer had to deal with the legitimate anxieties of the revolutionary syndicalists, who feared that by aligning themselves with the Communist International they would run the risk of seeing the unions transformed into mere subsidiary organisations under the control of the communist parties. In his speech to the founding congress of the RILU Rosmer defended the political role of the communist parties, but at the same time rejected the Second International model whereby the unions were subordinated to the political parties and confined to purely economic questions:

> The party is the soul of the working class. I do not mean to say thereby, that the trade unions should be subordinated to it. Absolutely not. The party must show a particular willingness to meet the unions halfway. The unions must serve as a point of support to the party in the realisation of socialism. Here there are no second-class 'comrades', and we cannot tolerate any arrogance by one group of fighters towards another. The syndicalists are just as good communists as we are. We must, however, vigorously reject what has been called 'the theory of the equality of the parties who are in agreement'. This theory does not correspond to the truth. This is the direct legacy of the decrepit, thoroughly rotten and mendacious Second International, whose principle was as follows: 'You shall concern yourself with political matters and we with economic matters; don't stick your nose in our affairs and we won't worry about yours'. No. We must tear this theory out by the roots from the consciousness of politically aware workers. (Rosmer 2000: 8–9)

Rosmer rejected the idea that politics should be excluded from the trade unions, something patently absurd in a potentially revolutionary situation. At the same time he made it clear that the unions must not be bureaucratically manipulated by communist parties. It was the job of communists to fight within the unions for their positions and to win support by persuasion. He invoked the example of the Russian Communist Party before the revolution:

> Its members had to be in the front ranks of those fighting for the proletariat, wherever that struggle might be. They had to permeate all the labour organisations. Its members strove to achieve the dominant influence in the unions, and their claim to do so was completely justified and normal.
>   The representatives of various tendencies, movements and parties, the different groupings fighting inside the unions, all make efforts to win a dominating influence. That is perfectly justified and acceptable.[10] (Rosmer 2000: 9)

The contradictions of leadership

Serge and Rosmer were both unambiguous partisans of the Bolshevik Revolution and of the Leninist style of leadership. Precisely because of this, they were highly sensitive to dangers within. Both observed that alongside Lenin's style of leadership, based on patient persuasion and constant interaction with the rank and file, a quite different sort of leadership was being practised within the Bolshevik Party and the International, one based on manipulation, bureaucratic manoeuvres and ultimately on that very principle of authority which both men had rejected in their youth. As Rosmer put it:

> Even before Lenin died a split had occurred inside the leadership of the Communist Party. On one side were the men who wanted to continue his work,

to maintain his policy of free discussion inside the party, of revolutionary audacity with the possibility of mistakes which could be corrected. On the other side were those who claimed that such a policy was no longer possible, that it involved too many risks, in short that it was too difficult. (Rosmer 1987: 251)

Discussing theses drafted by the Bolshevik Radek for the Second Congress of the Comintern, Rosmer noted that their style was such that they 'could not convince, only provoke' (Rosmer 1987: 87). The antinomy encapsulates the two approaches to leadership current in the International.

In the Comintern sections outside Russia, where the traditions of the Bolshevik Party did not exist, the situation was even worse. Serge in Germany noted the presence of what he called 'the Communist N.C.O. type, neither a blockhead nor a thinker: obedient only'. With such leadership 'corruption, servility, intrigue, backstage tale-bearing, and the official mentality began to assume an increasing role in the functioning of the International' (Serge 1967: 162, 166).

Manipulative leadership practices had existed in the Comintern from the beginning, and anti-communist historians have been able to make great play of them. But it was only when the revolutionary wave began to subside that they became dominant. Serge quotes a remark by Georg Lukács which effectively summarised the relation between leadership style and historical context: 'Marxists know that dirty little tricks can be performed with impunity when great deeds are being achieved; the error of some comrades is to suppose that one can produce great results simply through the performance of dirty little tricks ...' (Serge 1967: 186).

If the antithesis to Lenin's leadership methods had to be summed up in a single name, that name was Zinoviev. From his first encounter, Serge noted the weaknesses of Zinoviev's character, his vanity, irresolution and demagogy. But after Lenin's death and the failure of the German Revolution, Zinoviev showed the full dangers of bureaucratic ultra-left leadership:

> He refused to acknowledge the German defeat. In his eyes the rising had been only delayed and the K.P.D. [German Communist Party] was still marching to power ... I felt that he was obsessed by the error in his otherwise sensible judgement which had led him in 1917 to oppose the incipient Bolshevik Revolution; in consequence, he had now swung into an authoritarian and exaggerated revolutionary optimism. 'Zinoviev,' we used to say, 'is Lenin's biggest mistake.' (Serge 1967: 177)

Serge's account leaves many questions unanswered. Zinoviev had been a Bolshevik since 1903, and his methods had roots in the complex and contradictory history of Bolshevism. Nor will it do to blame Lenin, hard-pressed for able assistants, for letting Zinoviev hold positions of power for which he was not fit. But, for Serge, if Lenin represented what was best in Bolshevism, Zinoviev represented what was worst.

Rosmer concurred in this negative judgement of Zinoviev's methods of leadership. He had already clashed with Zinoviev in 1920; when it was decided to address an appeal to the reformist Amsterdam International Federation of Trade Unions, 'Zinoviev merely let fly a broadside of insults, often in pretty bad taste, against "Messrs. Scab leaders", etc.', showing total ignorance of the labour movement and the principles of united front activity (Rosmer 1987: 97).

In *Lenin's Moscow* Rosmer quoted in an appendix Lenin's last speech to the Communist International, in which he stressed the need for communists in every country to study reality rather than simply imitating Russian models (Rosmer 1987: 242–4; Lenin 1966). Zinoviev's 'Bolshevisation' (which led to Rosmer's expulsion from the French Communist Party) was the exact opposite of this approach. In an article written in 1926 Rosmer summed up the damage he believed that Zinoviev had done to the International:

> Zinoviev is the supreme demagogue, incapable of any constructive effort or of any organisational work. When the history of the Comintern is written, it will be seen that he bears the main responsibility for the lamentable way it has worked. Not up to his job, he is always careful to surround himself with mediocrities, for fear of being eclipsed and ... replaced. It was he who aroused and maintained for so long the distrust of syndicalists and serious militants with regard to the Comintern, by the way he shouted his mouth off in speeches marked equally by the absence of ideas and the triviality of form, revealing total failure to understand the labour movement in Europe.[11] (Rosmer 1926: 1–2)

Conclusion

Zinoviev paved the way for Stalin. In his *Portrait of Stalin* Serge showed the final stage of a style of leadership based on authority, distrust and manipulation: '[Stalin] is afraid for the system whose extraordinary fragility he is aware of. Afraid of the lies he reads in every eye. Afraid of the ghosts which his fear gives birth to ... When he passes the elite guard from the special detachment who is watching his door – and whose predecessors have been shot, as a precaution – he must be expecting a bullet in the back of his head' (Serge 1940: 182).

The distrust of authority that Serge and Rosmer learnt in their early years ensured that they never fell into the trap of confusing Stalinism with any kind of socialism. Both remained intransigent anti-Stalinists till the day they died. But both, in their writings, bore witness to what the Russian Revolution had been and what model of leadership it had represented.

Serge wrote in the year he died: 'So many changes have taken place in this chaotic world that no single Marxist – or for that matter socialist – idea which was valid in 1920 could be applied in practice without essential adjustments to bring it up to date' (Serge 1997b: 256). History does not repeat itself; all revolutions are surprises. Rosmer and Serge survived their surprise at the Bolshevik Revolution and went on to provide a model account of how revolutionaries learn from history.

The account of Bolshevik leadership contained in their works diverges so sharply from the dominant orthodoxy that many will naturally be sceptical of it. Yet it is worth remembering that neither sought to pursue a political career after the triumph of Stalinism; both remained, often at considerable personal cost, independent historians and commentators with no factional axe to grind, merely an overriding concern to see that the truth was not buried for ever by the apologists of Washington and Moscow.

In their writings Serge and Rosmer show how a generation of anti-authoritarian revolutionaries encountered Bolshevism; how they put their ideas to the test of reality and revised them where necessary; yet how they found in the Leninist model much of what was best in their own traditions. They discovered that revolutions create leaders rather than leaders creating revolutions, and that effective leadership must listen to and learn from those it aspires to lead. Their testimony deserves to survive and be studied.

Notes

1   Alfred Griot (1877–1964) (known as Alfred Rosmer) was born in New York, but came to France in 1884. After an initial period of anarchism, he became associated with Pierre Monatte on the syndicalist journal *La Vie ouvrière*. One of the few to oppose the First World War from the first day, he became a fervent supporter of the Russian Revolution. From 1920 to 1924 he held leading positions in the Comintern, the Red International of Labour Unions and the French Communist Party, but in 1924 he was expelled from the Communist Party. He was briefly involved in the early Trotskyist movement, but broke with it politically, while remaining a lifelong friend of Trotsky. He remained an intransigent revolutionary, and devoted the rest of his life to writing, mainly to producing a historical record of the 1914–24 period.

2   Victor Kibalchich (1890–1947) (known as Victor Serge) was born in Brussels. He moved to Paris and became involved in the anarchist movement; he was jailed for five years for defending the anarchist bank robbers of the Bonnot Gang. He took part in the Barcelona insurrection of 1917 before going to Russia, where he became a communist and played an active role in the Comintern, both in Russia and Central Europe. He became a supporter of the Left Opposition, was sent into internal exile and then expelled to the West. With the Nazi occupation of France he took refuge in Mexico where he died in 1947. He broke with organised Trotskyism, but remained a fierce left critic of Stalinism, both in his political writings and in the novels which he wrote in the latter part of his life.

3   There is a selection of Rosmer's political writings from all stages of his career in *Revolutionary History*, 7, 4 (2000).

4   See also the ensuing debate between Haberkern and the present author in Birchall 1998; Haberkern 1998b; Birchall 1999; Haberkern 1999.

5 Zimmerwald was the first international meeting of socialists and trade unionists opposed to the First World War. It was held in Switzerland in September
1915.

6 The term 'incorruptible' had obvious echoes of Robespierre. Time and again in
his writings on the early years of the Revolution, Serge drew parallels with the
French Revolution, and saw the Bolsheviks as the direct heirs of the Jacobins
(Serge 1997a: 50).

7 For a discussion of this problem of the shortage of leadership, see Cliff 1978
and Birchall 2000.

8 Rosmer's use of the term was not gender-specific; in fact he went on to recall
the valuable assistance with translation given by a Menshevik woman, a striking example of the way in which shortage of personnel required the Bolsheviks
to give positions of responsibility to their political opponents (Rosmer 1987:
110).

9 An English translation with additional material not included in the French
volume was published by Redwords in 2000 under the title *Witness to the
German Revolution*.

10 Rosmer's position therefore coincides with the position on trade union work
adopted by the Third Congress of the Communist International:

> The best measure of the strength of any Communist Party is the
> influence it really exercises over the working masses in the trade
> unions. *The party must learn to exercise decisive influence in the
> unions without subjecting them to petty control.* It is the union
> cell, not the union as such, which is under the authority of the
> party. It is only by patient, devoted, and intelligent work by the
> cells in the unions that the party will be able to bring about a state
> of affairs in which the unions as a whole will readily and joyfully
> follow party advice. (Degras 1971: 277)

11 Ironically, Rosmer went on to argue that 'Stalin is a man of very different
quality. His temperament and determination are those of a revolutionary'
(Rosmer 1926: 2).

4

Leadership, political opportunities and organisational identity in the French anti-racist movement[1]

Robert Gibb

Introduction

This chapter examines the relationship between leadership, political opportunities and organisational identity in the French anti-racist movement. In the first section, I argue that the 1993 legislative elections altered the political opportunity structure for social movements in France by bringing about a significant change in the configuration of power on the left. I show, in particular, how an opportunity subsequently arose for the president of the anti-racist organisation SOS-Racisme to participate in the formal political process, through an invitation from a centre-left party to stand as a candidate on its list for the 1994 European elections. This proposal was debated by SOS-Racisme's National Council at a special meeting held in Paris in April 1994. The chapter's second section analyses in detail the action of SOS-Racisme's president before and during the meeting, discussing it in terms of the Italian sociologist Alberto Melucci's (1996) recent analysis of the role of leadership in social movements. In the third section I suggest more generally that the exchanges which took place at this meeting revealed important differences between the leadership and grassroots activists, both in the assessment of political opportunities and in the definition of the nature and identity of the organisation itself. The chapter then concludes by reviewing the implications of this episode for the development of future leadership strategies within the French anti-racist movement.

The specific arguments advanced in this chapter are informed by two more general theoretical assumptions. The first is that the study of leadership involves an examination of two types of relationship: on the one hand, that between 'leaders' and 'followers' (Edinger 1967: 15); and, on the other, that between 'human agency', the purposive activity of individual leaders (and their followers), and 'political structure', the opportunities and constraints which shape such action (Cole 1997: 166). The second, and related, premise is that analysis of political opportunity structures must take into account not only 'objective' factors, such as the nature of the electoral system, but also the ways in which different actors *perceive* the political opportunities available to them (Tarrow 1988: 430). Leaders and grassroots members of social movement organisations, for example, do not always share the same perception of the potential costs and benefits of a particular course of action. As in the case considered here, fundamental differences in the evaluation of political opportunities may exist which threaten to undermine organisational unity and the legitimacy of a leader's position.

Changing political opportunities for anti-racism in France

One of the most important developments in the field of social movements research over the past two decades has been the steady growth of interest in the politics of collective action. This has led researchers to focus increasingly on the role of social movements in the political process. Indeed, much recent work has centred on the relationship between social movements and the state, parties and other more institutionalised forms of political action (Buechler 2000: 163–83). In particular, there has been a widespread concern to identify and compare the ways in which different political systems constrain or provide openings for social movement activity (Tarrow 1988, 1994).

The concept of 'political opportunity structure' has proved a useful tool for analysing the influence of political and institutional factors on the emergence and development of social movements (see Della Porta and Diani 1999: 9). Theorists have usually defined the concept in terms of a number of distinct variables. Kriesi (1995), for example, has used the notion of political opportunity structure to refer to the formal institutional structure of a state (including the degree of centralisation and concentration of power), the procedures and strategies employed by authorities to exclude or integrate external demands, and the configuration of power within and between political parties. This conceptualisation of political opportunity structure has provided the framework for a recent comparative analysis of the relationship between political systems and social movements in Western Europe (Kriesi *et al.* 1995).

An overview of the main features of the political and institutional context (the 'political opportunity structure') in France in 1993–94 provides a useful framework for discussing the events described in the present chapter. The 1993 French legislative elections transformed the third aspect of the political opportunity structure highlighted by Kriesi and his colleagues: the distribution of power amongst political parties, particularly those on the left. In May 1988, François Mitterrand was re-elected as President of the Republic and this was followed a month later by a Socialist victory at the legislative elections, albeit 13 seats short of an overall majority. Over the next few years, however, the Socialist government's popularity declined dramatically as a result of a series of scandals, public displays of internal party rivalry and a widely perceived failure to tackle rising unemployment (Machin 1993: 599). This culminated in a crushing defeat for the Socialists at the March 1993 legislative elections. The Socialist vote was halved (to 17.62 per cent of votes cast), with the party's parliamentary representation reduced from 276 to only 70 deputies. The electoral system ensured that with 44 per cent of the vote, the centre-right RPR-UDF coalition took 80 per cent of the seats (Hanley 1993).

The Socialists' disastrous results at the 1993 elections added fuel to the debate about the future of the party and its links with other progressive forces which former Prime Minister Michel Rocard had launched in the run-up to the poll (Hanley 1993: 420). Arguments about 'the reconstruction of the left' continued throughout the campaign for the 1994 European elections. A significant development, in this regard, was the decision by a centre-left party, the Movement of Left Radicals (MRG), to present its own list of candidates for the European elections rather than ally itself with the Socialists as it had done on previous occasions. The MRG list, entitled 'Radical Energy', was headed by Bernard Tapie, the popular, if somewhat controversial businessman and president of the football team L'Olympique de Marseille (OM). Tapie had entered politics in 1988, when he was elected as a deputy in the Bouches-du-Rhône *département* (comprising the area around Marseilles). He subsequently held a ministerial post, albeit briefly, in the 1992 Socialist government, prior to joining the MRG in the spring of 1993 (see Bouchet 1992, 1994). Shortly before campaigning for the European elections opened, Tapie was placed under investigation on charges of corruption, and although these eventually led to his imprisonment (*Libération*, 5 February 1997), nothing officially prevented him from standing for the European Parliament in 1994.

The announcement that Tapie would head a separate MRG list for the European elections provoked intense political argument in France. There was widespread speculation that the President of the Republic, François Mitterrand, was acting behind the scenes to promote Tapie, as a way of 'torpedo-ing' the presidential ambitions of his long-term rival within the Socialist Party, Michel Rocard (*Le Nouvel Observateur*, 28 April – 4 May 1994; *Libération*, 29 April 1994). The MRG stated publicly that its aim was 'to facilitate the emergence of a "reformist pole", independent of the Socialist Party, before the 1995 presidential election' (*Le Monde*, 3 May 1994). In line with this, Tapie actively sought to win over prominent left-wing figures to the MRG, inviting them to stand as candidates on its list for the European elections. Among those who accepted were a former Socialist minister, an Ecologist, a leading feminist and a trade unionist (Buffotot and Hanley 1995: 3).

One key figure whom Tapie was, however, unable to rally to the 'Radical Energy' list was Fodé Sylla, the president of the anti-racist association SOS-Racisme.[2] Sylla subsequently confirmed that Tapie approached him on 11

April 1994 with the offer of a place on the MRG's list of candidates for the June elections (*L'Événement du jeudi*, 12–18 May 1994). The association's executive committee or National Bureau discussed Tapie's proposal at a meeting in Paris on 27 April 1994; its members were reported as being generally favourable to the idea (*Le Monde*, 29 April 1994). A meeting of SOS-Racisme's National Council was then called. This comprises representatives from the association's committees all over France and is its ultimate decision-making body.

On 29 April 1994, members of the National Council duly assembled in an amphitheatre at the University of Jussieu in central Paris to consider whether Sylla should accept Tapie's invitation. It quickly became apparent that an important section of the membership was extremely hostile to the proposal. Indeed, even before the meeting took place, the association's Parisian headquarters had received telephone calls from provincial activists, voicing their opposition to Tapie's offer and, in some cases, threatening to leave SOS-Racisme altogether were it to be accepted. The National Council debate provided further evidence of significant divisions within the association. In particular, it highlighted major differences between part of the leadership (*direction*) of SOS-Racisme and many grassroots activists in relation to the perception of political opportunities, the definition of organisational identity and the conception of the nature of the leadership role in a social movement organisation. The chapter's next two sections discuss these disagreements and show how, in order to avoid provoking the departure of a large number of activists, the leadership was forced to reject the offer of a place on Tapie's list for the 1994 European elections.

Tensions and contradictions in leadership action

Thus far, I have described how moves to reconfigure the French left in the wake of the 1993 legislative elections created an opportunity for members of certain progressive movements, including the president of the social movement organisation SOS-Racisme, to participate in the formal political process. In Kriesi's terms, changes in the political opportunity structure temporarily made the French state less 'closed' to social movements by increasing, albeit partially, formal access to the party system. It is interesting to note here that a similar series of events occurred during the campaign for the 1989 European elections. On that occasion, the incumbent president of SOS-Racisme, Harlem Désir, was offered the fifth place on the Green Party's list of candidates. This was rejected by Désir on the grounds that he intended to constitute his own 'autonomous' slate for the elections (*Le Monde*, 31 March 1989).

Although the idea of a separate list was later abandoned, it reflected the leadership of SOS-Racisme's growing sense of frustration with the apparent imperviousness of the French public administration and party systems to

external pressure from social movements. Angered in particular by the failure of the Socialist Party, with which the association has always had close
links, to act on its recommendations concerning immigration and
intégration policies, Désir asked in 1990: 'Is the creation of a political party
the only means we have left of making our voice heard?' (*Politis*, 26 April
1990). The launch of a new political organisation did indeed subsequently
appear to Désir and other members of SOS-Racisme's leadership as the most
effective way to overcome the state's perceived unresponsiveness to the association's actions (*Le Monde*, 17 June 1992).

The proposed constitution of an independent list for the 1989 European
elections and the creation of a new political movement in 1992 can both be
interpreted as attempts by SOS-Racisme's leadership to maximise the association's 'means for action' (Melucci 1996: 339). This, as Melucci has
explained, is a key aspect of the leadership role in social movements (see
below). Confronted with a situation in which SOS-Racisme's capacity, as an
association, to influence the political process appeared extremely restricted,
its leadership engaged in a search for additional ways of accessing and having an impact upon the political system. As I shall now argue, the favourable
reaction of many members of SOS-Racisme's National Bureau to Tapie's
offer of a place on his list of candidates for the 1994 European elections
reflected a similar preoccupation.

The rest of this section draws on Melucci's (1996) recent work on leadership in social movements in order to begin to analyse the exchanges between
leaders and grassroots members at SOS-Racisme's National Council meeting
in April 1994. Although Melucci's analysis of the leadership role is open to a
number of objections – one of which is that he does not clearly distinguish
between leadership of 'movements', 'groups' and 'organisations' (see
Melucci 1996: 339–40) – it does provide a useful framework for the material
presented here. In the following section, I focus specifically on the competing
tasks which leaders of social movement organisations like SOS-Racisme
inevitably face and how their own legitimacy can be called into question,
depending on how they make a decision or respond to particular needs on
the part of the membership. Building on this, the final section presents a
more general discussion of how leaders and followers within SOS-Racisme
debated political opportunities and organisational identity at the meeting.

According to Melucci, the leaders of social movements typically perform
five main tasks (see Melucci 1996: 339–40). First, they define the movement's objectives; these can be of two kinds, either general (ultimate or long-
term goals) or specific (more immediate aims or means to the general ones).
In Melucci's view, leaders play an important role in adapting such objectives
to take account of changes not only within the movement itself but also in
the wider society. A second component of the leadership function is providing 'the means for action' (Melucci 1996: 339). For the movement to achieve
its objectives, leaders must channel members' talents and energies effectively,

as well as secure additional resources through contact with, for example, the state and political parties. Third, leaders are faced with the task of maintaining the movement's structure and cohesion. This involves regulating tensions within the movement as well as responding to adversaries' attempts to undermine or destabilise it. As Melucci emphasises, a crucial factor here is a leader's ability to control the circulation of information and to manage the effect of external 'stimuli' (e.g. pressure from other organisations or political opponents) on the movement (1996: 339–40). A fourth key leadership role is that of mobilising members' support for the movement's objectives. Leaders must act in such a way as to ensure members' continued investment in the movement and agreement about its aims. Finally, Melucci suggests that leaders have an 'expressive' function which is central to the process of collective identity construction. They present members with an image of the movement's identity which can form the basis of solidarity, identification and 'affective gratification' (1996: 340).

As Melucci emphasises, the different aspects of the leadership role which have just been distinguished become 'intertwined' in the daily life of a social movement (1996: 340). In so doing, they may pull leaders in opposite directions by making contradictory or irreconcilable demands. It follows that 'the fulcrum for leadership action is the *decision*, that is, the capacity to choose between alternatives and reduce uncertainties' (1996: 340, emphasis in original). Leaders must, in other words, be able accurately to weigh up the potential costs and benefits of particular courses of action, taking into account the needs and priorities of members. This is precisely what was at stake in the meeting of SOS-Racisme's National Council in April 1994 which I will now examine. The president of SOS-Racisme, Fodé Sylla, was confronted with a potentially explosive situation which forced him to choose between several competing options and leadership tasks. In the event, he decided to privilege the organisation's unity and cohesion over an opportunity to access new means and resources for action. He did so after failing to mobilise an adequate support base among the membership in favour of a specific, short-term goal (going forward as a candidate on Tapie's list for the 1994 European elections). To rebuild unity, he closed the meeting by explicitly voicing his agreement with an image of the association's identity presented by a previous speaker who had led opposition to the proposed action.

The National Council meeting began with a short opening address by Sylla. As a form of leadership action it exemplified the first task described by Melucci, that of articulating a movement's objectives. In his remarks, Sylla attempted to define both the specific aim of the meeting itself and the wider goals of the organisation. With respect to the first of these, he stated several times that the meeting had been called with a view to debating Tapie's proposition in the 'democratic structures of the association' in order to arrive at a 'collective decision'. He asserted that Tapie's proposition had raised the question of the association's 'autonomy' and 'independence', and this needed to be discussed. However, what became increasingly clear in the course of his intervention was that he personally was not in favour of accepting the offer. Moreover, the impression he gave was that it had already been rejected. This was highlighted by his statement that the National Council meeting should discuss in general terms, rather than in relation to Tapie's specific offer, how propositions of this sort should be dealt with in the future.

To all intents and purposes, Sylla's opening statement removed the rationale for the meeting. It reflected two days of telephone calls and debate between the provincial committees and the National Bureau in Paris, during which it had become clear to the leadership that Tapie's offer threatened to split the association down the middle. As Sylla himself stated, he would only accept Tapie's invitation if he had the whole association behind him, and this was manifestly not the case. Nevertheless, the way in which he redefined the objective of the meeting from the specific to the general left some grassroots members perplexed: 'Are we here to discuss the future presence of the president of SOS-Racisme on the European lists or not?', asked one member immediately after Sylla's opening address. Furthermore, although Sylla's admission that he was in favour of rejecting the offer can be viewed as an attempt to reassure members deeply opposed to it, and head-off a major confrontation, the redefinition of the purpose of the meeting only increased some activists' dissatisfaction with the leadership. A Parisian activist interviewed after the meeting declared:

> What was a bit scandalous was the fact that ... there was no consultation....
> So, in fact, the decision which was due to be taken – supposedly all together –
> was a sham because Fodé Sylla knew even before the meeting that he wouldn't
> belong to [Tapie's] list. [There was] no democratic debate. Really, it was done
> ... It was a struggle for power, a struggle of the apparatchiks between them-
> selves, but without the grassroots activists being adequately informed about
> the situation.

In the above passage, members of the National Bureau are dismissively referred to as 'the apparatchiks' and are presented as primarily concerned with their own internal power struggles to the detriment of the interests of the rank and file. According to this interviewee, everything had already been decided behind closed doors, before the meeting had even taken place. He went on to claim that Michel Rocard had put pressure on Julien Dray, one of the founders of SOS-Racisme and a Socialist deputy since 1988, to persuade Sylla not to stand as a candidate on Tapie's list. This sense of behind-the-scenes manoeuvring was shared by another member I interviewed, who commented that 'you had the impression that there had been a discussion at a higher level, pressure from above ...'. (Various rumours to this effect were, in fact, circulating in the press at the time. For his part, Dray admitted only that he had advised Sylla against accepting the offer [*Le Monde*, 29 April

1994], while the latter strenuously denied that prominent figures in the Socialist Party had 'intervened' [*L'Événement du jeudi*, 12–18 May 1994].)

Leaving aside the question of the influence exerted by the Socialist Party in this matter, it is clear that Tapie's proposition was initially attractive to Sylla and other members of SOS-Racisme's National Bureau for reasons related to a second aspect of the leadership role: the mobilisation of resources enabling a movement to realise its objectives. As Melucci notes, a leader 'must procure the maximum amount of resources available in the environment by entering into relations with other groups and organisations and with the society at large' (1996: 339). Both in Sylla's initial address and in the interventions of a number of National Bureau members during the meeting, emphasis was laid on the resources which acceptance of the offer would make available to the organisation. A succession of National Bureau members, for example, repeated that Sylla's election to the European Parliament would give SOS-Racisme a 'platform' from which to promote anti-racism at a European level and lead the struggle against the far right. One member of the National Bureau added that the association was currently experiencing difficulty in getting its ideas taken up, and that its mobilisations lacked credibility; this implied that new means for action were needed in order to ensure the organisation's long-term survival and effectiveness. It was pointed out that more mundane resources would be forthcoming as well, such as information but also the salary associated with the post, a not negligible consideration given that the association's state subsidy had recently been reduced (after the return of the right to power in March 1993).

While the leadership's initial attraction to Tapie's offer can be viewed in this light, as a way of maximising the SOS-Racisme's means for action, entering into any sort of agreement with Tapie was bound to be controversial, given the nature of the individual involved (as I have already noted, numerous allegations of corruption surrounded his business dealings). For opponents of the offer, in fact, the nature of this attempt to maximise resources smacked of opportunism and 'scheming'. The leadership opened itself up, in particular, to the accusation that it was putting political expediency before genuine anti-racist politics. This was one of the main arguments advanced in an article on the meeting published in the weekly paper of the Trotskyist organisation the Revolutionary Communist League (LCR), some of whose members were then actively involved in SOS-Racisme. The article criticised:

> all the past and present digressions aimed at subordinating the anti-racist struggle to extraneous concerns, ones which correspond more closely to self-seeking manœuvring, machinations even, than to a desire to advance the construction of a collective framework capable of exerting an influence in favour of equal rights. (*Rouge*, 5 May 1994)

In a similar way, a grassroots activist based in the Paris region stated in an interview:

Well, what struck me the most about this episode was the lack of political awareness of a certain number of my comrades, notably in the National Bureau. It makes them prepared to form all sorts of alliances and ends up as a certain opportunism. As in when they say: 'Yes, but Tapie, he is popular in the suburbs [*banlieues*].' Yes, but well, just because a number of people are taken in, it doesn't mean that the association should follow suit.

What the incident revealed, for this activist, was the political naivety of a section of the leadership. As I have already indicated, Sylla had stated in his opening address to the National Council meeting that he personally was against accepting Tapie's offer. During the remainder of the meeting, however, a series of National Bureau members intervened to argue in favour of a more positive response. They did so by highlighting Tapie's popularity among the type of young urban people the association itself was attempting to attract (see below). In the activist's view, however, this was not a sufficient reason for the SOS-Racisme to become involved with Tapie, and instead reflected an opportunistic approach rather than a principled political position.

Viewed from Sylla's perspective, however, the central question was the contradiction or at the very least the tension which existed between two of his tasks as president of SOS-Racisme. The first was that of maximising the organisation's resources with a view to increasing the effectiveness of its action and ability to realise its objectives. The second was the need to maintain the organisation's structure, cohesion and unity. As his opening address made clear, Sylla had decided that to seek to maximise resources through accepting Tapie's offer would be to risk provoking a split in the organisation. In particular, it appeared likely to prompt the departure of those associated with the Revolutionary Communist League as well as other members not directly affiliated to any political party. There was, in short, a balance to be struck between two key components of the leadership role.

In coming to a decision, Sylla had to assess the membership's reaction and the strength of opposition to the proposition. A key aspect of the leadership's attempt to maintain the cohesion of the organisation in the meantime was control over the circulation of information. A reminder of the time-scale involved illustrates this point. As Sylla later confirmed in an interview, Tapie had made the offer on 11 April (*L'Événement du jeudi*, 12–18 May 1994). It was not, however, debated by the National Bureau until 27 April, and it was only then that the decision was taken to call a meeting of the National Council two days later. In so doing, the leadership was obviously attempting to 'manage' and contain the potential effect of Tapie's invitation on the membership at large. Nevertheless, grassroots activists were subsequently to regard the leadership's failure to inform the membership sooner and to give adequate notice of the National Council meeting as evidence of a lack of transparency and internal democracy. Thus, when asked later about the meeting during an interview, one Paris-based activist commented:

> For a start, what was serious about this episode was that ... the National Council meeting which took place, people were informed about it the day before. That is to say that three quarters of the activists from outside Paris, including those from Toulouse who were among those who had strongly expressed their opposition to the project, had enormous difficulty in coming to Paris ... to participate in this decision. I personally was informed the day before by telephone.

The issue raised here is the extent to which the late announcement of the National Council meeting prevented representatives of SOS-Racisme's provincial committees, as well as grassroots activists from the Paris region, from attending. Thus, while the leadership's control over channels of communication may have successfully limited controversy over Tapie's invitation to the two-day period leading up to the meeting, it only served in the longer term to increase dissatisfaction with the National Bureau on the part of sections of the membership. It was even claimed that the leadership only resolved to consult the rank and file when reports of negotiations between Tapie and Sylla were published in the press (*Rouge*, 5 May 1994).

Thus far I have analysed the action of SOS-Racisme's president and National Bureau at the National Council meeting in terms of the first three components of the leadership role described by Melucci: defining objectives, mobilising resources and maintaining structure and cohesion. To conclude this section, therefore, I want briefly to consider examples of the remaining two leadership tasks: mobilising a support base and reinforcing identity. With respect to the first of these, the National Council meeting can be interpreted as an attempt by the leadership to persuade grassroots members that the potential benefits which would flow from accepting Tapie's offer outweighed any costs. A common theme running through the interventions by National Bureau members in the course of the evening was that the association was in the process of 'missing an opportunity', that it risked 'missing the boat'. Indeed, members were encouraged to accept that the association had to adapt to a changing environment and take advantage of an opening that was presenting itself. In this way, the leadership sought to secure members' identification with the short-term aim of fielding a candidate for the European elections as a means to the association's more general objectives, such as the struggle against the far right.

However, both during the meeting and in the course of numerous telephone conversations beforehand, the leadership's bid to mobilise a consensus in favour of Tapie's proposition came up against the determined opposition of several of the most important provincial committees as well as that of influential Parisian activists. As I indicate in the next section, the opposition of many grassroots members was based on the view that the association would change its identity by accepting the offer. It was not simply a 'fear' of the political field (as certain members of the National Bureau suggested during the meeting) which prevented such activists from accepting the offer, but rather an often complex and sophisticated distinction between (party) political action and associative action.

Finally, SOS-Racisme's president was constrained at the end of the meeting to work towards a reinforcement of the association's identity, in order to limit the damage caused by the whole incident. The threat to its cohesion represented by the potential departure of a significant fraction of the membership required the leadership to attempt to rebuild unity. Sylla did this at the close of the meeting by projecting an image of SOS-Racisme with which members on both sides of the argument could identify. During the debate one of the most vocal opponents of an agreement with Tapie had argued that 'The offer to appear on Tapie's list is a sign that our association is worth a lot and that is a tribute to you, Fodé, and to the association. Nevertheless, my view is that the association is worth more than M. Tapie can afford …'. In his closing address Sylla referred explicitly to this statement, claiming that it neatly summarised the message which members should take away from the evening's debate. He repeated the phrase that SOS-Racisme was 'worth more than Tapie could afford', an action which appeared designed to reinforce a positive, valorising image of the association as well as to imply that it (and the leadership) could not be 'bought'. In so doing, Sylla was endeavouring to ensure that the meeting ended with a measure of consensus and unity over the association's identity.

As I will indicate more fully in the next section, the definition of SOS-Racisme's identity as an anti-racist organisation had in fact been an important stake in the meeting itself. Speakers on both sides of the debate had projected a number of different images of the association's identity in support of their arguments. In particular, those against the proposed action sought to mobilise opposition to the leadership by appealing to a historically important and consensual idea of SOS-Racisme's specificity. Part of the negotiation or 'transaction' (Melucci 1996: 334) between leaders and followers at the meeting, in other words, centred on the meaning and nature of the association itself.

Debating political opportunities and organisational identity

In this section I turn to examine how the definition of political opportunities and the identity of SOS-Racisme as an organisation were key stakes in the debate between the leadership and grassroots at the National Council meeting. Following Melucci, I want to argue that leadership must be viewed as 'a form of interaction' (Melucci 1996: 333) during which crucial types of social movement activity occur. These include the negotiation of a collective identity and the development of a shared understanding among actors of the political and institutional environment (the political opportunity structure, in other words) in which they are operating.

As will become apparent in what follows, both leaders and grassroots members were engaged during the meeting in a cost-benefit calculation of the advantages and disadvantages associated with accepting Tapie's offer. Ideas about the nature of SOS-Racisme as an anti-racist organisation and its relationship to the political sphere (or, more precisely, the sphere of party politics) were also at stake. Although the leadership suggested at the time that members were reluctant to accept the offer simply out of a 'fear' of the political field, or because of a 'lack of maturity' of debate within the association, subsequent interviews with grassroots members revealed rather complex conceptions of the relationship between associative and (party) political action. In particular, interviewees tended to exhibit not an apprehension of politics but rather a strong, deeply held commitment to SOS-Racisme's independence and freedom from political party influence.

The debate which Tapie's proposition provoked revealed the extent to which opinion differed as to the conditions under which (if at all) SOS-Racisme should enter the field of party politics. This divergence co-existed, however, with significant agreement among members about the nature of the relationship between the association and young people. Arguments in favour of accepting the proposition for the 1994 European elections tended, for example, to suggest that there was a close relationship between Tapie and young people, on the one hand, and between SOS-Racisme and young people, on the other, which in turn implied a convergence of interests between Tapie and SOS-Racisme. Although other representatives disputed the appropriateness of viewing Tapie as the champion of young people's interests – and thus rejected the equation advanced by those favourable to the proposal – they appeared generally to agree with the idea that SOS-Racisme voiced the aspirations and convictions of young people. Nonetheless, as interviews I conducted with activists later confirmed, less of a consensus existed concerning the position which SOS-Racisme as such should adopt with respect to political party competition.

The issue of Tapie's appeal to young people was raised early on in the National Council meeting by one of the association's co-founders. He referred to a series of reports which had appeared in the French daily newspaper *Libération* that very morning (29 April 1994). These revealed that Tapie's level of popularity was highest among young, left-wing people, especially in the suburbs (*banlieues*). The newspaper also provided evidence that support for Tapie among these young people was indicative of their disaffection with other parties on the left such as the Socialists and the French Communist Party (subsequent analysis of voting behaviour at the election itself suggested a similar conclusion, see Grunberg 1995). Citing these reports, the speaker argued that even though fellow activists might not find Tapie a particularly congenial figure, they couldn't simply reject him out of hand or ignore his appeal to a significant proportion of the French electorate. In particular, the fact that Tapie drew his support from the very section of the population – urban young people sympathetic to the left – which SOS-

Racisme sought to involve in its campaigns was, in the view of this activist, an important reason for considering the proposition seriously. A member of the National Bureau subsequently reiterated this point as a major reason for accepting Tapie's offer.

A degree of confirmation of these newspaper reports of Tapie's popularity among 18–25 year olds was provided by an activist from Marseilles who emphasised that Tapie represented hope for disillusioned young people in the suburbs (*banlieues*). Later, another member of the National Bureau added that Tapie's appeal derived to a large extent from the fact that both his 'ordinary' background and use of vernacular language distinguished him from the rest of the French political class. By virtue of these characteristics and links with an important football club, Tapie was, he concluded, 'not a politician like the others' in the eyes of many young people.

As these comments make clear, for a number of National Bureau members as well as representatives of the Bouches-du-Rhône group (comprising the area around Marseilles), Tapie's popularity among young people was an important reason for giving his proposal serious consideration. An important corollary of this argument, which certain speakers took for granted or implied rather than stating explicitly, was that SOS-Racisme should be regarded as an association which was not only composed primarily of young people but also sought to reflect their interests directly in its campaigns. A former vice-president, for example, prefaced his intervention in the debate with the statement that: 'SOS is one of the few organisations today which is in touch with young people'. In short, an argument in favour of accepting the proposition was built up gradually by the assertion of two separate links (Tapie/youth, SOS-Racisme/youth) which together suggested a third (Tapie/SOS-Racisme).

However, activists opposed to entering into an agreement with Tapie questioned the extent to which he was actually concerned with promoting young people's interests. Another co-founder of the association and (at the time) member of the Revolutionary Communist League, for example, dismissed as 'populism' Tapie's much-publicised comment that he would make unemployment illegal for those under 25 and require firms to hire hundreds of thousands of young people (cf. Buffotot and Hanley 1995: 5). According to this activist, the fact of the matter was that Tapie pursued his own commercial interests, not those of young people. Despite his undoubted popularity among this category of the population, the activist claimed that Tapie had long advocated policies detrimental to young people. In an important intervention in the debate, he added:

> Tapie has a programme which is *anti*-young people. His policies would not solve the problem of unemployment but would actually make it worse. In my view, it is clear that Tapie is for the interests of big business, for 'the winners'. Is that our ethic [*morale*]? No, this association has a tradition of arguing for equality. Then there is the matter of the corruption allegations against Tapie.

> These are not side issues. Tapie represents the anti-model of the moral genera-
> tion. For that reason, I recommend that we don't get mixed up in this at all. It
> would be a step backwards for our movement ...

What is particularly interesting here is the speaker's description of Tapie as
'the anti-model of the moral generation'. In the mid-1980s, the phrase 'the
moral generation' was coined in France as a way of referring to the group of
young people who had reached adolescence in the period since the election
of Mitterrand and the left at the start of the decade. These young people
were supposed to have abandoned political 'ideology' (i.e. the revolutionary
ideals of the 1960s and early 1970s) in favour of a set of core moral values
such as equality, democracy and solidarity (Joffrin 1987; cf. Reynaud 1980).
The young members of SOS-Racisme were widely regarded as emblematic
figures of the so-called moral generation (see Joffrin 1987: 59–70; Dray
1987), and it is this image of the association to which the activist is appealing in the passage quoted above. Rather than highlighting a potential convergence of interests between Tapie, young people and SOS-Racisme (the
strategy adopted by a section of the leadership), the activist in question
emphasises a divergence of identity. He argues against accepting the proposition by emphasising the contrast between SOS-Racisme, a symbol of the
moral generation, and Tapie, a politician/businessman surrounded by
corruption allegations.

A similar definition of SOS-Racisme's identity in terms of morality and an
ethical stance was articulated by other activists during interviews conducted
subsequently. An activist based in Paris, for example, acknowledged the potential benefits which the organisation would have been able to draw from
Fodé Sylla's election to the European Parliament. Nevertheless, he insisted
that this would have been outweighed by the damage inflicted on SOS-
Racisme's image. He summarised his position on Tapie's proposition as
follows:

> I personally was totally opposed to it. That is to say that if this business had
> gone ahead, I would have left [the association]. I have an image of moral con-
> duct [*la morale*] which I associate with SOS-Racisme, even if there are strug-
> gles for power and so on (which seem to me to be rather inherent in the nature
> of things in the political realm). This was in total contradiction with the image
> of Tapie, which is, in my view, an image of utter dishonesty, bad faith ... In no
> way could it be acceptable, as far as I was concerned.

What is interesting here is the way that the activist contrasts the image of
SOS-Racisme as principled and 'moral' with the image of Tapie as dishonest
and corrupt. He too brings into play a historical image of SOS-Racisme (as
part of the 'moral generation') in order to justify his opposition to the
proposition. This emphasises once again how the assessment of political
opportunities by activists was inextricably bound up with conceptions of the
association's identity and public image.

For a number of activists, therefore, accepting Tapie's offer of a place on his list of candidates for the 1994 European elections would have the negative effect of destroying SOS-Racisme's image as part of 'the moral generation'. The question of identity was also central for other activists, albeit in a slightly different way. As an activist from the Paris region stated in an interview, a key concern was SOS-Racisme's future identity *as an association*:

> If Fodé [Sylla] joined Tapie's list, that would mean, as far as I'm concerned – and it's what I said within the association at the time – that SOS [-Racisme] would change its nature. It would no longer be an anti-racist association: an *association* would become a *political movement*.

For this activist, then, the implications of accepting Tapie's offer would be fundamental and far-reaching for the nature and identity of the organisation. The involvement of the association's president in the political field as a member of the European Parliament would change the way in which the association would be viewed by potential members. Instead of being an association, she argues, SOS-Racisme would become a political movement. The danger of this would be that the association would thereby cut itself off from sections of the population. A first issue for this activist, therefore, was the possibility that accepting the offer would restrict the association's appeal and undermine its potential for becoming a mass movement. Second, however, there was a suggestion that associating SOS-Racisme with Tapie would not simply alter the reasons why people would join in the future; it would also fundamentally alter the nature of the organisation itself. As she argues in the above quotation, the association would change its nature and become a political movement. Later in the interview, she used a fascinating analogy in order to clarify the difference between associative and more narrowly (party) political activism:

> There is a saying which goes that an activist in an association is in the zone of the prophet and the political activist is in the zone of the king. So there is one who enlightens, who makes statements, who expresses values and convictions and so on, and there is another who carries things out, who acts ... It's not at all the same role. And personally I want SOS [-Racisme] to continue in the role of a prophet because ... SOS [-Racisme] was a reference-point [*un référent*] in society, it still is a reference-point. A reference-point for moral values, it has defended certain things, moral values. If you enter politics [*le jeu politique*], the reference is no longer the same.

The distinction here is between two different kinds of activity: on the one hand, action in an association which involves the expression and defence of moral values and convictions; and on the other, political action which is presented as more pragmatic, the putting into practice of certain policies or orientations. Both can be seen as part of the political process in the widest sense, but the distinction or separation of roles is crucial for this activist.

As the material examined in this section has demonstrated, the meeting of SOS-Racisme's National Council in April 1994 was the site of an important debate about the definition of political opportunities and the nature of the association's identity and public image. The section of the leadership favourable to Tapie's proposition for the 1994 European elections and those strongly opposed to it drew on and discussed a range of ideas about political and associative activism as well as SOS-Racisme's links with young people. Resistance to any form of agreement with Tapie was so strong among the grassroots members, for reasons I have highlighted, that the leadership was in the end forced to abandon any hope of realising this objective.

Conclusion

The five years since the events discussed in this chapter have witnessed a dramatic upsurge of social movement activity in France. The massive public sector strikes of November–December 1995 (Mouriaux and Subileau 1996) have been followed by a series of further protests by French workers (Wolfreys 1999), as well as hunger-strikes and occupations by undocumented foreign residents or *sans-papiers* campaigning for residence permits (IM'média/REFLEX 1997), AIDS activism (Martel 1999: 285–359) and the winter 1997–98 movement of the unemployed (Royall 1998). Against this background, the 'autonomy' of social movements from party political 'leadership' has emerged once again as a key issue for both activists and social scientists (see Aguiton and Corcuff 1999; Brochier and Delouche 2000: 163–78).

As far as leadership and autonomy within the anti-racist movement are concerned, two main conclusions can be drawn from the analysis presented in this chapter. First, the different components of the leadership role distinguished by Melucci can create competing if not contradictory demands for leaders in concrete situations. The continued legitimacy of their own position and the movement's unity more generally may both depend on a leader's capacity to evaluate the potential advantages and disadvantages of particular courses of action and to assess members' needs and priorities accurately when coming to a decision. Second, significant differences can exist between leaders and grassroots members of social movements over the nature and definition of political opportunities and collective identities. On the basis of the material examined here (and the more recent events alluded to above), future leadership strategies within the French anti-racist movement must acknowledge the importance attached by many grassroots members to 'autonomy' from political parties and the specificity and distinctiveness of associative activism. How to increase the anti-racist movement's political influence, while recognising this desire for independence, is a challenge which leaders will continue to face for some time to come.

Notes

1   The fieldwork on which this chapter is based was conducted in Paris over an
    18-month period (1993–94), as part of a Ph.D. in the Department of Social
    Anthropology, University of Edinburgh. It was funded by the Economic and
    Social Research Council of Great Britain (Award Number: R00429234105). I
    am grateful to those members of SOS-Racisme who permitted me to share in
    the life of their local committee and who gave freely of their time and patience.
    With the exception of SOS-Racisme's president, Fodé Sylla, all names of activ-
    ists in the association have been either changed or omitted to preserve their
    anonymity.
2   SOS-Racisme was founded in 1984 by a group of Paris-based students and
    political activists committed to fighting the rise of the far-right National Front
    (FN) party in France (see Le Gendre 1990). It has the legal status of an associa-
    tion, as defined by the 1901 law on the freedom of association. For analytical
    purposes, however, this chapter follows Jan Willem Duyvendak in defining
    SOS-Racisme as a social movement organisation (see Duyvendak 1994: 235).

5

Struggles over leadership in the women's liberation movement

Carol Hanisch

Introduction

The first independent women's liberation groups began to emerge in the United States in late 1967, inspired by the civil right movement and other great upsurges for freedom around the world. Women came into the women's liberation movement (WLM) with ideas about leadership formed in groups ranging from hierarchical churches to anarchistic counter-culture hippie communes. Its early leadership came mostly out of political organisations that fell somewhere in-between: civil rights, peace, free speech and student movements. Many had ties with the New Left, the Old Left or both. Many were in rebellion against what they perceived as oppressive 'male' leadership, meaning that they were often left out of the decision-making process, while doing most of the clerical and other support work. This diversity of experience – much of it unpleasant and some of it outright oppressive – made fractiousness over leadership inevitable.

This chapter explores some of the theoretical and ideological struggles over leadership in the women's liberation movement during its heyday – including my own experience, sometimes as follower, sometimes as leader. It will show that when the growth of the movement called forth a need for more structured organisations with accountable leaders, it was met with a resistance that contributed greatly to radical feminism's inability to unite, fight and survive.

My account of the first year of the women's liberation movement focuses largely on New York Radical Women (NYRW), partly because, as a member, I have first-hand knowledge of its history. Also NYRW was one of the hotbeds in which many of the theoretical and strategic questions that marked 1968 were debated and developed, including consciousness-raising, 'the personal is political' and 'the pro-woman line', and where much practical independent WLM activity was organised, from the Miss America Pageant Protest to the journal *Notes from the First Year*. Other women's liberation groups went through similar experiences with local variations.

Beginnings: New York Radical Women

NYRW, one of the earliest independent women's liberation groups in the US and the first in New York City, was called together in late 1967 by Shulamith Firestone and Pam Allen. Initially the group was small enough to meet in the tiny apartments of its members. Unlike some early women's liberation groups, members of NYRW were not attached to any university community as either students or professors, so were not as heavily influenced by the academic milieu. Most worked for a living and did not identify as students, though some were or had been active in, or supported, the Students for a Democratic Society (SDS) and other student organisations. Neither were they the mates of 'left' male leaders, as were the founders of WLM groups in some cities.

All the founding members of NYRW had leadership experience in some form, though certainly with differing degrees of expertise in various capacities. NYRW members had felt hampered in attempts to exert – or in some cases be recognised for – leadership in mixed groups of men and women, not just in 'the Movement', but in society in general. However, there was no concrete theory of leadership explicitly discussed in the WLM in its very beginnings. It was tacitly agreed that the off-putting abstract, theoretical speeches and 'revolutionary' posturing that many 'left' men engaged in was not what we wanted for leadership in the WLM. We wanted a movement that was concretely related to our lives at all times.

On 15 January 1968, less than two months after its first meeting, NYRW held an action at the Jeanette Rankin Brigade, a large women's peace march held in Washington DC to protest against the Vietnam War. NYRW's plan was to convince the old-line women's peace activists, such as Women's Strike for Peace, that 'playing upon the traditional female role in a classic manner' of mother and wife was not a very potent means of achieving peace. NYRW called upon women to unite to fight their own oppression and achieve some real power because 'it is naive to believe that women, who are not politically seen, heard, or represented in this country could change the course of a war by simply appealing to the better natures of congressmen' (Firestone 1968: n.p.).

Whatever struggles over leadership erupted among radical feminists at the Brigade action were more faction against faction over contending political lines than against individual leaders or against leadership *per se*. A few may have grumbled at the content of her speech, but, as far as I know, no one condemned Kathie Sarachild for being a leader when, representing NYRW, she addressed a post-march convention in which she first used the slogan 'Sisterhood Is Powerful'. When some 500 women broke off in disgust from the convention into a more radical counter-congress, the feminists were taken by surprise. In her assessment of the Brigade action in *Notes from the First Year*, Firestone showed recognition of what happens when leadership is not prepared to step into a situation and provide direction. She wrote that 'we were not really prepared to rechannel this disgust, to provide the direction that was so badly needed.... [We] learned the value of being able to size up a situation and act on it at once, the importance of unrehearsed speaking ability' (Firestone 1968: n.p.).

Consciousness-raising and leadership

From its inception, NYRW had operated with no formal structure. However, leaders of those advocating various strategies quickly emerged following the Jeanette Rankin Brigade action when it became necessary to decide what the group would do next. Some wanted to study the status of women by reading various books, a sort of study group. Others clamoured for an immediate action, but could not find one compelling to the group. Still others wanted to study women's situation and build women's liberation theory from the ground up by studying the experience of our own lives. So many falsehoods had been written about women, we argued, that we must test everything by our own life experiences, discussing and analysing our feelings as a guide to the truth.

Leadership at this point was a matter of having enough vision to point the way and enough verbal agility and persistence to convince others to take the same path. The faction advocating consciousness-raising won out, though not without ongoing dissention. Some women formed study groups and action groups on the side, but most also continued to participate in the weekly NYRW consciousness-raising meetings. Women's liberationists were under constant pressure from the SDS and other left organisations to prove themselves as revolutionaries, and consciousness-raising came under attack as so much 'navel-gazing'. It took a good deal of courage and determination not to respond to that pressure.

As NYRW set about developing consciousness-raising as a tool for both organising and advancing women's liberation theory, the group's structure and decision-making remained informal. Meetings were freewheeling, yet amazingly productive. We did soon institute the practice of going around the room to answer the consciousness-raising question, not only to encourage everyone to speak, but, more importantly, to keep focused on the topic at hand. The only rules were to tell the truth and not to discuss someone else's testimony outside the group. Consciousness-raising proved an effective method to unite women as it broke down the isolation so important to the authority of male supremacy. As women learned that there was a pattern to their oppression and no longer saw their problems as personal, they developed political solidarity and were motivated to try to change their conditions.

Those who could best vocalise their own personal experiences with insight and analysis and/or had the facility to draw out and make astute political observations and analysis from the often conflicting testimonies of others were doing the work of leading. And it was, indeed, hard work. At this point, attacks on leadership began to emerge in the form of complaints that some of these women 'talked too much' and that it was more important to 'hear from the quiet women'. Others objected to having their experiences analysed and questioned at all, even though that was necessary for successful consciousness-raising. To a large degree, these criticisms came from those who wanted 'small groups' with 'free space' to 'heal and restore ourselves to wholeness' (Allen 1970: 15) because women were supposedly 'damaged' by their oppression. This focus on individual psychology represented a major ideological split from those who maintained that women were oppressed, not damaged, and needed a theory and strategy to free women from oppression.

Sometimes, of course, some women did 'talk too much' without saying anything new or interesting. Once the dam of silence was broken, it was hard for some women to control their desire to talk. Sometimes other women really did want to know what 'the quiet women' thought. More often, however, the complaints against the 'women who talked too much' and 'dominated the group' were actually a veiled criticism of the political conclusions being drawn from the testimony, an early form of the challenge to leadership that would eventually become so destructive to the movement.

This ruse became personally apparent to me one evening when we were talking about manual labour. A woman recounting her experience in a back-to-nature commune declared that women got more respect from men in situations where women did manual labour, like carrying water. I blurted out that my mother, as a farmer's wife, had done a tremendous amount of physical labour and all it had gotten her was callouses and old before her time, not respect. Because I was considered one of the 'quiet women', I, and almost everyone else in the room, was shocked when the woman who had been advocating manual labour as the route to women's liberation turned to me and said sharply, 'You talk too much'.

Barbara Leon described the effect of some women demanding that others shut up so they could 'hear from the quiet women' as follows:

> I was really interested in the discussions of male supremacy although I didn't contribute much – at times out of indecision, not knowing where I stood on certain issues and wanting to hear more before I made up my mind, at other times because of [the] conflict over how involved in this movement I wanted to be. But what made me really uncomfortable were the discussions on 'what was going on in the group.'
>
> There were women in the group who seemed to be supporting me. They criticized others for being dominating and monopolizing the meetings. In the middle of a discussion, they would break in to say that those talking were not giving others a chance and would then add, 'Let's hear from the quiet women.' I knew that that meant me. I felt that I should be grateful and yet I would wince every time I heard that phrase.... It got to the point where I didn't even

trust my own perceptions of what was happening. I *felt* angry and patronized
by the women who were claiming to represent my interests. I felt attacked
whenever another woman was accused of dominating me – since that implicitly meant I was easily dominated, weak, damaged, etc. Yet I continued to
believe that it was for my own good and to wonder why it only made me feel
worse. I also ignored my positive feelings toward those women who were
supposedly 'dominating' me. (1972: 13)

Since the act of following often leads others, following as well as leading
came under attack because being 'second through the door' often shows others the way. Even one person unifying with a leader makes it easier for others
who actually agree with the leader's position but hang back until they see the
numbers grow. Agreeing with a leader who was being attacked could mean
being labelled her 'dupe' by those who wanted to stop the group or movement from going in the direction she was advocating. This was a put-down
of both the leader and her perceived supporter, and made it necessary for
both to stand up to these charges in addition to defending their political
position. Because feminist theory was so new to me in the early days of the
movement (I hadn't even heard of Simone de Beauvoir, while many of the
leaders in NYRW had already read *The Second Sex*), I was often 'second
through the door' and often referred to as a 'dupe'. Besides smacking of anti-
communist cold-war McCarthyism and its 'guilt by association' overtones,
this is perhaps more insulting to the 'follower' than to the leader. It assumes
the 'follower' has no mind of her own and, once presented with the arguments, is too stupid or gullible to make a wise decision. Who, under that
definition of a follower, would want to admit to being one?

By the spring of 1968, some 30 or so women were packing the weekly
NYRW meetings, which had outgrown living rooms and were being held at
the office of the Southern Conference Educational Fund (SCEF), a progressive organisation for which I then worked. Out of necessity, we had progressed to meeting in a central place on a regular basis where other women
could find us. Still operating without a formal structure, the group was
admittedly noisy and difficult at times, but it remained fascinating and productive. The larger size meant a broader range of experiences was fed into
our consciousness-raising hopper. Some women, however, still agitated for
smaller, more intimate groups. Those who thought women's oppression was
a political problem and were determined to build a mass women's liberation
movement welcomed the larger meeting with its broader perspective, despite
its difficulties.

In the late spring, Shulie Firestone decided it was time to get some of our
ideas down on paper for distribution to other women and proposed that we
write and publish *Notes from the First Year*. There was no committee or
editorial board charged with overseeing the publication, though Firestone
did much of the editorial pulling-it-together work. It was pretty much open
to anyone in the group who wanted to write something, though there was

some group debate on some items. Nevertheless, through a good deal of cooperative work, it was mimeographed in time for Firestone to take it to Paris in June, where she hoped to deliver a copy to Simone de Beauvoir. Again, I don't recall anyone complaining about Firestone's leadership on this project. We were excited about disseminating our ideas and letting others know about our group and what we were doing.

Leadership and the protest against the Miss America Pageant

As the WLM became more public, friction over the issue of leadership sharpened. What went on within the group was one thing; how the group would be represented to the public became a much more serious matter. The entry of the mass media into the stir meant major difficulties as well as new opportunities. The September 1968 protest against the Miss America Pageant, with its need for spokespersons both during and after the action, took the internal struggle over leadership to a new level and greatly exacerbated tensions.

New York Radical Women, which spearheaded the protest, decided that no one would talk to male reporters. This was partly because some felt the protest was more likely to get favourable coverage from a woman and partly because we wanted to force the media to send women journalists, who in 1968 were relegated to the society pages and rarely sent out on assignments. A few women with some amount of celebrity and media connections felt they did not have to abide by the decisions of the group and spoke to the press at will. This set them up as spokespersons, not only for the protest, but also as favoured media contacts for the future. Since we failed to designate spokespeople from amongst our own ranks, the self-appointed ones were able to speak for the group with impunity.

Some women had joined the protest at the last minute and had not been in on the earlier discussions of why we opposed the Miss America Pageant and our decision to make sure that contestants would not be made the target of the protest. It somehow never crossed our minds to write up NYRW's official position in a flyer to give to the protestors who joined us as well as to the observers. This would not have guaranteed compliance, as a number of the posters and anti-woman[1] slogans, such as 'Miss America Sells It' and 'Miss America Is A Big Falsie', came from women who had attended the meetings. However, it could have been cited as the official position of the group. Instead, the anti-woman faction wrote up its own flyer, which was distributed without feedback from NYRW.

The experience of our first major action aimed at the general public forced us to focus on some of these leadership problems. Practice was making necessary some reconsideration of our loose approach to organising. In 'A critique of the Miss America protest', written soon after the action, I wrote:

A spirit of every woman 'do her own thing' began to emerge. Sometimes it was because there was an open conflict about an issue. Other times, women didn't say anything at all about disagreeing with a group decision; they just went ahead and did what they wanted to do, even though it was something the group had definitely decided against. Because of this egotistic individualism, a definite strain of anti-womanism was presented to the public to the detriment of the action.

We tried to carry the democratic means we used in planning the action into the actual *doing* of it. We didn't want leaders or spokesmen. It makes the movement not only seem stronger and larger if everyone is a leader, but it actually *is* stronger if not dependent on a few. It also guards against the time when such leaders could be isolated and picked off one way or another. And of course many voices are more powerful than one.

Our first attempt was not entirely successful. We must learn how to fight against the media's desire to make leaders and some women's desire to be spokesmen. Everybody talks to the press or nobody talks to the press. The same problem came up in regard to appearances on radio and television shows after the action. We theoretically decided no one should appear more than once, but it didn't work out that way. (Hanisch 2000a: 378)

Although many of us were not yet ready to give up our utopian ideal of a leaderless movement, it began to become clear in the aftermath of the Miss America protest that this hope was itself part of the problem.

Until then, most resistance to leadership in the group had taken the form of sniping complaints that some women were 'dominating the group', 'talking too much', 'being too judgemental', and 'acting like men' by interrupting and not giving everyone a chance to speak. Conversely, the 'quiet women', like myself, who were often learning from what was being said by those who 'talked too much', and were not yet always able or ready to enter the fray, were set upon for being 'too feminine' and 'too passive'. Frustrating and painful as the various charges were, the group managed to continue to function. Attacked in other struggles as 'Commies', 'Nigger-lovers', 'traitors', and so on, these seasoned activists might have weathered this also had the success of the Miss America protest not brought about new conditions for which the group, unstructured and without a chain of command and rules for participation, was not prepared.

After the Miss America demonstration, NYRW was asked to send a representative to appear on the popular David Susskind television talk show. Because of our lack of a quick and unified decision-making structure, the show, not NYRW, managed to select the spokesperson, based largely on her attractiveness. This caused additional rancour in the group, not because we felt their choice represented us badly, but because the decision was taken out of our hands. The woman they chose had not been present at the protest, while the woman many in the group wanted to have represent us had been instrumental in its planning and had helped hang the women's liberation banner from the balcony during the live coverage of the pageant. Even though the protest had been my idea and I, too, had helped hang the banner, I was relieved that I didn't have to be the spokesperson. Although by then I had a much better grasp of feminist theory and had begun to speak up and contribute more in NYRW, I had no illusions that I would do well on a live talk show.

We were also inundated with letters, many of which never got answered because we had not set up enough structure even to handle the mail. Many of us never saw the letters or even knew they existed until much later, and then discovered they had not even been saved for history.

The desire to include all women and a fear of being 'elitist' and 'undemocratic' stopped us from setting up any kind of membership criteria. Women unknown to us began to show up at our meetings and tried to impose their own agenda. Some were from left sectarian groups who had come to realise that the women's liberation movement had tapped into a possible new constituency with revolutionary fervour. They attempted to redirect the WLM away from fighting male supremacy and to use it as a recruiting ground. Some of the new women who came in during this period had little or no previous movement experience and were easily confused by the struggles they witnessed. Furthermore, newcomers trailed well behind the group's knowledge and we often had to spend time repeating and explaining what was already understood by the rest of the group, which was inefficient and caused resentment.

Most critical, however, was that the leadership ante was raised with the advent of the media's newly found interest in the group. Many who had played around on the edges of the WLM, who had been reluctant to be *infamous* feminists, were suddenly quite willing to be *famous* feminists, when rewards of money and power were offered. Some realised that the more outrageous their statements, in the name of the new movement, the more press attention they could garner. Others were happy to 'interpret' the new movement with their own personal spin. Opportunism on a grand scale was gathering strength, as was interest on the part of the governmental powers. In the last days of planning for the Miss America protest, we saw police cars parked outside our meeting place where they had never been before. We assumed they were listening in on our meetings.

Together all this was enough eventually to swamp the radical feminist agenda and cause chaos, like a disorganised army being routed. Without an agreed upon and recognised chain of command that could genuinely speak for the movement and muster our forces from groups scattered across the country, we were unable to fight back effectively. To make matters worse, what had been an anti-leadership tendency began to erupt as a full-blown ideology.

The structuralist takeover

The structuralists were the proponents of an idealistic ideology insisting on a 'structureless' (non-hierarchical) movement with no leaders and absolute equality within the groups. They were called 'structuralist' by their opponents to point out that they were actually not only in favour of structure, but were trying to enforce an anarchistic, ultra-egalitarianism structure that pushed for individual development over changing the objective conditions for the masses of women. This anti-leadership ideology rapidly gained credence in the WLM. (It also had currency in the New Left and the counter-culture, where it took on various forms.) Attacks on leaders for leading became common, supplanting what could have been instructive debates on the political directions which those leaders represented and what kind of leadership was needed for greatest effectiveness. Hidden leadership meant it was difficult openly to assess and judge a leader's work on political grounds, thus making personal attacks the easiest means of challenging her.

Although the legitimate aversion to the patterns of leadership women had experienced both in the left and in general society and the very real problem of opportunism needed to be addressed, questions about how to have effective, representative leadership were ignored. Instead, many proclaimed leadership itself to be 'male'. As Catha Mellor and Judy Miller argued in 1969:

> In every group or grouping we've been in, those women who by some chance have acquired the typical 'male' traits of aggressiveness, forcefulness, articulateness, loud voices, and especially public self-confidence, have become the leaders. This reinforces the female tradition of expecting leadership to always have these qualities. Those who are more typical 'feminine' (i.e. passive, not self-confident, inarticulate, 'illogical,' soft spoken) don't see themselves as leaders any more than they did in the male oriented student movement. To compete with such 'male' leadership as already exists in WL would be difficult until the whole problem is out in the open and those who unconsciously lead because they have more of the above-mentioned traits pull themselves back. New styles and definitions of leadership then emerge from the more passive 'feminine' women. (1969: 154)

The structure devised to be the 'great equaliser' of this perceived inequality was the lot system. Rather than making a logical assessment of who was the best person to do a particular task – and what was best for women's liberation – the group simply drew lots.

The lot system made its first appearance in New York Radical Women shortly after the Chicago Women's Liberation Conference, held during the Thanksgiving weekend of 1968 in Lake Villa, Illinois. By then, NYRW had grown to a solid core of about 20 to 30 women who came regularly, with weekly meetings reaching 50 to 60 or more. Some women thought the group unwieldy and wanted to split into smaller groups by drawing lots. Almost all the founders wanted to keep the large group, or split along lines of the people one wanted to work with, if such a split was really necessary.

It was decided by a majority vote that the group would split – and split by lot – in the name of democracy. Many were afraid it was 'elitist' to want to work with certain women with whom they shared a common political direction. The result was the first division of the original militants into several groups where they were less effective. This was a victory for those who favoured the disconnected, random, therapeutic small group devoted to individual self-development ('change yourself') over the more political consciousness-raising cell devoted to building theory and developing feminist consciousness ('change the world') as the organising form of the movement. Many women eventually decided to ignore the lot that they drew, but there was no reverting to the old NYRW with its large and lively political debates and challenging political thought that had resulted in so much important theory and activity.

One of the groups that formed out of this breakup of NYRW was not a lot-assigned group, but one made up of some who drew the lot and others who went to the group anyway. Later to take the name Redstockings, it continued to build on the radical consciousness-raising tradition of NYRW, putting out literature that further developed the earlier group's radical analysis of the condition of women, including the pro-woman line. It led some major innovative actions that put consciousness-raising principles and practice to use in a public way, including disrupting a New York State legislative hearing on abortion composed of 14 men and a nun. Redstockings proclaimed women were the experts on abortion and soon afterwards held their own famous speakout in New York City, where women testified in public for the first time about their abortions – then still a crime. These actions were a critical spur to passage of the liberal New York State abortion reform law of 1970.

Making a step toward greater organisation, Redstockings established a set of principles, a statement of purpose, and orientation sessions for new members, all in the hope that only those women who were in political agreement would join. But those who disagreed to the point of wanting to change the group's direction came anyway, including the structuralists who succeeded in imposing the confining lot system so that the pro-woman radical feminist politics that the group was formulating could effectively be kept from the public.

Some of these structuralists joined Ti-Grace Atkinson, who, though a well-known media spokeswoman herself, had left the National Organisation of Women on the same anti-leadership grounds to form The Feminists. The group operated strictly on the lot and disk systems of anti-leadership rules and regulations plus several more, including a rule that only a third of the membership could be married or in a relationship with a man, a foreshadowing of the separatism that would soon help decimate the WLM. The Feminists described their system in a handout to prospective members:

The Feminists is an organisation without officers which divides work according to the principles of participation by lot. Our goal is a just society all of whose members are equal. Therefore, we aim to develop knowledge and skills in all members and prevent any one member or small group from hoarding information or abilities.

Assignments may be menial or beyond the experience of a member. To assign a member work she is not experienced in may involve an initial loss of efficiency but fosters equality and allows all members to acquire the skills necessary for revolutionary work. When a member draws a task beyond her experience, she may call on the knowledge of other members but her own input and development are of primary importance. The group has the responsibility to support a member's efforts, as long as the group believes that member is working in good faith. A member has a responsibility to submit her work for the group – such as articles or speeches – to the group for correction and approval.

Members who [are experienced in writing and speaking] are urged to withdraw their names from a lot assigning those tasks. [Those] who have once drawn a lot to write or speak must withdraw their names until all members have had a turn.

Each member is guaranteed, and in return is responsible for, equal development on all levels by the lot system and is expected to participate in equal amounts, both as to tasks and hours, with all other members in all the activities of the group. (The Feminists 1970: 115)

Had the structuralists confined the lot system to their own groups, the damage would have been limited. But they sought to impose it on the WLM as the test of what was radical – or even feminist. At the Second Congress to Unite Women in New York City, held on 1 May 1970, The Feminists distributed a leaflet demanding that all participants accede to the lot system or they were not real feminists:

[The lot system] says women – all women – are capable of power – of leadership – but that we no longer want the male values imposed on us – that of hierarchy. It also says that – unless controlled – women – in an anarchic situation – will grab control – and dominate others – become 'stars' – cater to the press – and enter into a position they could not have outside the movement – on top!

Only you're on top of us. So get off our backs. Become Feminists! (leaflet in author's collection)

Leadership also became tied to class in an artificial and sometimes self-serving way. A group called 'The Class Workshop' was organised as a caucus in the New York WLM. It included many members of The Feminists. While visiting New York in 1969 or 1970 (I had moved to Florida to organise women's liberation groups in the South), I was allowed to attend one of their meetings, since I came from a rather poor background. In order to dictate absolute equality, the group not only used the lot system to assign tasks, but they handed out disks at their meetings to make sure nobody talked more often than anyone else. Each person received an equal number of disks to be thrown into the centre of the group each time she spoke. When the disks were gone, the member could no longer speak.

The meeting was boring and awkward and at its end most of my disks were still in my hand. I could not see how one could develop one's speaking abilities in such tightly controlled conditions that did not at all resemble the rough and tumble of the real world. The disk system actually structured consciousness-raising in such a way that it lost its dynamism. Debate, judgement and even comments on what someone said – all critical to political development – were not allowed. There was little of the to and fro of debate which gives people a chance to build on their knowledge by truly investigating an idea. Consciousness-raising under the disk system was deadly for theoretical progress, an imperative for motivating and stimulating members politically.

I was also disturbed that speaking ability could be so completely linked to class. Though I considered class a factor, and I often envied the poise and self-confidence with which the more affluent and secure seemed to move in the world, I knew it wasn't the whole explanation. I remembered the eloquence of Fannie Lou Hamer, who addressed the whole country on national TV during the 1964 Democratic Convention, and many other of the poor, uneducated – even illiterate – leaders of the Mississippi freedom movement who would rise to the occasion with wonderful speeches. Although I felt uncomfortable sometimes as a 'rural hick' among well-educated, urban members of the WLM, I had learned that something besides class background gave people the ability to speak in the language of revolution. It had a lot to do with clarity of direction and purpose and the ability to put into words thoughts and feelings that spoke simply of the actual conditions and hopes of the oppressed. It also had to do with being dedicated and willing to take a clear and firm position on the issues and to take risks.

Fighting the 'tyranny of structurelessness'

Fed up with the attacks and aware that the movement was losing its political depth and forward thrust because it was unable to speak with an organised, powerful voice, some women began to fight back publicly against the anti-leadership ideology. In the spring of 1971, for example, Lynn O'Connor, in declaring the establishment of a group built around *The Woman's Page*, a West Coast feminist newspaper, wrote:

> Hidden leaders have just as much power as acknowledged leaders but they don't have to be responsive to the rest of the organisation. A leader who is not recognized as such, openly, is free to abuse his or her power and not take any responsibility. This is one kind of insidious, destructive leadership running rampant in the left-wing and women's movement today. It follows a distinct pattern. First there is a great deal of liberal talk about the evils of leaders, and the

organisation proudly spreads the word 'we have no leaders in OUR group.' Then, slowly, the individuals who are very serious about their work, who take initiative and feed energy into the organisation, are driven out. They are told that their hard work and initiative are 'elitist', 'arrogant', and inhibiting to others. In fact, this tactic serves to remove all of the real ('indigenous') leaders from the group and leaves it wide open for the opportunistic concealed leaders who then manage to keep the group from moving at all.

Another kind of leadership that has been working against our interests in the left-wing and women's movement is the 'star' who does nothing but public self-promotion via the press, and passes as a representative of the movement but in fact represents no one at all (except fellow strivers) and prevents those who might really represent people from appearing in the public eye. Consequently, the information passed out to the public is usually the bullshit of a petty opportunist star type who has nothing but contempt for most people and manages to convey that contempt and drive away potential allies.

In order to pursue our real work, strong responsible leadership is an absolute necessity.... Masses of people who the left runs down as 'apathetic' will be full of energy and work effectively and well with real leadership behind them, but to allow that to take place, we must be rid of the opportunistic striving prison-guard type leaders who make it their business to stop real work and make people feel inadequate. (1971: 5)

Woman's World, a New York-based radical feminist newspaper edited by Kathie Sarachild and Barbara Leon, reprinted 'The prison guards stand in my way' in its first issue in April 1971 and carried several other articles decrying the suppression of leadership. Other feminists who had been attacked for leadership also briefly united with the California group. Sifting out the truths within the ranting style of *The Woman's Page* was often difficult, however, and its sectarian approach made it impossible for many good feminists to join them. The paper's counter-attack on 'prison guards' – of both the anti-leadership and opportunist varieties – eventually cut such a wide swath in the WLM that few feminists were left standing. The alliance fell apart when accusations of prison guarding were extended to its allies and eventually to its own members. The common bond of having been trashed as leaders was not enough to hold the alliance together in the face of major political differences, including over the direction in which feminism should go. *The Woman's Page* eventually declared itself a vanguard group (a tendency also happening with groups on the left) and clerical workers to be the vanguard of the working class. It then metamorphosed into *The Second Page*, becoming a group of both women and men concerned mainly with fighting capitalism, leaving feminism as a secondary concern.

Among others who fought back against 'The tyranny of structurelessness' was Joreen Freeman, whose paper by that name was published in 1972–73:

To strive for a structureless group is as useful, and as deceptive, as to aim at an 'objective' news story, 'value-free' social science, or a 'free' economy. A 'laissez faire' group is about as realistic as a 'laissez faire' society; the idea becomes a smokescreen for the strong or the lucky to establish hegemony over others ... because the idea of structurelessness does not prevent the formation of informal structures, only formal ones.... For everyone to have the opportunity to be involved in a given group and to participate in its activities, the structure must be explicit, not implicit. This is not to say that formalization of a structure of a group will destroy the informal structure. It usually doesn't. But it does hinder the informal structure from having predominant control.... We cannot decide whether to have a structured or structureless group, only whether or not to have a formally structured one. (1972–73: 152)

The lesbian vanguard

Another challenge to the leadership of the original, militant radical feminists came in the form of lesbian separatism. Lesbians, and sometimes proponents of celibacy, began to complain in consciousness-raising groups that women talked too much about sex and relationships with men, and the attendant issues of abortion, housework and child care, crucial topics that had grabbed the attention of masses of women and caused the WLM to mushroom. Instead they pushed for discussions of 'divisions among women', and often for the abandonment of consciousness-raising itself. 'Straight women', wrote Julia Penelope Stanley, 'even those who call themselves "feminists," are still tied to men and dependent on their tolerance and goodwill, which is why they cling to issues like equal pay and birth control. A woman who has no vested interest in men wouldn't bother' (1975: 9).

Most early feminists had supported lesbians, at least as one of the ways women lived their lives under male supremacy. Since any woman who is a feminist is assumed to be a lesbian by many anyway, it seemed important to most radical feminists to do away with discrimination against lesbians. There were very few tensions between lesbians and so-called 'straight women' until late 1969 when some lesbians began to create a separatist theory and movement in which lesbian*ism* began to supplant femin*ism* by claiming that women who were – or wanted to be – in relationships with men were 'sleeping with the enemy' and 'male-identified'. The conclusion of this argument was that women who wanted men for mates couldn't possibly be *real* feminists and had no place in the WLM, especially in its leadership. Charlotte Bunch proclaimed lesbians to be the vanguard of the feminist movement: 'Lesbianism is the key to liberation and only women who cut their ties to male privilege can be trusted to remain serious in the struggle against male dominance' (Bunch 2000). Or as one slogan put it, 'Feminism is the theory; lesbianism is the practice'.

By the early 1970s, the women's liberation movement was giving way to lesbian vanguardism and to the rising tide of cultural feminism. Many movement women turned to an all-woman alternative culture, with lesbianism at its core, where men were simply irrelevant and to be ignored. The era of the collective fight against male supremacy was supplanted by the era of attempting to escape from it. 'Liberation' was deleted from the women's liberation movement. The 'women's movement' stood in its stead, with no definition of itself, except perhaps in the self-serving and age-old rhetoric of women's natural superiority to men. A woman with whom I shared a panel in the early 1990s pointed to the progress of the 'women's movement' by stating gleefully, 'Feminism today is anything a woman says it is'.

The liberal takeover

By the time some women's liberationists had begun to figure out and combat the anti-leader tendency, organised and well-funded forces had moved into the leadership void with their own 'leaders' and agenda. This rush by the media – and, to a debatable degree, government counter-insurgency organisations[2] – to fill the leadership gap with their own spokespersons effectively cut off the original, radical movement from its constituency.

The media had not only singled out certain spokespersons, they 'promoted' women from within their own ranks to speak for the WLM. As Kathie Sarachild pointed out in *Feminist Revolution*, a book published by Redstockings in 1975, which exposed this takeover as part of its analysis of the decline of the WLM:

> Many media women themselves were becoming the movement's representatives to the media, whether self-arranged or picked by the men in control. Most notable and powerful among these is Gloria Steinem, who started as a reporter for *New York,* the magazine which then backed the first preview issue of *Ms.* magazine. But there were others who first reported on it, then joined it, and then became the main source of feminist opinion instead of the founders they used to quote. They suddenly found the anti-leader line convenient whereas formerly they had searched for leaders to write about, attacking women who resisted uncontrolled exposure as examples of alleged female passivity. But suddenly a means of establishing authentic [leadership] – that is, chosen leaders and groups that actually represented themselves – would threaten their unique and newly acquired position of access to media channels themselves. Gloria Steinem, so clearly the main feminist political leader chosen from the media and for the media, began to come out for 'leaderlessness,' using her position as leader to enforce that trend for others. (1975: 31)

Although Gloria Steinem has occasionally come out with some good feminist soundbites, she has never broken new ground or been accountable to any women's liberation group and is truly a media phenomena. What's more, when authentic leaders, like Betty Friedan, a founder of the National Organisation for Women, and Redstockings have pointed this out, they have been accused, even by other feminists, of merely being jealous of Steinem's looks or fame. Attributing political criticism of leadership – or perceived leadership – to psychological motives has also contributed to the favouring of celebrity spokespersons over authentic leaders.

Gil Scott Heron used to sing 'The Revolution Will Not Be Made on Television', but even many radicals have forgotten that they cannot depend on the corporate media to carry their ideas out to the public in their original form. As the definition of leader has narrowed to mean public 'speaker' and 'writer', the invaluable, but often less glamorous, work of organising and theorising – and the dozens of other crucial skills women have to offer – are no longer acknowledged and supported and have fallen off the movement's radar screen.

As the early radical feminist ideas, and the leaders behind them, were pushed aside to make way for a safer, less demanding, individualistic feminism, the development of groups into organisations prepared to deal with the very real power of the ruling classes – both economic and sexual – was blocked. The creativity of both the authentic leaders of the movement and the masses of women they had been rousing to action was cut off. The 'celebrity leadership' that filled the void raked in support and money that should have gone to further development of women's liberation groups that were actually organising women to fight for their liberation. Instead, groups and individuals who survived the takeover more or less intact have run into roadblocks at every turn and have great difficulty getting their ideas out to a broad audience.

With the original leadership, work and ideas of the WLM no longer readily available, the revisionist 'interpreters' of the movement have been free to remove it from its exciting, radical roots of fighting male supremacy. The feeling that the impossible might be achieved through knowledge, clarity, unity and struggle has suffered a staggering setback.

Conclusion

By 1975, thousands of women had dropped away from the women's liberation movement, in large part because it no longer spoke to their needs and their hopes. Not wanting to abandon feminism completely, some joined – or went back to – the more liberal groups, such as the National Organisation for Women, because their hierarchical structures and financial bases had allowed them to survive. Many of the leaders who had given the movement its impetus dropped away, discouraged and disgusted by both the personal attacks and the disruptive, blocking tactics of those who have made it nearly impossible even to hold a public meeting that focuses on male supremacy and women's liberation.

Loose decentralisation can accomplish much under certain conditions, such as during the great consciousness-raising period of women's liberation when groups sprung up like grass. The genius of these early radical feminist consciousness-raising groups was that, though anarchist in form, they were at least partially democratic centralist in function. The raw data gleaned from the experience of all women in the group was analysed and formulated by a leadership (however unacknowledged) and immediately fed back for further discussion. Even with only mimeograph and ditto machines – instead of the Internet – ideas spread like wildfire across the country and around the world in newsletters, position papers, journals and letters, and through word-of-mouth, conferences and progressive organisations.

Consciousness-raising groups used broad democratic participation to bring about unity of thought and deep agreement among members. These loosely structured groups taught women that their problems were political, not personal, that even the differences among women had political roots. This knowledge built unity where competition had previously flourished.

'A hundred flowers bloomed' as ideas and theories contended. Some of the ideas turned out to be invasive weeds, however, and these informal groups were not organisations capable of taking on the repressive apparatus of either men as a class or the state when the inevitable backlash set in. Consciousness-raising groups did a fairly good job of fulfilling the first part of Chinese revolutionary Mao-Tse Tung's advice to 'divide our forces to arouse the masses; concentrate forces to deal with the enemy', but the anti-leadership ideology helped dismantle attempts to move to the second part.

The history of the women's liberation movement shows that more structured forms are necessary to assure the development of the organised strength needed to accumulate and eventually take power – assuming the goal is to take women's fair share of power to meet the needs of all, not just to 'empower' individuals.

It also shows that, although structure and organisation are necessary, over-structuring a situation can also be detrimental. For example, when too many rules were applied to consciousness-raising (disk systems, being non-judgemental, no interruptions), the democratic spontaneity necessary for creativity was lost, and the leadership, which did much of the analysing and formulating, was suppressed.

Of course there were many reasons, in addition to 'the leadership problem', that the women's liberation movement fell apart, but without leadership, organisation and the discipline that goes with it, no gains for women can be defended and furthered. Sometimes I wonder if those of us in nations spoiled by the fruits of imperialism, and now trying to understand and adjust to our current financial fall from grace, are ready for that kind of discipline, for even as we call for it, we often do not practice it. We need to acknowledge that the competitive system of capitalism has a thwarting effect on even the most dedicated among us. In 'The double standard of organisation', Elizabeth Most contrasted our resistance to structure with the well-organised opposition:

> What the individual is most afraid of, must avoid at all cost, is organisation. Organisation calls up regimentation, the specter of automation, blue ants. The worst enemy of individuality is structure.... A glimpse through Alice's looking

glass to the other side, seeing the double standard at work, may help turn us 'little' Americans around. The 'big' Americans are organised within every inch of their roles and careers. They are companies, corporations, combines, consortiums, conferences, cartels, and conglomerates. (1975: 160)

Creating the organisational structures, theories and formulas to attain our goals is no easy task and one that cannot be learned by any preordained short cut. We can't know ahead of time *exactly* what forms of organisation will work under present world, national and local conditions or *precisely* how to go about building them, but we now have experience of our own, as well as much useful history from past revolutionary struggles. Fortified with this knowledge, we need to get back to organising, to uniting women around a programme for liberation.

We may find that 'one size fits all' doesn't work for all situations and all stages of struggle. An elected hierarchy and Robert's Rules of Order may not always provide the best solution. We will no doubt also find that structure does not solve all the problems of leadership and democratically selecting our leaders does not solve all the problems of opportunism. But many of us have learned that leadership is necessary to win, and that it is crucial that leaders be democratically chosen, acknowledged, valued, encouraged, supported – and held accountable. We now face the challenging task of creating the organisations, structures and leadership to get us where we want to go.

Notes

Several of the sources used in this chapter are out-of-print, including the book *Feminist Revolution,* which was first published by Redstockings in 1975 and by Random House in 1978. *Feminist Revolution* and many early WLM documents are available from the Redstockings Women's Liberation Archives Distribution Project, P.O. Box 2625, Gainesville, FL 32602-2625 USA or on the web at www.afn.org/~redstock.

1 'Anti-woman' and 'pro-woman' refer to two competing political lines in the WLM. Anti-woman means the theory that women are damaged, brainwashed, conditioned and consent to their own oppression. The pro-woman line says that women are not damaged and do not consent to their oppression, but act in certain ways in order to survive or cope with their oppressors, as in 'women are messed over, not messed up'. Anti-woman here refers to those who blamed, attacked, or made fun of the contestants. For a further discussion of the 'pro-woman line', see Hanisch 2000b: 113 and Leon 1975: 66.

2 In 1975, Redstockings publicly questioned Gloria Steinem's sudden positioning as spokesperson for the WLM, given her involvement as founder and director of a CIA-funded front group, the Independent Research Service, which recruited and sent anti-communist young people to the world youth festivals in the late 1950s and early 1960s. The extent of US government interference in the WLM has still to be fully documented, but there is no doubt that it existed. For example, the Rockefeller Commission Report of June 1975

exposed an executive branch counter-insurgency programme – aptly named 'Operation Chaos' – which listed the WLM among its targets. FBI files obtained under the Freedom of Information Act show that many individual feminists and WLM groups were spied upon.

6

Self-emancipation and leadership: the case of Martin Luther King[1]

Alan Johnson

> For several hours he listened as the young men talked about the conditions in which they lived, especially the absence of jobs for youths of their age, race and education. King argued that non-violent protest offered the only possible course for substantially changing their conditions. The gang leaders who had been impressed by King's forays through the streets listened respectfully to his tactical argument. After a lengthy dialogue, King convinced Richard 'Peanut' Tidwell, the twenty-year-old leader of the Roman Saints, to accept his point. Tidwell joined him in telling the other gang chieftains to give King's proposals a try, and the discussion went back and forth in the early-morning hours in the sweltering apartment ... King's arguments won over more and more of the gang leaders. Finally at 3:00 or 4:00 a.m. the entire group agreed to tell their members to avoid further violence. (Garrow 1988: 496)

Self-emancipation is a political process in which the oppressed author their own liberation through popular struggles which are educational, producing a cognitive liberation, and instrumental, enabling the defeat of their oppressors (Draper 1977: 213–34; 1992b; Geras 1986; Johnson 2000a). To 'lead' a process of self-emancipation is to empower the oppressed to liberate themselves by self-controlling, mass, collective action. Democratic leadership is a *conversation*, spoken *within* the movement, sustained by leader and follower, concerning the *goals* both can agree to pursue, pragmatically, in light of their changing interpretations of circumstances and experience, and the *means* to achieve those goals against an adversary (Johnson 2000b). In this conversation the functions of 'leading' and 'following' are not the exclusive possession of particular actors. Actors possess both 'leading' and 'led' selves, and, like Martin Luther King, Jr. and Richard Tidwell, can shift repeatedly, during the conversation, between moments of leading and following.

This chapter examines Martin Luther King's leadership of the civil rights movement in the United States from 1955 to 1968 as a case study in the leadership of self-emancipation. I do not claim King as a model of such leadership, but rather seek to explore his *struggle with* democratic leadership for clues about its character and conditions. The first part of this chapter critically appropriates what remains useful and important in some old stories about King's leadership, but urges a dialectical approach in which King is understood as *both sculptor and marble*. The second part of the chapter evaluates King's contribution to the process of self-emancipation from 1955 to 1968, highlighting his communicative leadership of cognitive revolution and his generalship of movement struggles, paying particular attention to the leadership skills and followership skills he possessed, and those he lacked. Finally, I examine the transformation of King's leadership after his political radicalisation and adoption of new goals in 1967–68. I employ the philosopher Alasdair MacIntyre's insight that actors 'can only answer the question "What I am to do?" [once they] can answer the prior question, "Of what story or stories do I find myself a part?"' (1985: 216). I show King was a purposeful and reflective agent who *learnt* from his experiences in a mass movement of self-emancipation, and so began to tell himself a different story about America and, therefore, about his own leadership.

Some old stories about King's leadership: a critique

Stories about 'History'

The Russian Marxist philosopher Plekhanov, in his famous essay 'The role of the individual in history' (1940), reduces the individual leader to the *determined product* of 'the social needs of the given epoch', only able to influence the short-term and individual features of events. This story about leadership has been retold by Isaac Deutscher (1963), and by Ernest Mandel, who saw the 'cunning of History' expressed through 'larger social forces', which shape the individual leader 'as sculptors hammering away at blocks of marble' (1986: 74).

This story is useful in locating King as one of a layer of new black leaders who emerged in the context of the socio-economic shifts which transformed the US class structure, created a black urban working class, and undermined the social relations and politico-cultural structures of 'Jim Crow'. This layer represented, but also helped produce, the 'new Negro' whose struggle overturned the system of legalised southern racism in the decade from 1955 to 1965 (McAdam 1982; Bloom 1987: 120–54; Carson 1999: 88–99). King's development of the 'cognitive praxis' of the civil rights movement (its worldview, sense of self and Other, goals and tactics) occurred within shaping contexts of articulation: historically specific political cultures and institutional traditions (Eyerman and Jamison 1991: 62).

Indeed, according to Aldon Morris, the very 'quality and success of King's leadership stemmed from the interaction of large social and historical factors with the unique combination of qualities that were deeply rooted in his own personality' (1993: 35). Morris blends the large-scale and structural with the personal and contingent, to establish that 'the times were ready for King' and 'King was ready for the times'. He identifies several shaping contexts, both 'political opportunities' and 'mobilising structures', for King's leadership, from the racist system of domination in the south to the urbanisation of the black population; from institution building in black urban communities to the impact of the Cold War on a Federal government claiming leadership of the free world; from decolonisation abroad to the technological development and expansion of the mass media at home; and, of course, the inheritance of a rich black protest tradition transmitted across generations.

But Morris also insists that the socialisation King received from a rich interlocking network of family, church and college decisively shaped his leadership. First, it equipped him with highly developed personal leadership *skills* of self-control, discipline, a remarkable ability to communicate, and a deep sense of social obligation. Second, it instilled in him a *philosophy* mixing the social gospel, personalism, Hegalian ideas, and socialistic politics, which not only wedded him to the oppressed, but led him to understand the oppressed as capable of self-change through struggle. Third, it gave him *knowledge* of the black protest tradition, of non-violent civil disobedience, and of the scope and meaning of the colonial revolution. Fourth, it provided him with a social *location* atop a resource-rich, mass-based, independent black institution: the church. These socially conditioned and historically specific skills, resources, locations and knowledges combined in such a way that when Rosa Parks refused to stand up for a white man on a bus in Montgomery, and the southern black revolt began, 'they had a leader in their midst' (Morris 1983: 58).[2] Ernest Mandel's concept of 'social sifting mechanisms', those class- or group-specific institutions through which leaders are selected and tempered, is a valuable development of Plekhanov's framework, and highly relevant to understanding King's leadership, which was socially sifted through the indigenous structures of the black community and church, and tempered throughout the 1955–56 Montgomery Bus Boycott (Mandel 1986: 70–3).

However, while it is essential to place King's leadership in broader historical contexts, the historian must avoid *reducing* it to those contexts until, as with Mandel, the leader is a mere block of marble sculpted by History. Ironically, the Hegel-reading King initially wrote himself into this very story (see Garrow 1988: 61, 68, 218–19, 377, 428). In Montgomery, in 1955, he declared to a mass meeting, 'If M.L. King had never been born this movement would have taken place. I just happened to be here. You know there comes a time when time itself is ready for a change. That time has come in Montgomery, and I had nothing to do with it' (in Garrow 1988: 56). This story has been retold many times, in tones both sacred and profane. But the danger of this story of a metaphysical sculptor, whether God or History or Movement, to which King stands as merely a 'representative', is three-fold: the very idea of democratic leadership is obscured as the role King's leadership played, for good and for ill, fades out of the picture; it makes it impossible for us to grasp that his leadership evolved through abrasive conversations with a mass self-emancipatory movement which refused to sanctify him; and it has no vocabulary to describe King's attempt, after 1966, to *shift* History onto other, more radical tracks.

Stories about 'the movement'

The New Left rejected the tropes of the 'Great Man' and the 'Laws of History' in favour of the view of the civil rights leader Ella Baker that 'The Movement made Martin, Martin did not make the Movement'. The historian and civil rights activist Clayborne Carson has insisted that King was 'the product of the social movements that he has come to symbolise', and has urged us to reject the idea of leaders as 'decisive elements in historical processes'. Indeed Carson claims that 'if King had never lived, the black struggle would have followed a course of development similar to the one it did' (1993: 241, 246). Robert Parris Moses, the Student Non-Violent Coordinating Committee (SNCC) leader, when asked to weigh the contribution of King's leadership to the civil rights movement, argued King was just a wave on the ocean and advised us to 'shift our attention from the wave to the ocean' (1993: 73). But this metaphor, like Mandel's, invokes the natural world as a model for the social world, and so, in its own fashion, also brackets out individual human agency, reflection and praxis. Against his own intentions Moses also stops us thinking about how to practice leadership democratically, as a 'conversation'.

Stories about 'Destiny'

Finally, our historical memory is often frozen by *that* image of King on the steps of the Lincoln Memorial, on 28 August 1963, arms out-stretched, voice tremulously calling us to his dream of a new moral geography. This King is cast in the role of Carlyle's Hero as Divinity, a 'natural luminary shining by the gift of heaven' (1995). In our less self-confident times this trope takes the form of a 'chosen' man 'bearing his cross'. This lacks the Nietzscheanism of Carlyle but remains just as metaphysical. King's greatness is still 'on loan' from a higher power or place. Thus, the historian David Garrow sees a personal religious experience dividing King's leadership into two clear-cut periods. *Before* his 'vision in the kitchen', on 27 January 1956, the 'reluctant leader' is gripped by feelings of fear and inadequacy. *After* this 'most central and formative event in his life' (when, in answer to desperate prayer, a personal God told King to carry on the fight), the 'strong and dedicated' leader emerged, with an understanding of 'his role, his mission, and his fate' in 'rather a complete form' (1993: 14, 18–19).

The value of Garrow's story, of course, is that it captures the humanity of the leader. Under constant physical threat, and dragged into a leadership position he never actively sought, by a movement he felt he could not deny,

King placed his (endangered) self into a bigger story authored by his God. As Huggins says, following William James, the story of the vision in the kitchen helped King construct a unified, from a divided, self (1993). Richard H. King is surely right that the story was 'the way [King] had of explaining himself to himself and to others and of giving coherence to the story of his public life' (1993: 146).

But this story risks reducing King's complex and protracted *growth through learning* in the context of a mass insurgent movement of self-emancipation, to a simple and unitary moment of *transformation through revelation* in the context of spiritualised isolation. Indeed the story reproduces, as historical narrative, one of the main limitations of King's leadership in practice: a tendency to treat that leadership as a sanctified and personal destiny. For King, the story endangered the conversation between himself and the movement, for a man bearing a cross is rarely talkative. For us, it risks obscuring the dialectical relationship between leader and movement.

Each of these stories tells us much about, respectively, the structural context, popular determination, and personal meaning of King's leadership. But to think about his leadership *dialectically* we need to insist on its importance *and* de-divinise it – to view it as practised within an ever-changing relationship between leaders, followers and goals. Our sense of the structural conditioning of movement leadership can be enriched by a sharper awareness of the ways leaders are central to 'the active construction of group cohesion and the conscious definition of group interests', as they shape 'interaction of and within collectivities', via their 'words and actions' (Bloom 1987: 9). A concern for such interactive, or dialogic, processes will help us *see* leadership, de-sacrilise it, and rediscover its communicative and artistic character (C. Barker 2001). Our attention will turn first to the role of both followership and leadership skills in the conversation of leadership (Johnson 2000b).

Leadership skills and followership skills

Leadership skills 1: cognitive revolution and the communicative leadership of self-emancipation
The leadership of self-emancipation is, *above all else*, concerned with the resolution of a paradox. Without a cognitive revolution of the oppressed (self-changing) then the idea of structural social change (the changing of circumstances) being authored *from below* is unviable. Yet, if the existing social relations and structural disparities of power condemn the oppressed to not only material but also *ideological* subordination, then how can a cognitive revolution take place at all? In 1845 Karl Marx founded a new politics by giving an entirely new answer to this paradox. He wrote, 'the coincidence of the changing of circumstances and of human activity or self-changing can be conceived and rationally understood only as revolutionary practice'

(Marx 1975: 422). Hal Draper found in this thesis 'the "philosophic" formulation by Marx of the principle of Self-Emancipation', and 'a rejection of the whole humanitarian-philanthropic attitude towards the masses of the people', which had dominated thinking about leadership until that point (1992b: 258).

King's leadership helped resolve the paradox of self-emancipation by marrying a viable protest strategy to a refocusing of the black church tradition (Bloom 1987: 137–50). By facilitating mass participation in struggle, King *fused* the moments of self-changing and the changing of circumstances. Non-violent direct action was a new language, a 'strategic frame', through which popular forces could envision and speak themselves in a new way, and defeat their adversary (see Marable 1998: 192–3; McAdam 1996). The settings in which this new language was spoken were the church, mass meeting, the freedom song, the citizenship school, the courthouse, the march, and the jailhouse (R. H. King 1996: 41–3).

Leadership was vital to this process because no automatic relationship exists between economic change and political identity and action. The conditions of emergence for the 'new Negro', speaking a new discourse, may well have been the tectonic post-war socio-economic shifts, but the political skills of movement leaders were central to the construction of an emancipatory subject and the development of a viable protest form to defeat the adversary. In McAdam's terms King was a 'master-framer' with a 'genius for strategic dramaturgy' which reinforced the purely ideational content of his communication (McAdam 1996: 348).

With King in mind, Eyerman and Jamison have highlighted this first, *communicative* aspect to the leadership of self-emancipation. Their concept of the 'movement communicator' sensitises us to the leader who 'In mobilising a sense of collective will, as well as in articulating felt needs ... thematizes in speeches, tracts, articles, and books the rudiments of a new collective identity. Central to this process of self-formation is the construction of an Other against which the budding movement will interact' (1991: 101).

The communicative leadership of self-emancipation involves the translation, generalisation, and selection of language in the social setting of a mass movement. First, King self-consciously *translated* vocabularies which had seemed incommensurable, enabling different audiences to hear, and begin speaking to, each other. He enabled communication across generations, 'races' and organisations, creating a relatively unified movement. King could speak to an AFL-CIO convention until 'that great crowd of hardened unionists – most of them white – stand up and cheer and cheer', but he could also move a poor black rural church audience to action (Oates 1982: 186). He could defend the movement to a president or, in *Letter from a Birmingham Jail,* the circulation of which reached one million before he was released, to a hostile white clergy. But he could also talk with gang members on street corners and pool halls.

Second, as Stokely Carmichael pointed out, King was also 'a true teacher' able to stretch the political understanding of his audience by *generalising* the particular struggle, tracing its connections to other struggles, suggesting broader alliances and wider goals (in Hampton and Fayer 1995: 348). For example, King framed the 1955 Montgomery Bus Boycott to its participants – after their élan and creativity had suggested new possibilities to him – as part of a world-wide anti-imperialist revolt of the helots: 'We must oppose all exploitation. We want no classes and castes. We want to set everybody free.' King told Bayard Rustin that he was working 'to *instil within the minds of the people* [that] it is much larger than a bus situation' (in Garrow 1988: 71, 79, emphasis added).

Third, King grasped the political importance of linguistic *selection* in movement discourse. The dialogist Volosinov argued that it was the task of the leader of self-emancipation to respond 'strategically and creatively to the problems which ... people pose for themselves in the contest over alternative futures [and] helping to provide and develop the symbolic, cultural and organisational resources with which they themselves can provide answers' (quoted in Collins 1996: 86–7). King argued that 'a leader has to be concerned about the problem of semantics. Each word ... has a denotative meaning – its explicit and recognised sense – and a connotative meaning – its suggestive sense' (in Carson 1999: 321). King's careful critique of the slogan of 'black power' demonstrated his leadership. He warned that the slogan, despite its ability to instil pride, could, unless articulated with wider agencies and programmes, 'confuse our allies, isolate the Negro community and give many prejudiced whites ... a ready excuse for self-justification' (in Carson 1999: 322).

Charisma and self-emancipation

Was the charismatic form of King's communication compatible with self-emancipation? According to Aldon Morris, 'King had precisely the type of personality that Weber conceptualised as charismatic': 'he was viewed as extraordinary by large numbers of people; he was competent at his tasks; many people identified with his vision of a "beloved community" devoid of racism; and King had the talent to articulate this view forcefully through powerful oratory' (1984: 279).

King's charisma was, in part, the result of training, informally at the feet of his preacher father in the black Baptist church, and formally at black institutions such as Crozier College, where he took courses in preaching and public speaking. The Roman statesman Cicero defined the *rhetor* (orator) as one trained to embody rhetoric, communicating not only through words but through the entire persona. Garry Wills has observed that King's education, formal and informal, reprised that of the *rhetor* of the Greek and Roman empires (1994). The results were witnessed by C. T. Vivian: 'Doc really communicated on other levels than just the intellectual. He communicated on the emotional level too, so that you didn't have to understand his words to understand what he meant. That's why the No D's and the Ph.D.'s could be moved by the same speech' (in Oates 1982: 289).

Are such emotive forms not hostile to the self-reliance we associate with self-emancipation? When we find in the speech of some poor southern blacks the expression '*the* Martin Luther King', or when we hear Donie Jones, a bus boycotter in Montgomery in 1955, recalling that 'I'm telling you the gaddam truth, you had to hold the people to keep them from gettin' to him. Reverend King was a God-sent man', we might feel we have travelled far from a process of self-emancipation (in Hampton and Fayer 1995: 24). The true picture, I would suggest, is more complex.

In the context of the black south the preacher's charisma was a social and cultural relation rather less elitist, and rather more demotic, than one might expect; in important respects it was quasi-contractual, marked by rough forms of accountability to the congregation. Moreover, King's charismatic leadership and church base played 'a crucial role in the mobilisation process'. Self-emancipation in the south had to pass through the portals of a radical refocusing of the black church tradition. King was, as Aldon Morris puts it, 'the master of this refocussing process [and] a model for activist clergymen across the South' (Morris 1984: 7–10, 93, 98).

King infused the emotive-participatory traditions of the church with a new, more radical content, unlocking the psychological door to mass black participation in political protest in the south. As he filled the messianic style with a new content, he developed what Bayard Rustin described as 'tremendous facility ... for giving people the feeling that they could be bigger and stronger and more courageous than they thought they could be' (Oates 1982: 112). King used *his* force of personality, his schooled and socially sanctioned 'charisma', to help make *self*-emancipation possible. One biographer, Oates, has described the peak of the civil rights movement, in 1965, as 'a time of self-liberation when they stood and marched to glory with Martin Luther King' (1982: 372). A young black leader has recalled that King 'made it possible for them to believe that they could overcome' and Morris rightly argues this was the 'most profound contribution he made to the black protest movement' (Oates 1982: 372; Morris 1993: 56).

Leadership skills 2: defeating the other – the generalship of self-emancipation
And yet, to 'lift the slave before his Lord', to quote Shelley, is only half the job. The other half is the engagement, and defeat in battle, of the adversary. As Perry Anderson has put it, contra Habermas, 'The danger of conceiving democratic life as dialogue is that we may forget that its primary reality remains strife' (1994: 43). In consequence the leadership of self-emancipation involves *generalship*, which we can define as the authoritative strategic direction and tactical coordination of the movement in its conflict with the enemy, in such a way that the oppressed develop their collective capacity to

author their own liberation. Indeed McAdam has argued that King's genius lay precisely in 'the compelling dramaturgy of his tactics' which, as much as his oratory, did the work of cultural framing for the movement (1996: 354).

Generalship involves the translation of the goals of the movement into negotiable demands in the arena of the established political culture, the coordination and direction of forces in pursuit of those goals, the management of rapid shifts from advance to retreat, and the timing of compromises in light of assessments of the movement's strength and momentum. Generalship is a historically variable activity reshaped repeatedly in light of changing social relations and cultural purposes (Keegan 1987).

Judgements on King's generalship are mixed. It is clear that he was knowledgeable about its arts. He knew that 'each situation had to be studied in detail: the strength and temper of our adversaries had to be estimated and any change in any of these factors would affect the details of our strategy' (in Carson 1999: 278). His strategy of non-violence reassured whites and emboldened blacks. It was a vital part of their cognitive liberation because it unlocked the door to collective political protest. In King's response to the call from Robert Williams for armed self-defence we can find a hard-headed strategic insight highly relevant to self-emancipation, as much as a religious sensibility: 'There is more power in socially organised masses on the march than there is in guns in the hands of a few desperate men' (in Bloom 1987: 143). King was flexible enough to call for a re-think about non-violence after the state response to the Selma protests of 1965. As he learnt more about his adversary he began to speak of the need for more direct and coercive forms of non-violence (see Garrow 1978).

Moreover, in his understanding of the aesthetics of protest, and of the need to dramatise the underlying issues for the new mass media, King was, according to Oates, 'better than any Negro leader of his generation' (Oates 1982: 178). The socialist Michael Harrington judged King to be 'a genius at improvising' (in Hampton and Fayer 1995: 458). Ved Mehta linked King with Gandhi as the two great 'imaginative artists' of protest, 'who knew how to use world politics as their stage' (in Oates 1982: 290). And, as generalship depends upon the ability to make clear judgements when 'under fire' from the enemy, King's personal bravery was an important leadership skill. Harrington was struck by King's 'emotional strength and maturity', which enabled him to carry on the conversation of leadership at 'the eye of the storm, calm and self-possessed, while a tempest whirled about him' (Harrington 1972: 114). Even King's ability to coordinate leadership teams, often noted in the memoirs of the Southern Christian Leadership Conference (SCLC) staffers, is part of the art of generalship.

But King's generalship was also the object of sharp criticism from the movement. For example, at Birmingham in 1963, Fred Shuttlesworth was infuriated when King negotiated a local truce without winning guarantees or properly consulting local leaders, and told him 'you're mister big but you're soon to be mister nothing' (in Garrow 1988: 256–7). At the Democratic Party convention in Atlanta in 1964, King failed to back fully the black delegates of the Mississippi Freedom Democratic Party, in order to preserve his access to the Democratic Party and Administration. One delegate witnessed the anger of SNCC leader Bob Moses, who 'tore King up' (quoted in Branch 1998: 474). In both instances King's generalship confused and demobilised the movement, 'cashing in' its strength in ways which eroded its self-reliance, confidence and combativity. To lead a process of self-emancipation is to use established political institutions and processes while viewing the source of change as the clarity of consciousness, organisational strength, and self-reliance of the emancipatory subject.

These examples demonstrate that while generalship can enable or hinder self-emancipation, it is an *inescapable* part of social movement practice. This is because social movements are built by the oppressed not merely for expressive purposes, but also for instrumental purposes; not only for self-changing, but also for the changing of circumstances. These two moments of self-emancipation are inseparable: winning changes the self and circumstances, while defeats lead to a general retreat, to old selves as well as old conditions. Generalship is an indispensable condition for victory because the basic *capacity* of the oppressed is its collectivity. This capacity, while being built in struggle through democratic dialogue and cognitive liberation, can only be *deployed* in the form of coordinated thrusts at the enemy, brought to bear upon 'circumstances' – structures of domination and exploitation – *so as to change them*.

However, for generalship to enable collective empowerment, and not merely individual or sect aggrandisement, then leadership must sustain a democratic conversation within the movement in which the initiative, innovation and experience of the ranks is fully present. And here we arrive at another paradox. To be a democratic leader requires *followership skills*.

Followership skills

To associate leadership exclusively with the 'leading self' is a mistake. Democratic leadership involves an equilibrium between the leading and the led self of an actor. As such it is defined not only by dynamic initiative but by *an openness to being acted upon*, a quality William Wordsworth called 'wise passiveness', and John Keats 'negative capability'. I call these qualities 'followership skills' and suggest that it was because King possessed them that he was open to learning and growth as a movement leader. Where his followership skills failed there lay his biggest failings as a democratic leader.

What were King's followership skills? First, Aldon Morris has identified King's 'absolute identification with the poor, oppressed black masses' as the foundation of his leadership (1993: 57). Second, Richard King has highlighted the 'metaphor of maturation' at the heart of King's thought, the conviction that collective political action was able to produce a transformation of the self, and a development of the human virtues of courage and solidarity (1993). Third, as Marable has pointed out, King remained open to new ideas and new experiences. 'Unlike nearly all his contemporaries King consistently challenged himself to draw new correlations between poverty, racism and war' (1992: 207).

These three followership skills – commitment to, faith in, and willingness to learn from the struggle – were visible in embryo in his first speech to the Montgomery Bus Boycott. We are struck not only by King's impact upon the audience, by the *leader's* ability to 'sense ... the mood ... and articulate ... the unspoken and inchoate feelings of the audience', but also by the impact of the audience upon King, by the *follower's* ability to be acted upon: 'My heart was full ... The unity of purpose and esprit de corps of these people had been indescribably moving' (Fairclough 1990: 21).

It is important that we tell ourselves, with Adam Fairclough, that 'the response of the black community ... transformed King's life', rather than think that a solitary religious experience left King 'bearing his cross' (1990: 16). With Greg Moses we should conclude that King's ideas were 'distilled from long experience with struggle', drawn from the 'rougher texture of lived human experience', rather than imagine his ideas and his courage were breathed into him metaphysically (1997: xi, 18). With Cornel West we should judge King the most successful organic intellectual in US history *because* he was 'ensconced and enmeshed' in the world of 'common, ordinary people' (1993: 115–16).

Moreover, we can extend West's insight to begin thinking about the *limits* of King's followership skills. For the world in which King was 'ensconced and enmeshed' was a patriarchal one, in which the preacher-congregation relationship positioned him as a messianic figure. These legacies were never fully sloughed off by King and deformed his leadership in decisive ways, interrupting, at times stopping altogether, the conversation which lies at the heart of the leadership of self-emancipation.

When the talking stopped

Ella Baker famously argued that King offered a model of the 'leader-centred movement', when what was really needed for self-emancipation was 'movement-centred leaders' (Oates 1982: 123–8, 243). Charismatic leadership and the preacher-congregation style, she insisted, blocked the development of self-reliance, political growth and leadership skills further down. Complaining of the 'Moses' quality of King's leadership (Fairclough 1990: 54), she proposed a democratic, participatory leadership style which was more suited to the dynamics of self-emancipation:

> Instead of 'the leader' – a person who was supposed to be a magic man – you would develop individuals who were bound together by a concept that benefited larger numbers of individuals and provided an opportunity for them to

grow into being responsible for carrying out a program. (quoted in Morris 1984: 104)

And, for a brief shining moment, under Baker's influence, the young militants of SNCC put some flesh on these ideas. As Carson puts it:

The most successful SNCC projects unleashed the power of communities, allowing residents to become confident of their collective ability to overcome oppression ... The most effective organisers of the 1960s realised their job was to work themselves out of a job. They avoided replacing old dependencies with new ones. (in Marable 1998: xv)

In sharp contrast, King struggled with the legacy of the preacher-congregation model of leadership. SCLC, at its centre, was more a court than a democratic organisation. Proposals could fall or be taken up on the strength of King's approval. Indeed C. K. Steele recalled that 'Dr King was the last word on everything. I don't remember any time that Dr King made a proposal that we did not accept' (in Morris 1984: 93). Virginia Durr complained that King 'cannot stand criticism and has to be a leader of the sheep not a real democratic worker along with the others' (in Fairclough 1987: 50). In 1962 Emery O. Jackson, Birmingham newspaper editor, was moved to complain that 'An itinerant leadership which floats in and flows out of a city is not the correct approach. There must never be allowed to develop a let-King-do-it attitude ... No exotic leadership with a medicine show type of exhibition is likely to get the job done.' As late as 1965, in Selma, the SNCC Project Director, Silas Norman, was moved to complain that 'SCLC pushes the idea that local people need leaders like Martin Luther King'. Norman counterposed to this SNCC's preference that 'local people build their own leaders out of their own communities'. In similar vein, Dave Dennis, a leader of the Congress of Racial Equality (CORE), thought SCLC made no effort 'to really involve indigenous leadership' (in Garrow 1988: 201, 396, 370).

Moreover, Baker argued that SCLC, in replicating the fluid and charismatic relationships of the church, failed to open up the organisation to those with a different culture and practice. When Bayard Rustin suggested to King that he had failed to think through his Chicago campaign to abolish the ghetto, had not understood the power-structure there or formulated any clear goals, King's response was to walk off and pray, to Rustin's understandable fury at 'this business of King talking to God and God talking to King' (in Garrow 1988: 455). It is little wonder that King was referred to irreverently by some SNCC staffers as 'De Lawd' (Oates 1982: 309). Even a writer as sensitive to his strengths as Aldon Morris has concluded that King 'believed that the leader should have the last word because that is the way they ran their churches' (1984: 224). R. H. King judges King's Moses self-image to have 'hindered the emergence of political independence and autonomy in the black communities where he conducted campaigns' (1996: 116).

Son of a preacher man

Two further limits to King's ability to practice leadership democratically, as a conversation, can be traced to his inheritance of the messianic tradition of black leadership. First, his southern Baptist idiom and religious sensibility, while crucial to cognitive liberation in the south, often failed to translate to the more irreligious black communities of the north and west. Moreover, it could be a *substitute* for the kind of strategic thinking the movement needed from its leaders. As R. H. King observes: 'By overriding intellect with rhetoric, by preferring to deploy ideas for their effects rather than to analyse ideas for their plausibility, King prefigured and helped perpetuate the development of a type of black leader who all too often substitutes rhetoric for ideas, repetition of phrases for analysis of situations' (1996: 113).

Second, the patriarchal traditions of the church led King to exclude women from leading roles in the civil rights movement. Bluntly put, King struggled to see women outside the rigid categories of the biblical tradition (see Oates 1982: 44–5, 283, 470–1; Garrow 1988: 375–6; Fairclough 1987: 50). He surrounded himself with male staffers because, as James Lawson noted, 'Martin had real problems with having a woman in a high position' (Garrow 1988: 141). Ella Baker left SCLC amid bitter complaints that she was never treated as an equal by the younger and less experienced King.

While women had a 'disproportionate presence and importance' in the civil rights movement, there was no independent organisation of women which might have contested the teachings of a patriarchal church tradition and offered leadership to King (R. H. King 1996: 44; Robnett 1996). Only organised, political, social movements can render the tacit and experiential knowledge of the oppressed in a politically effective form. When a delegation of women leaders from the National Welfare Rights Organisation (NWRO) visited King in 1968 they sharply criticised his ignorance. King fell silent and just listened, thanked the women *for leading him* and then persuaded SCLC to endorse the NWRO's leading policy demands (Garrow 1988: 595). Movement leaders are, in part, *made* wisely passive, open to being acted upon, by movements which alter their cognitions. Indeed this structuring of leadership by social movements is the subject of the third and final section of this chapter, where I consider how King's leadership 'changed as a result of [his] involvement in a movement in which tactical and strategic ideas disseminated from the bottom up as well as from the top down' (Carson 1993: 247).

The re-education of Martin Luther King

The grammar of strategy structures the conversation of leadership. In other words, while leadership is a set of skills which can be learnt, and a relationship between people, it is also inseparable from strategic questions such as how and when to act, who to ally with and for what goals – questions which are answered in the light of relatively abstract conceptions of the nature of society and the possibilities for change within it. As new experiences produce new (and plural) answers to such questions, then the character, meaning and purpose of 'leadership' can shift quite rapidly.

Such is the case with Martin Luther King's leadership from 1955 to 1968. Every time he encountered a situation in which democracy remained, for the poor and oppressed, merely formal (or as he expressed it, 'thin paper not thick action') – from Selma to Chicago, Watts to Vietnam – he deepened his understanding of the nature of the adversary until there took place a kind of Kuhnian scientific revolution in his thought. Over time, he found himself a new part in a different story.

Movements educate leaders
A dialectical approach to leadership will have at its heart the dynamic inter-action between leaders and movements. We cannot hope to capture the hurdy-gurdy of this relationship with a static model derived from exchange-relations and the crude categories of 'leader' and 'support-base' as Melucci tries to do (1996). Movements educate and form leaders as much as leaders constitute movements. Leadership goes *all the way down* a movement (Robnett 1996).

Examples of King learning from the movement are ever-present in the history of his leadership of the civil rights movement. In 1956 the draft of his book about the Montgomery Bus Boycott was sharply criticised by his clos-est political adviser, Stanley Levison. Not only had King given the impres-sion 'that everything depended on you' but had also included a lengthy paean to black self-help. Levison rebuked King: 'the section on Negro self-improvement is undesirable ... The goal should be to activate and organise people toward the main objective rather than appeal for change of character separated from the pursuit of social goals' (in Garrow 1988: 105). W. E. B. Du Bois, an important influence on King, criticised his neglect of the class interests of black workers (see Marable 1998: 117, 125). In 1958–59, Ella Baker and Fred Shuttlesworth continually pressed King for a better organ-ised and more crusading SCLC, and demanded he play a more engaged role in its affairs. Soon after, he left his Dexter Avenue ministry (Garrow 1988: 120–3). In 1960 and 1961 he was acted upon by the student sit-ins and Freedom Rides which 'challenged his imagination' and 'led him forward' to more militant forms of leadership (Fairclough 1990: 64; Garrow 1993: 172). Julian Bond and other SNCC activists badgered King to join the Atlanta sit-ins and get arrested (Bloom 1987: 167), while King's refusal to join the Freedom Riders in 1961 provoked sharp rebukes from the students. Even a memo from SNCC activist Diane Nash, criticising movement leaders who served bonds rather than served jail time, can be seen as instrumental in changing King's attitude to that question (Garrow 1988: 202).

Moreover, as Bloom has pointed out, SNCC changed the conditions in which King exercised his leadership, the constituencies who entered the civil rights coalition, and, in consequence, the demands to which his leadership had to give expression (1987: 170). During the fight to desegregate Birmingham in 1963, King's willingness to lead mass direct action confrontations was due to the pressure of student militants; but from the experience of Birmingham he learnt that his ability to move the Federal government depended on the insurgency of a mass movement. As he worked to unleash 'the biggest wave of black militancy since Reconstruction', he learnt that 'the geometric growth of black militancy was a phenomenon of such elemental force as to defy the control of any individual leader or group of leaders' (Fairclough 1990: 82, 87). By 1964, accepting the Nobel Peace Prize, he defined the civil rights movement as a mass movement of self-emancipation driven by 'the direct participation of the masses in protest, rather than reliance on indirect methods which frequently do not involve the masses in action at all' (Garrow 1988: 365).

When the ghetto riots/uprisings introduced another 'voice', angry and inchoate, to the movement's conversation, King visited the riot-torn Watts area of Los Angeles in 1965 and returned 'absolutely undone', receptive to Bayard Rustin's advice that not just a politics of civil rights, but a class politics, was needed. Garrow detects Rustin's 'tutelage' in King's statements that 'social peace must spring from economic justice', and that Watts represented 'a class revolt of the underprivileged against privilege', in which 'the main issue is economic' (in Garrow 1988: 439).

When King turned SCLC north to fight the slums of Chicago, in 1965–66, he was turning the movement's conversation around to this angry urban voice. But his *experience* of Chicago, where the protest methods of the south failed to make any impression on the structural economic inequalities and sophisticated political machines of the north, drew him toward more radical political conclusions than the social-democratic ameliorism of Bayard Rustin. King began to air his accumulating uncertainties in mass rallies: 'We stand at the gate of a new understanding of the dimensions and depths of our struggle with racial injustice in this country, dimensions not limited by geographical boundaries or adequately addressed by civil rights laws' (in Garrow 1988: 436).

And, as the Vietnam War escalated, other leaders led King to see the inner connections of war, racism and poverty. Even an apparently flippant aside to King by Stokely Carmichael can be read as the deliberate conversational leadership *of* King. Talking of the death in Vietnam of a mutual friend, Carmichael addressed King's led self:

> You told him to be non-violent in Mississippi. He didn't get shot there. You should have told him to be non-violent in Vietnam. That's what your problem is. You didn't carry your stuff like you said you're supposed to carry it. (cited in Hampton and Fayer 1995: 340)

All these experiences and conversations persuaded King to 'reassess his basic assumptions about American society'. He concluded that racism, poverty and militarism were parts of a totality, in the face of which the movement had won 'at best surface changes' (Fairclough 1990: 109–10). With this thought he placed his leadership resignedly, but definitely, into quite a different story. No longer 'serving History', he now aimed to shift History onto new tracks. 'A genuine leader is not a searcher for consensus but a moulder of consensus' (in Garrow 1988: 506).

The theory which is of value to a social movement, said Leon Trotsky, is that which is 'not inseparably linked with the practical tasks contemporary to it, but rises above them, that has the gift of seeing ahead, [and] is able to prepare to link itself with the future practical activity and to train people who will be equal to future political tasks' (quoted in Rees 1998: 268). King sought just this projective distance in his last years, to 'link the movement with the future'. The only fruit of this revolution in his thought was the Poor People's Campaign.

The Poor People's Campaign

King organised the Poor People's Campaign because he had concluded that the goal of the movement should be poor people's power. He told the SCLC board in 1967 that 'the evils of capitalism are as real as the evils of militarism and the evils of racism' and constituted a totality, a 'system'. King ended up a democratic socialist, a revolutionary of sorts: 'I have found out that all that I have been doing in trying to correct this system in America has been in vain ... I am trying to get at the roots of it to see just what ought to be done. The whole thing will have to be done away with' (in Garrow 1988: 552, 580).

The depth of King's radicalisation is rarely recognised. For instance, in a reading inspired by Hannah Arendt, R. H. King has suggested that King carried on a tradition of American radical liberalism by fighting for democratic rights and political participation – for access to the 'space of appearances', in Arendt's terms – for African-Americans (1996: 103). In fact the Poor People's Campaign embodied King's realisation, like Dewey's before him, that it was impossible either to keep open the 'space of appearances', or to render it meaningful, while 'profit motives and property rights are considered more important than people' (in Fairclough 1983: 121). It was precisely the scale of King's own cognitive revolution which forced him to the conclusion that he would have to 'build a new political movement virtually from scratch' (Fairclough 1990: 120). The Poor People's Campaign of 1968 was his first, experimental stab at creating such a movement, and reflected his new radical consciousness at the levels of strategy, coalition, organisation and leadership.

First, King was under no illusions that the goal of poor people's power demanded a fundamental reappraisal of the *strategy* of the movement: '"For years I laboured with the idea of reforming the existing institutions of the society, a little change here, a little change there", King told Halberstam. "Now I feel quite differently. I think you've got to have a reconstruction of the entire society"' (in Garrow 1988: 562). King felt his leadership had to respond to the failure of the civil rights movement to produce enough substantive changes to the material lives of the black poor. The 'performance gap', as Greg Moses has termed it, was being filled by 'black power', the inchoate anger and despair of the riot, and by a retreat into electoralism and the Democratic Party. King's innovative strategic response, the Poor People's Campaign, was arguably a form of transitional politics, in which the fight to achieve practical reforms would be integrated with the fight to transform social and economic structures, by the organisation, education and growth of an independent, mass opposition to 'the system'. In King's conception, the Poor People's Campaign would bring Washington to a halt by the mass, coercive, non-violent protest of the poor, shift public opinion, and wrench an Economic Bill of Rights from Congress. He also pushed SCLC into 'a serious campaign that involved them in strikes and union organising in Atlanta; Memphis; Detroit; Birmingham; St Petersburg; Florida and Charleston, Georgetown and Florence South Carolina'. He hoped a class programme would stimulate black and white unity, force reforms, and so end the desperate isolation of the black struggle (Bloom 1987: 213).

Second, the radical goals that King now adopted helped to rupture the civil rights *coalition* on which his leadership had been based. Fairclough has summed up the dynamic at work:

> When King adopted a radical agenda ... raising the issue of economic justice and challenging cold war orthodoxy – former white supporters moved to cut him down to size. The President withdrew his favor; northern mayors attacked him as a trouble-maker; the press wrote him off; the Supreme Court upheld his 1963 conviction for 'parading without a permit'. (1990: 138)

When, in 1967, King finally came out in active public opposition to the Vietnam War, key advisers like Rustin, and the leaders of other black organisations, such as Roy Wilkins and Ralph Bunche, opposed him publicly (Garrow 1988: 438). He was described as 'the crown prince of the Vietniks' by Harry McPherson, an aide to the President (in McKnight 1997: 16), and as 'an instrument in the hands of subversive forces' by the FBI chief J. Edgar Hoover. Black columnists now denounced him as no longer 'the selfless leader of the late 1950s'. The 'artist of protest', so adept at using the mass media, now suddenly discovered that 'they have all the news media and TV' (in Garrow 1988: 555, 576, 445).

Third, the new goal of poor people's power challenged King to rethink the kind of *organisation* he needed to build. At a rhetorical level he did register that the poor had to develop 'the ability, togetherness, the assertiveness, and the aggressiveness to make the power structure respond' (in Oates 1982:

460). He knew that 'when people are organised they become a greater political force', and expressed his desire to 'organise this total community into units of political and economic power' (Garrow 1988: 466). But he never translated this rhetoric into a new organisational form, and was still groping towards a model in April 1968.

With the goal, strategy, coalition and organisation which had formed the coordinates of his old leadership style in crisis, it is not surprising that the nature of the leadership he offered to the movement was transformed. After the Voting Rights Bill was passed in 1965, and the first reforming phase of the civil rights movement drew to a close, the struggle to define King intensified. Stanley Levison advised King that he was now 'one of the most powerful figures in the country – a leader now not merely of Negroes, but of millions of whites', adding the warning, 'America today is not yet ready for a radical restructuring of its economy and social order' (in Garrow 1988: 418–19, 420). In similar vein, Bayard Rustin argued King should not, for the sake of the long-term prospect of realigning the Democratic Party, publicly oppose the war in Vietnam. Indeed, Wofford has suggested that 'Rustin ... acted as if King were a precious puppet whose symbolic actions were to be planned by a Gandhian high command' (in Fairclough 1987: 39).

By 1967, the radical King began to intervene directly in this conversation about his leadership. 'Too often when you're called a responsible leader, it means you're an Uncle Tom leader' (in Garrow 1988: 561). Declaring himself 'more than a civil rights leader', King now sought to *make* America ready for radical change, seeking greater projective distance from the movement in order to lead it toward a new goal. 'We must be hammers shaping a new society', he said. In the new story he told himself about America, his part as a leader was not to service historical necessity but to shift History onto new tracks. In 1968 he said, 'The leader has the responsibility to find an answer. I have been searching for ... the last eighteen months' (Garrow 1988: 609).

Conclusion

The idea of self-emancipation, in liberating people from the need for liberators, can seem to deny the need for leaders at all. It certainly denies the necessity for a Power From Above to deliver liberation to the poor benighted subjects below. Yet there are two reasons why we can't get rid of leadership so easily: unevenness in the consciousness of the emancipatory subject, and the organised opposition of the adversary. *Leadership – as communication and as generalship – is a necessary and democratic response to both realities.*

First, leadership is an expression of the unevenness in organisation, experience, consciousness and combativity of the emancipatory subject. Self-emancipation is a messy, profane, human activity, with no guaranteed outcome. It involves a rough and ready simultaneity between acts of *trans-*

formation of the world and the self and acts of *redescription* of the world and the self. For the emancipatory subject, the process is necessarily a collective endeavour and is therefore inter-subjective. However, as persons do not share uniform interpretations or experiences, talents or skills, then acts of persuasion, and acts of being persuaded, will always form the warp and weft of collective action. As Lukács pointed out, in what remains the most profound treatment of the relationship between self-emancipation and leadership, it is 'the prevailing disunity, the differing degrees of clarity and depth to be found in the consciousness of different individuals, groups, and strata' which makes leadership necessary, and which defines its primary task as the raising of the consciousness of the emancipatory subject as a whole until self-emancipation is possible (Lukács 1971: 322).

Second, leadership is a necessary response to the brute fact of highly organised opposition on the part of adversaries to emancipation of any kind, and the necessity of their defeat in battle. Generalship, the art of winning the battle, is therefore necessary to win. The contemporary hostility to the notion of generalship usually reflects the failure of cultural politics to engage in those kinds of collective action, whether against the state or the employer, in which one learns why generalship matters. The quietistic alternatives of textual deconstructions of the adversary, or the living out a personal ethic in a corrupt world, do not require generalship. Real social struggles do.

The need to overcome these two obstacles to self-emancipation – of uneven consciousness and organised opposition – dictates the form democratic leadership must take. In the most general sense, it must balance 'insidedness' (to avoid getting too far in advance of the life and current vocabulary of the subject, and hence becoming unable to influence it) and 'outsidedness' (to avoid merging with the current state of consciousness of the subject, and hence becoming unable to lead it forward). This balancing act seems to constrain the leadership of self-emancipation in three ways. First, it dictates that leadership must be a *collective*, whether an organisation or a network, composed of the 'large numbers of individuals' that Ella Baker spoke of, rather than being vested in a single charismatic or gifted individual. Second, it dictates that those individuals will be composed, in the main, of the most active, resolute and conscious members of the self-emancipatory subject itself, rather than any outside social force, however well-intentioned. Only a leadership organic to the emancipatory subject can sustain the conversation and raise the subject up as a whole. Third, it dictates that the prime task of those individuals is to 'work themselves out of a job', as Carson put it, by raising the emancipatory subject as a whole to the level of its most advanced elements.

I have suggested in this chapter that if we can get past the tropes of 'The Great Man', 'The Laws of History' and 'The Man of Destiny', then we will see more clearly Martin Luther King's *struggle with* democratic leadership. As we study the efforts of movement leaders – here succeeding, there failing

– to *be* democratic leaders we can learn much about democratic leadership's nature and dynamics, the skills of leadership and followership necessary for its practice, and the social and organisational contexts in which those skills are developed, or blocked. We can sharpen our understanding that in social movements, which are neither armies to be drilled nor the passive reflections of social structure, collective action is undertaken in a pragmatic and experimental spirit, 'given a try' as the gang leader Robert 'Peanut' Tidwell put it. Democratic movement leaders must be 'conversational', persuasive, and attentive to the movement's experience, always ready to follow in order to lead, to balance the 'leading' and 'led' self, until they 'unite in themselves the leader and the comrade and servant' (Barratt-Brown 1938). And, as each new experience of struggle is processed by the movement in an inter-subjective interpreting babble, the democratic leader is the one who tries to keep the conversation *and* the struggle going, enriching the one with the other, while remaining porous to the influence of both. Just before his assassination, in his combination of intellectual openness and practical determination, King struck the authentic note of the democratic leader. 'I am still searching. I don't have all the answers and I certainly have no claim to omniscience' (Fairclough 1987: 383).

Notes

1 I am grateful to Debbie Williams for her detailed comments on the chapter. I also benefited from criticism from Colin Barker, Carol Hanisch, Michael Lavalette, Kent Worcester and, especially, Joanne Landy and Jesse Lemisch.
2 Rosa Parks was of course a leader in her own right, a 'bridge-leader' as Robnett (1996, 1997) puts it, and an illustration that leadership goes *all the way down* social movements.

7

Defending the 'Sefton Two': contested leadership in a trade union dispute

Michael Lavalette (with Nigel Flanagan)[1]

Introduction

On 29 July 1994, several hundred trade unionists, socialists and movement activists gathered outside the High Court in Manchester. Inside, two officers from the Sefton branch of the trade union Unison[2] were on trial, charged with contempt of court. Both officers had been served with a writ at a union mass meeting, prohibiting the branch from taking strike action. The officers had informed the meeting of the contents of the writ, but urged defiance and the strike went ahead. In the aftermath, management within Sefton Metropolitan Borough Council (a hung council within which Labour was the largest party) decided to invoke the powers of the court against the union. Thus the officers were called to appear before the High Court, but so were the union's national officials – they too faced the same charge but (unlike the branch officers) denied guilt. They had tried to stop the strike; they had repudiated the branch's actions and argued it was the local officers not the national union that had broken the law. The potential consequences were dramatic. The union faced the prospect of a heavy fine, the branch officers a possible two-year gaol sentence and costs as great as £100,000. Later that day the judge gave his verdict: Unison was fined £5,000 and the two officers £1,250 each. The officers avoided a custodial sentence and the fines were 'paltry', easily paid for out of the solidarity fund that the branch and its supporters had created.

The decision was a great victory for the branch officers but for the national officials and the local managers in Sefton it was less welcome. Over the previous year the council managers had tried various methods to 'police' the union branch. The decision to invoke the authority of the courts against the officers was part of their strategy to control the union and let their managers manage – the court decision was a setback in these terms. The national union officials also saw the branch (and its officers in particular) as being 'out of control', under the influence of socialist political organisations (in particular the Socialist Workers Party [SWP][3]), rejecting the authority of regional and national officials and threatening the legitimacy of the union by its actions (which the court case seemed to prove). The outcome seemed to strengthen an oppositional rank and file in one of their branches – a rank and file which had over the previous 18 months shown its independence and willingness to reject the authority of the national officials.

The Sefton episode provides a useful case study of the contested process of leadership within collective action. During a series of events which included a workplace occupation, several unofficial strike days, various union mass meetings and the court case and its aftermath, various groups argued and competed over 'what should be done', 'how' and 'why'. In doing so each group asserted differing conceptions of leadership: who has the right to make decisions, who should be listened to, whose 'authority' is to be accepted and whose strategic and tactical advice should be followed.

There were three key participants in the contest: the regional and national officials of the union, the locally elected branch officers and the SWP. They all brought with them their own political perspectives and goals and from this flowed a set of 'political logics' that shaped their actions and intervention in the events. Such logics were not entirely exclusive; each group shared a commitment to saving jobs, for example, and each was supportive of organised marches and demonstrations as a means of exerting pressure on Sefton council. Yet each had a way of seeing and interpreting the world that had a direct impact on its involvement in the protest actions, promoted different sets of strategic impulses and prioritised certain forms of action or protest while deprioritising, or even precluding, others. As the conflict developed, the shared common ground became squeezed as the battle over strategy and goals became exacerbated.

These competing 'logics' are, in part, derived from the contradictory nature of trade unionism. Trade unions are 'an organisational expression of the irreconcilability of labour and capital', but they embody 'a politics of accommodation to … capitalist society' (Lane 1974: 25). In other words they struggle 'both *against* capitalism and *within* it' (Darlington 1994: 26).

Trade unions provide an organisation that can make effective the power of the working class at the point of production. They mobilise workers' 'collective strength and stop the employers riding roughshod over them, and through their experience of trade union struggle workers can develop their confidence, organisation and political consciousness' (Darlington, 1994: 26). But the unions also contain fundamental limitations. First, as organisations built on particular trades or industries, they mirror the divisions imposed on workers by capitalism and thus they divide workers (as well as offering the potential for unity). Second, their organisational objective is to improve the position and employment conditions of workers within the existing framework of capitalism. Third, they reinforce the conception that there is a sharp division between politics and economics – they are reform organisations. As Callinicos notes: 'Put most crudely, this leads to an attitude which sees unions concerned with the economic struggle over wages, conditions and the like, while the [social democratic] party concerns with politics in parliament on workers' behalf' (1995: 13–14).

The contradictions of trade unionism create a wide space within which various different politics of trade union action operate – from a 'narrow' concern with negotiations over pay and working conditions, to a 'broad' conception based on notions of class solidarity and the 'irreconcilability' of labour and capital, to revolutionary perspectives which try to bridge the 'artificial' divide between economics and politics and build on the 'broad' view to pose the question of the need for revolutionary change to society. These differing perspectives underpinned the clash of 'logics' in the Sefton episode and shaped the leadership contest.

For the national and regional officials the conflict operated within set boundaries within which they were the formal elected leadership of the union, custodians of a tradition and heritage, whose authority should be recognised by the membership. In general, trade union leaders have a distinct social position operating between capital and labour to negotiate reforms and economic improvement for their members (Cliff and Gluckstein 1986). As Callinicos notes: 'the trade union bureaucracy … is … a social layer made up of full-time officials with a material interest in confining the class struggle to the search for reforms within a capitalist framework' (1995: 16).

For trade union leaders, demonstrations and strikes can, *in certain circumstances*, be a useful pressure to exert on employers. But it is their responsibility to assess 'the circumstances' and condone or curtail any collective action in the interests of the union as a whole – and any such judgement involves an interpretation of what the 'best interests' of the union are. Importantly this includes protecting the union's funds and day-to-day activities, operating within the confines of existing law, maintaining their links with the Labour Party (in Britain) and not 'rocking the boat' – the perception in Britain that union–management conflict and militant trade unionism may threaten the Labour Party's electoral credibility.

Thus, the actions of the national and regional union officials of Unison were shaped by two goals. First, they *cooperated* with the local branch officers in the early stages of the campaign to defend jobs and conditions. But second, as the movement developed and the union got embroiled in a political campaign over the legitimacy of wildcat strike action, their goal became extricating the union from the threat of legal sanction and distancing themselves from rank-and-file militancy. This led them *to confront* the branch officers and *to compete* with them inside the union branch over who had legitimate authority. Their conception of leadership was one in which they led and others were *expected* to follow. They viewed the membership as an essentially passive group, which was being led in an inappropriate, confrontational direction by its local officers and the SWP, an illegitimate political organisation with no place inside the union.

The second group involved in the leadership contest was the elected branch officers (and the activists in the union branch). They shared a number of goals with the national and regional officials: to save jobs and protect services, to extend union influence and protect the union from outside interference and state regulation. The activists devoted a considerable amount of time and energy to union work and being 'good union activists' was a central part of their social identity (Reicher 1996b). For the local activists the union also provided a forum for members to discuss an array of economic and political issues affecting their lives. Branch democracy – the right of members to discuss, vote and make decisions affecting the branch and its members – was viewed as fundamental. 'Active involvement' by as many members as possible was constantly fought for – and hence members were viewed not as passive but potentially direct participants in meetings, demonstrations, disputes, pickets, etc. The national leaders were expected to carry out their members' wishes and defend the branch against interference from employers, the law and the state. Thus, in significant respects the branch activists had a different – although overlapping – conception of trade unionism from the national and regional officials.

Thus, the events in Sefton partially reflect the clash between two conceptions of trade unionism, with the consequence that as the events progressed the formal authority and leadership of the national union officials was rejected. The branch and its officers followed a path that rejected the compliance to the law favoured by the union officials in favour of a strategy of defiance and confrontation with the local management and the courts. The various decisions of branch mass meetings provided the legitimacy for such a strategy: the branch officers repeatedly claimed that they were following their members' democratic decisions – and thus leadership involved not only the process of strategising but also convincing members in open debate that the proposed strategies were appropriate and could obtain the movement's goals. The branch officers' conception of leadership was not a simple one of 'leaders' and 'followers'; it was based of having *to convince* the membership *to follow knowingly and actively*. In this conception of leadership the membership is a critical and engaged group – or at least, if the branch leadership is to be successful in its competition with the regional and national officials, it must convince the members to be active and critical and not passive and disengaged.

The branch leadership's decisions and strategic turns also reflected, *in part*, the influence, politics and practical solidarity offered by the third group, the SWP. As an organisation of revolutionary socialists with a minority presence in the branch, the SWP was able to pose questions that exposed the differences between the two conceptions of trade unionism held by the branch activists and the national and regional officials, bringing out the 'conflict of logics' held by both groups.

SWP members shared the commitment to defend jobs and protect and expand union influence and this provided them with the necessary credentials to gain access to the branch members. They were able to generate significant support from within the labour and trade union movement for the branch and hence show 'practical solidarity', while the actions of the national and regional officials offered the SWP an opportunity to lead politically a campaign in defence of two trade unionists and to generalise the campaign to one which covered the right to strike and defiance of 'unjust' anti-trade union laws, the nature and role of the trade union bureaucracy, and the role of the state and government in modern capitalist society.

Hence SWP members were able to pose a series of wider general political questions – the 'cosmological' role of leadership described by Eyerman and Jamieson (1991) – in a conflict that required their 'world-view' to be translated into a practical, concrete set of activities. Thus the events presented an opportunity for the organisation to engage with movement activists on three levels: *ideologically*, by emphasising the roots of their grievance within the totality of social relations within society; *politically*, by arguing for strategies which involve the greatest possible number in the campaign; and *practically*, through their activity, attempting to build the movement and 'prove in action' how their political philosophy, direction and action could bring success. In other words the SWP members sought to lead *by winning political hegemony within the movement* and this involved them arguing and convincing as many activists as possible that their strategies and goals were appropriate and could be successful. Here Alan Johnson's conception of the active 'led selves' is useful (see Chapter 6). It emphasises that following can be a knowing, active and positive expression of commitment to particular goals, strategies, values and outcomes.

The Sefton events emphasise the importance of individuals and minority groupings in shaping social conflict. They do so not in any Blanquist or Bakuninist sense of a small minority imposing their will on the majority in the name of some supposed greater good (Draper 1990; Wheen 1999), but by articulating the justness of their cause and providing practical steps and advice to take events forward. In this sense, leaders frame questions in ways that can convince participants to follow actively.

Phase 1: DLO not DOLE![4]

In October 1993 the Secretary of State for the Environment wrote to Sefton council to enforce the closure of the council's Direct Labour Organisation (DLO), with the loss of 360 jobs. As soon as the notice of closure became public, the 'Sefton Joint Trade Union Committee' (SJTUC), an *ad hoc* organisation of all the main unions representing workers in the council, held an emergency lunchtime meeting for workers in the main DLO where it was decided to occupy the depot. The workforce left the meeting, marched to the depot, closed and padlocked the gates and put a banner over the works entrance: 'DLO not DOLE – depot under occupation'.

Later that Monday evening various supporters (including local trade unionists and SWP members) attended the occupation. The SWP members brought a leaflet arguing that the workforce should spread the dispute to other depots and council buildings. Over the week the SWP members were an almost constant presence within the occupation and on several occasions were to make significant contributions to the unfolding events. The following day Unison had one of its regular joint shop stewards[5] meetings inside the occupation and the SWP leaflet formed the meeting 'agenda'. As Nigel Flanagan (Unison Branch Secretary) said:

> The leaflet presented the arguments very clearly. It argued against closure, emphasised the social consequences if closure went ahead and it presented a clear strategy over what we should do next: spread the action; involve other groups of council workers etc. We just adopted this as the agenda for our shop stewards meeting. One steward objected (out of 30) but the rest overruled him and we carried on.

There were daily mass meetings at which the SJTUC discussed tactics, gate rota and any other business. On the Thursday evening a full council meeting was being held to discuss the DLO closure. The mass meeting of those in occupation decided to organise a march to the Town Hall. Leaflets were hurriedly printed and distributed to local unions and to members of the public across Merseyside. Before the march started, the police met with representatives of the SJTUC and demanded that the march be re-routed to avoid the main street. The march had not obtained the appropriate permission and the police claimed it was an illegal obstruction of the highway. There was some confusion amongst the strike leadership until the SWP full-timer[6] intervened. As Nigel recalls:

> To be honest I didn't know what to do. He [Chief Inspector] was saying it was a safety issue, that it was a serious breach of the law, etc. Then Mark, the SWP full-timer, called me over, and asked me what they were saying. I told him, and he said: 'Tell them to fuck off, there's 500 people here, they can't arrest everyone, all they'll do is walk alongside the march like they do at all other demos'. I didn't exactly tell them to 'fuck off', but I did say we were sticking to our original plan.

The march set off down the main street with the police in front stopping and re-directing the traffic. When it got to the Town Hall 60 strikers went to the public gallery and the rest were ushered into another room to hear speeches from supporters. Earlier that day the SJTUC (on Nigel's initiative) had taken a decision that they would try to stop the councillors from voting on the closure issue. Among the 60 strikers in the council chamber public gallery were a number armed with whistles and bells – when the council moved to discuss the closure they would create a noise and their comrades would move to occupy the chambers. The plan worked perfectly. At the sound of the whistles and bells the strikers and their supporters rushed the chamber, while the councillors fled to another part of the building.

After an hour, Labour Group leader Dave Martin entered the chamber to ask those occupying if the council could reconvene. Once again the presence of the local SWP full-timer was important. As Nigel says:

> Mark was standing next to me. Dave Martin told me the Tory Group were demanding the police forcibly remove us from the council chamber or guarantee their safety in another room so they could vote on the closure. Dave was saying for safety reasons and to stop arrests we should leave the chamber. Mark simply said to me: 'Tell him we'll leave if they guarantee there will be no vote on the closure tonight'. I followed this advice, and made this announcement to Dave in front of the occupied chamber. Dave Martin was a bit taken aback and really put on the spot I think. After a few minutes he agreed to our demand and we left to go back to the depot.

The following morning the non-elected officials of the four manual unions met with their members and told them the occupation was hindering negotiations and they wanted it to end that day. After heated debated the membership agreed to their officials' request and informed the local Unison officers. The Unison members faced with a *fait accompli* agreed to finish the occupation at the end of the Friday workday, but at the mass meeting the Unison officers argued that if the occupation was ending it was important to have a clear objective. They proposed and won a motion arguing for a one-day strike of all council members on 14 October, the day the council was next due to meet and discuss the closure.

On 14 October there was a very successful unofficial strike across Sefton council. In the morning DLO workers were dispersed to join pickets at all council workplace gates and entrances. In the afternoon there was a large demonstration but this time the police were well prepared: the Town Hall was cordoned off and special riot police were held in reserve. The day ended peacefully, but the vote for closure of the DLO was passed. By March 1994 the DLO had closed with the loss of all 302 manual jobs, though Unison had managed to get Sefton council to re-deploy its members elsewhere.

Leadership in phase 1

At this stage in the events both the regional and national officials within Unison were very supportive of the branch and its officers – perhaps because Unison officers were playing the leading role in a joint union campaign. The regional committee donated money to the campaign against privatisation and the national officials were generally supportive of the campaign and the branch's role in it. As Nigel notes:

The regional official was summoned to Sefton by the Director of Personnel, who then tried to lecture him on the damage to good industrial relations caused by the branch's behaviour. But he firmly told her that it was not his job to police the branch and that in his view the bad industrial relations were caused by the council's behaviour.

Within their own union branch Martin Murphy (Unison Branch Chair) and Nigel had an established record as trade union representatives and, through their union and political work, they had built a strong and loyal following. In the DLO, however, Unison members were a small minority of the strikers, yet the Unison officers were quickly able to establish their leading role. This was partly a consequence of the political perspectives held by both the Unison officers. They were elected and accountable to their members – elected on a platform of protecting jobs and services in Sefton – and they rejected the legitimacy of union law. As Martin said: 'There's a time when you have to break the law. That's always been the history of workers' struggles' (Sefton Defence Campaign 1994: 5). And they shared a commitment to overcoming sectional interests amongst the workforce and emphasising the common concerns of both white- and blue-collar workers. They both viewed trade union militancy as the best way to defend their members' interests and stressed decisions had to be agreed by their members, or by those in occupation, in an open vote after a period of debate. Such debate created the conditions for the leaders to convince participants – via 'active listening' (Volosinov 1986) – of the plausibility of their strategies. They were, therefore, prepared to highlight and articulate the workforce's grievances and present political remedies by suggesting *appropriate* forms of action from the repertoire of contention (appropriate in the sense that they were practically 'do-able', realistically achievable and the leaders were able to convince others of these possibilities).

The leadership of Martin and Nigel was reflected in three complementary processes: first, the speed of their response to unforeseen events (they were confident of their arguments and were prepared to act on their own initiatives or those of others and recognised that practical leadership comes from reacting quickly and appropriately as situations develop and change); second, 'strategising' (thinking through the various possible strategies and tactics open to the SJTUC and the potential consequences resulting from each); and third, 'dialogical' engagement with the participants (that is, an ongoing process of political argument to convince participants of the validity of their strategic proposals and the possibility of winning). But dialogical engagement was not simply left to the mass meetings. It took place between meetings in the arguments presented in leaflets, in private or informal meetings, in the cars visiting other workplaces and on demonstrations – and it was precisely on such occasions that the arguments (the theory) could be tested practically by participants who could assess the level of support they had and make some judgement on the effect of their action.

But a final point to emphasise was Martin and Nigel's openness to debate and to engage with other groups who were not directly involved in the dispute. In particular Martin and Nigel (and the entire group of Unison shop stewards) were remarkably open to the SWP, which only had one member amongst the branch's 30 shop stewards at this stage. Anybody who was 'on the side' of the workforce was welcomed into the occupation, to take part in the discussions, but not, of course, to take part in the mass meetings. Here we see an example of 'followership skills' – the notion that active leaders listen to the advice and experiences of a range of (those they consider) legitimate actors, choosing whether to follow their strategic prognoses or not after a period of reflective consideration of the arguments.

For the SWP members the dispute created an opening from which they could relate to the workforce and the strike leadership politically, trying to convince strikers of their strategic arguments and generalise from these to debates over the wider political situation. Thus they were more than a support group and set out the lines of agreement and disagreement they had with the strikers. Their political leadership developed not from simply espousing the shared and agreed programme of the majority (in this case 'occupy the depot') but from pushing solutions and strategies in areas where there was uncertainty and/or confusion over the way ahead (spread the dispute, march down the main street, refuse to leave the chamber without a guarantee from the Labour leader).

But to win such arguments and promote such ideas the SWP had to be taken seriously and this involved practical activity. It was present throughout the occupation and had mobilised its members locally to support the occupation, provide speakers for the Thursday evening meeting, and both raise money and pass supporting motions in other unions in which it had members. It was this combination of practical and political engagement that meant that the SWP full-timer could have an influence on events by discussing immediate tactical problems with the occupation leadership and offering practical advice at key turning points. This activity also led Nigel and several other stewards to join the SWP – a factor that was central to events in 'phase 2'.

Phase 2: 'we are all Nigel Flanagan, we are all Martin Murphy'

Early in 1994, the Director of Personnel and the Chief Executive of the council formally wrote to Unison demanding that it control the branch and stop it taking unofficial wildcat strike action. Unison regional officials were present when the branch officers were summoned to the council's Chief Executive's office to explain these actions. While regional officials were broadly supportive of their officers, they became aware of the presence of the SWP within the branch. Nigel takes up the story:

Key regional activists and officials, signalling a change in attitude from the earlier support for the branch, made some hostile comments to me personally. I laughed it off at the time, thinking it would be of no consequence, but it gradually began to feel like we were on some sort of 'warning'. Politically they were, of course, much closer to the Labour councillors than they were to me and other SWP members. Consequently any claims we made about the behaviour or actions of the council were treated as 'propaganda'.

The council was increasingly concerned at the militancy being shown by the Unison branch. The national union was under pressure from the council to control its members. The branch officers continued to show independence of thought and action in dealing with their members' problems and attacks on their working conditions. And the SWP was becoming more visible, as a political force, within the branch, recruiting members and gaining an audience for its politics through sales of its newspaper, *Socialist Worker*, and through regular workplace bulletins and leaflets. All the elements were now in place for the second major confrontation in Sefton in less than a year. The spark was provided by the council's attempt to privatise services.

In an attempt to avoid a repeat of the government-enforced closure of the DLO, the council decided to pursue voluntary competitive tendering (VCT) – known as 'externalisation' – of the Technical Services Department. Technical Services were well represented inside the union branch and on 12 April 1994 the section voted to oppose the council's policy, a stand that was supported by the branch at a specially called meeting on 29 April. This meeting also requested a ballot for strike action if the council did not change its mind.

Over the next few weeks the branch made several requests to regional and national officials asking for a strike ballot, but the union prevaricated, rejected the request and made it known that it would sanction a ballot for strike action only by the Technical Services section and not the branch as a whole (National Executive Report, 1994).

On 27 June, 500 members attended a mass meeting to discuss what the branch should do. The branch officers proposed a one-day strike for the following day when the council was due to meet to make its decision. However, as the meeting was about to begin the two full-time branch officers were served with a High Court injunction. Despite this, the branch voted for strike action.

The consequences of the strike for the local branch and the two branch officers were dramatic. Having ignored the injunction, the two branch officers were summoned to the High Court in Manchester. To justify its use of the courts, the council attempted to 'politicise' the dispute by pointing to the presence of the SWP within the branch. The Chief Executive stated:

> Our decision to go back to the court was to ensure that the rules concerning strikes are complied with and that unlawful industrial action does not happen

again. This was the third such illegal action and enough was enough. It must
be recognised that this illegal action is more to do with the militant politics of
the Socialist Workers Party than the furtherance of a legitimate industrial dispute.
(*Southport Champion*, 27 July 1994)

The council clearly felt that by attacking the SWP and its involvement within
the union branch, it could divide the membership and stop any future unofficial actions. The council's action required an immediate response from
Unison nationally, the branch and its supporters.

The response of Unison national officials

Unison policy was very clear on the issue of externalisation. It was agreed
only months before at its National Local Government Conference:

> Unison ... believes that as a last resort industrial action might be necessary to
> prevent councils privatising departments, therefore full national and regional
> support and encouragement will be given to branches to campaign for and
> take action against privatisation. (Voluntary Privatisation of Technical Services
> Department, Conference Motion No. 59)

But as we have already noted, the officials' response was rather different. On
the day of the mass meeting the officials had received a copy of the injunction and made considerable (unsuccessful) efforts to contact the officers and
instruct them not to take strike action. The Regional Secretary faxed the
branch office stating that the action was 'to be repudiated', while the
General Secretary wrote saying:

> I ... *instruct* the branch to comply with the terms [of the injunction] as failure
> to do so could lead to the imposition of unlimited damages on the union ...
> please confirm immediately to me that any instruction to take industrial action
> has immediately been revoked. (Letter from the General Secretary, 27 July
> 1994, my emphasis)

After the strike day and the council's move to take the officers and the
union to court, the national officials responded by repudiating the branch's
actions and informing them that unless the two officers both apologised to
the court and gave an undertaking never to break an injunction again, they
would not provide them with access to the union's lawyers for their defence.
In adopting this approach the national officials referred to a letter the union
had received from the Personnel Officer in Sefton (4 July 1994) that stated:

> Our objective ... [in returning to court] is to obtain firm assurances that there
> ... [will] be no future occurrences of unlawful action. Rather than to be puni-
> tive ... we would wish to adopt a reasonable approach.

Management were willing to be 'reasonable', providing Unison national and regional officials brought the 'rogue' elements within the branch to heel and prevented future wildcat strikes. In response, the national leaders emphasised they would not sanction law breaking and considered the branch leaders to be acting illegitimately – despite the fact that they were following branch decisions (and union conference policy).

The national officials had a very clear conception of leadership. The branch had moved to forms of action that threatened the union's funds and reputation and thus they changed from cooperation with the branch to conflict with it. They attempted to impose a formal and bureaucratic leadership based on the assertion of their *authority*. In their terms, they had the power of the union vested in them. Their role was to negotiate with local managers and, at the same time, to control or police 'unruly' locally elected officials. In the final analysis, leadership meant local branches doing what they were told by national officials, because such officials represented the union, and followed a course that was in the best interests of the union nationally. Failure to accept the officials' authority would result in sanctions being imposed on the branch and its officers, even if this seriously increased the chances that the officers may be imprisoned for their actions.

The Sefton branch's response

Faced with the confrontation with the regional and national officials, the branch leadership had to explain to members why the officials were failing to support them, why they had refused the branch a ballot (for official strike action) and why they were not supporting its local officers. To answer these questions 'conversation', debate, discussion and argument were necessary between the branch officers, activists and members. The branch leaders emphasised the successes of the campaign, defended the branch's right to make democratic decisions and drew a distinction between their rights as trade unionists and ordinary Unison members and the social position and actions of the regional and national officials. The branch's newsletter (*Sefton Unison News*) was a key tool. For example, Alison, a steward in the Social Services Department, argued:

> Our branch officers have acted consistently and democratically by following the decisions reached at each Special General Meeting. In response, our regional/national officers have: 1. Refused our legal request to ballot, 2. Repudiated us at the time of the strike, and, unforgivably, in Court; 3. Refused to provide legal help, or any support whatsoever, to Nigel and Martin. (*Sefton Unison News*, September 1994)

Distributed to all branch members, the newsletter directly confronted the regional and national officials' arguments. But it also emphasised that the branch was obtaining support from other trade unionists and Unison branches across the country – that it was not alone but at the forefront of a wider movement. A range of branch activists wrote in the newsletter, not just the two officers, emphasising the unity and agreement of the shop stewards committee. But the newsletter was not enough. Stewards had to carry the argument at section meetings and through informal discussions in offices across the council. The two branch officers simply could not have undertaken all this work themselves – the officers had to mobilise the stewards and activists to take the political and strategic conversations down to office and departmental level.

The stewards argued that the 'illegal' action had been necessary, was a branch decision and should not have resulted in a threat of imprisonment of the officers.[7] In putting forward such arguments they were making a number of powerful appeals to their members. First, there was the 'broad' conception of trade unionism – asserting their right to discuss a range of political issues.

> One of the points of trade unionism is to fight inequality and injustice in society and make this fight a political issue – that is what we were doing. (John, Steward, Technical Services)

Second, and linked to this, was the justness of their cause – their grievance – and the failure of the national union to allow the branch to vote on strike action.

> I supported the unofficial strike. It was the ultimate demonstration and gave over the view that not all the workforce was going to stand by and be sold out. (Stuart, Steward, Technical Services)

> I felt that the strategy was right, illegal action was all that was left when a legal ballot was refused. (Ian, Steward, Public Protection)

Third, there was the notion of democracy – members had listened to the arguments, evaluated the positions and voted in a mass meeting for strike action. Here there is a very specific interpretation of union democracy as something embodied in ordinary members of the union. It involved asserting their 'rights' and 'freedom' to make such decisions – if necessary in opposition to the national leadership.

> I supported the strike, we had a democratic vote, it was a yes vote and we had to go with that decision, I was pleased with the outcome. (Ellen, Steward, Education Department)

Finally, they argued that the national and regional officers had betrayed the branch.

> The role played by regional and national officials was appalling. They refused to help at all and in fact supported the council in their attempt to victimise our officers. (Wendy, Steward, Social Services)

I resented the intervention by Unison's leadership, as it was negative. (Paula, Steward, Technical Services)

They [national and regional officials] tried to undermine the democracy of the branch. (John, Steward, Technical Services)

It is worth noting the terms in which the 'debate' was framed. The support the branch received emphasised the notion of 'class solidarity' that the activists used to counter claims that the branch was being run by a few political agitators, while 'justice', 'democracy' and 'freedom of political action' – powerful mobilising concepts within political discourse – were utilised to strengthen the branch's position and support its independence of action.

These elements – the failings of the national officials, branch democracy, the principled and just stand being taken – became the main points of the branch leaders' engagement with their members, to try and convince them of their case and to reject the regional and national officials' claims.

The events revealed a tension between two different conceptions of trade unionism. For the stewards (and other activists in the branch), while the 'national' aspect of the union was important and while a nationally sanctioned strike would have been better, the main role of the union and its branches is to fight injustice and carry out the wishes of branch members. If the national organisation stands in the way (as in this case by refusing to organise a strike ballot) then the branch has the right and the duty to follow the democratic decisions of its members and strike. While the branch officers, the local leadership, may have coordinated and organised the strike and may have personally ignored the court injunction, they did so as democratically elected officials carrying out the wishes of their members. The officers' leadership was not conspiratorial, authoritarian or elitist, but part of the democratic heart beating at the centre of the branch itself. This view was aptly summed up in the two dominant slogans created by the branch and its supporters as part of the defence campaign: 'You can't get us, we're part of the union' and 'We are all Martin Murphy, we are all Nigel Flanagan'.

The SWP and the defence campaign

The hostility of the national and regional officials to the branch meant that it needed to act quickly to protect its officers. Money was needed to mount a defence and the branch needed to pursue strategies that would generate support for its officers in the face of the gaol threat. It was decided to set up a 'Sefton Two Defence Campaign'. Central to building the campaign was the SWP.

The SWP did not arrive at the dispute with a simple 'collective action proforma' – a series of steps that participants must follow if they want to win – for collective action is too messy and unpredictable for any such guide to work. But the SWP's general political perspectives gave members particular strategic impulses or inclinations (to involve as many people as possible in the campaign, to generalise the issues involved, to look to the power of the organised working class, etc.) and a tactical 'flexibility' (to try a range of activities to maintain or muster support), which came from the party's experience of working within episodes of collective action. The openness of the branch stewards committee and the seriousness with which the SWP took its initial activity within Sefton Unison provided a platform from which the party could become more influential – and in this sense offer political leadership to the campaign.

The SWP moved quickly to build support for the Sefton officers. While defending and protecting one of its own members was clearly important to the organisation, the SWP based its intervention around defence of both officers, the right of unions to challenge and break 'unjust' laws, and the defence of any trade unionist or socialist facing imprisonment or fine from the courts. Rita[8] makes the point:

> Any trade unionist or activist who is threatened by the law or the courts must be supported. In the case of the Sefton Two, it was an attack on the whole socialist and trade union movement.

While Pete said:

> Nigel was a member and it is important we protect our comrades from attacks from the state ... but we would have acted just the same if it had only been Martin who was facing the court. Remember when Arthur Scargill [leader of the National Union of Mineworkers] was under attack ... it was the SWP who produced leaflets and factsheets defending him ... we were central to the defence campaign, but Scargill is not, nor ever likely to be, an SWP member.

The party engaged with the branch members ideologically and politically. At each turn it produced leaflets and carried articles in its paper arguing for a strategy which would confront the local employers (to defeat VCT) and challenge the activities of both the courts (to defend the right to strike against anti-union laws) and the national officials (to support the democratic decisions of the branch and protect workers against employers and the state). How this should be done varied in each particular instance. Thus at the original mass meeting the party and its members in the union argued for the one-day strike to defeat the VCT plans and to defy 'unjust' laws. When the branch officials were called back to court, they rejected the national leaders' prescription that they should apologise to the courts; instead they called for defiance and the organisation of a defence campaign to mobilise as many people as possible to attend the High Court in defence of the right to strike. They advocated a strategy of raising money and support across the trade union movement (and other movement campaigns) and attempted to mobilise as many people as possible to support the Sefton Two: to pass support motions in their unions, to raise a collection in their workplace or community, and/or to attend the demonstration outside the court.

But the SWP also attempted to *generalise* the issue, so that the defence of the Sefton Two was about the right to strike, about the unjustness of anti-trade union laws, about the protection of workers from employers and the courts, and about the responsibilities of unions to protect their members. Finally, party members practically attempted to show what could be achieved by raising money, petitioning, sending messages of support and bringing people to demonstrate in support of the branch and its officers. Andy describes what his party branch did:

> Whatever the circumstances it is important that we do as much as we can to raise solidarity with those in dispute or under attack. In the case of the Sefton Two we put motions of support through our own union branches, whether Unison or any other union; petitioned [for] support on the streets of our home towns and cities; raised collections at work and in the community and tried to get people to attend the demonstrations outside the court on the days when Nigel and Martin were there.

Once again we can start to identify the key elements of leadership – dialogical engagement with participants, strategic planning and the delivery of practical support 'to prove' the strategy can work. Such activities will not convince everyone, but they can start to have an impact amongst a layer of participants.

The (non-aligned) stewards had a clear view about the role of the SWP in the defence campaign:

> I think that left-wing groups should organise support during industrial disputes. The SWP organised petitions, lobbies, levies, etc. and these were very useful. (Wendy, Steward, Social Services)

> Without the support of the SWP there would not have been a proper campaign and fund-raising. (Martin, victimised Branch Chair)

> I thought that they were hijacking our dispute for their own ends – but I was grateful they got involved. (Ian, Steward, Public Protection)

> The SWP were very involved from the beginning and became even more so when it came to the Court. Their intervention was very direct and was generally welcomed. (Paul, Social Services)

The comments show general support for the SWP members from the stewards but also a degree of tension – they might have been 'hijacking' the campaign. This reflects at least three features. First, that the SWP members were prepared to disagree and argue with stewards and branch members and felt they had something worthwhile to say – they were not merely a 'support group' unquestionably following the strategies of the local activists, they were competing for leadership within the dispute. Second, the party was attempting to recruit members from the campaign. As Pat, one of the stewards who joined the organisation, argues:

> As well as helping the dispute win, we wanted to have some tangible gains from it, we wanted to recruit ... There isn't anything cynical about this. We want to recruit fighters. Struggles throw up good fighters time and again, but struggles go up and down. If the party locally and those involved in a particular struggle are to learn lessons from any dispute, and generalise these into the movement as a whole, we have to recruit the best of those involved. That isn't just about building the party; it's about the self-preservation of the best activists. Good fighters can be made, won and lost all in the course of a dispute. If they are to be kept for the movement as a whole, they need organisation. Conversely the party needs working-class cadres and the experience and connections that they bring.

While the party may be open about its attempts to recruit activists, there is little doubt that this can lead to tension as some activists interpret their actions as 'using the dispute' for the party's own ends. Finally, this theme fits with a more general, 'commonsense' perspective that all politicians are 'in it for themselves'. Nevertheless, while there was a degree of tension between the SWP and some activists, the successful outcome of the court case and the size of the demonstration outside the courts gave the SWP a high degree of validity in the eyes of many branch activists.

Phase 3: the aftermath – the union makes us strong?

After the court decision, a certain amount of weariness set in, and it was clear that many members wanted to see an end to the fight with the national union. Many members wanted a return to 'normal' industrial relations, while the SWP and its supporters argued that the conflict was likely to continue with the union nationally. This issue produced a significant split within the branch stewards committee, with some stewards arguing that the SWP members were prolonging the dispute for their own political interests. As Paula said:

> I did not realise at first the full extent of the SWP involvement and welcomed their support. However as things went on I felt that they had taken over and felt it was beginning to alienate people. (Paula, Steward, Technical Services)

Even Martin argued in reflection that:

> I was concerned that this dispute would be seen as a 'loony left' affair and that people would dismiss its importance because it was supported by the SWP.

Ironically it was the national officers who cured the 'split' by setting out to 'deal with' the branch. The branch called a meeting for 1 August at which it agreed to pay the fines of the two officers and to start a fund-raising campaign to pay the court and legal costs. National and regional officials opposed these decisions and launched an attack on the branch at both national and regional level. The General Secretary wrote to all Unison branches saying:

> It is essential for the protection of the union's funds and to allow it to continue to operate and fight successfully for its members' interests that all members and branches do nothing to support financially or in any other way the acts of Mr. Flanagan and Mr. Murphy that were admitted by them to have been in contempt of court. (Industrial Action in Sefton, Letter to all Branch Secretaries, 10 August 1994)

The General Secretary also wrote to all members of the Sefton branch urging them to overturn the decision to pay the fines on the grounds that it was putting the union's funds at risk. Regional officials wrote to all northwest Unison branches again attacking the Sefton branch for its actions (Letter from the Regional Secretariat to all North West Regional Council Delegates, 25 August 1994). Managers only too eager to prove that the union branch was out of touch with the rest of Unison circulated virtually all of this information around the council.

The national and regional officials clearly felt that the branch had managed to mobilise support amongst Unison branches and the local membership and it was necessary to counter this, not simply by edict, but by argument and persuasion through personal letters. Thus the officials attempted to go over the heads of the branch officers and appeal to the union loyalty of the membership. It would seem the officials had learnt a valuable lesson over the previous months – the loyalty of the union members to the national officials could not be taken for granted or enforced through edict. They would have to persuade the members of the unreasonable strategy being followed by the branch officers and their shop stewards. This strategy had some success when a senior manager in Sefton Finance Department organised a petition of 40 names to call a Special General Meeting (SGM) with a motion in support of the General Secretary's position. The meeting was scheduled for 15 September.

In order to put their case a reply was produced by the stewards and sent to all members of the branch. At the same time a letter was prepared and sent to all Unison branches, again outlining the branch's case, and calling for delegates to attend a solidarity conference on Saturday 17 September in Sefton. The branch therefore responded to the national official's letter in like fashion, but it also used the letter to build a collective forum – the solidarity conference – where it could emphasise the level of support it had from 'ordinary' trade unionists. The network knowledge and contacts of the SWP were again vital to the branch. Contacts within the union movement were urged to send messages of support and money to the defence fund. All this information was in place for the special general meeting on 15 September. Once again countering the officials' actions involved both a theoretical and practical input – responding to the letter, reiterating the justness of the cause and democracy of the branch's operations, while generating 'facts' (money, support, etc.) to emphasise the breadth of support they had.

At the SGM all those in attendance were given a list of all the Unison and other trade union organisations that had supported the branch. The SGM started with a delegate from Sheffield Unison (and an SWP member) handing over a donation of £700 and making a speech about why that branch supported the campaign. This helped to create an atmosphere of support and solidarity within the meeting, emphasising the successes of the summer's campaign. In this atmosphere the meeting voted against the motion to overturn the earlier decision to pay the branch officers' fines.

The outcome finally convinced the national officials of the union that it would not win the argument against the officers inside the Sefton branch itself. The following Saturday the solidarity conference was attended by 250 delegates from a range of campaigns and over 100 Unison branches. The atmosphere was euphoric and the defence fund well stocked. On 24 September the National Executive Committee decided at its meeting not to pursue any disciplinary investigations against Sefton branch, a decision that was no doubt partly due to the presence of 200 people on a lobby of the NEC that morning. To all intents and purposes the episode was now over.

Conclusion

Different conceptions of leadership were operating throughout the Sefton episode. For the national and regional officials, leadership was something they had as a consequence of their position within the union structure. In the early phases of the events they were happy to 'oversee' the branch's activities and support the officers in their campaign against privatisation; the contradictory social position of trade union leaders means that they must respond to pressures from below and sometimes this means condoning actions taken by local officers (Callinicos 1981, 1995). But this stance changed as the branch's activities impinged on their roles and threatened to drag the national union into a dispute with the courts. Now, their chief goal was to avoid confrontation with the law and preserve their organisation, finances and indeed their social status; for the leaders, the organisation is an 'end in itself' which must be protected at all costs (Cliff and Gluckstein 1986; Luxemburg 1964). At this stage, the political affiliation of one of the branch officers and several of the stewards was branded as problematic; they were identified as pursuing illegitimate political goals which were incompatible with the 'legitimate goals' of trade unionism. The officials then tried a mixture of edict, demand, instruction and denunciation to control the 'rogue' officers, who increasingly rejected their 'right to lead'.

The branch officers had a different conception of leadership. They saw themselves as representatives of the workforce, bound by their democratic decisions – but it would be wrong to view them as passive actors in this process. The evidence clearly shows their leadership in their ability to act speedily when faced with new problems, to strategise over what to do next and to argue with members over the relevance of their proposed solutions. Leadership, here, is about conversation, argument and debate (in mass meetings, section meetings, small groups, newsletter or personal letters), but it also requires practical evidence of success – theory and practice went together, testing each other, reflecting back on each, sometimes vindicating action, sometimes not.

Finally, the SWP members saw the events as an appropriate site for them to engage with the Sefton Unison members and branch stewards and officers over a series of political, strategic and tactical questions. Via a combination of political argument and practical support and advice they attempted to lead the dispute politically – to obtain hegemony within the branch for their strategic orientation and general political perspectives. In this sense the SWP did not compete with the branch for leadership but attempted to exert political leadership over the branch's activities.

These perspectives on leadership were played out over an 18-month period inside the Sefton Unison branch and emphasise that leadership need not be a static 'given' of social movement activity but can be a contested and moving element within a set of dynamic social processes. Competing 'leaders' or aspiring leaders may offer different conceptions of what should be done and why – but to be successful they must convince participants of their case, and show, in practice, the validity of their arguments. Leadership, in this sense, can be a central part of democratic social movement activity and contrasts sharply with conceptions of leadership that view it as something imposed, formal and bureaucratic – the type of leadership from above which the national and regional Unison officials tried, unsuccessfully, to impose on the Sefton workforce.

Notes

1   Michael Lavalette wrote this chapter and any inadequacies in argument, errors of fact or substance rest with him. The chapter could not have been written without Nigel Flanagan, who answered my questions, provided access to his personal library and managed to arrange a number of the interviews with participants – as the story unfolds it should be clear that Nigel was central to the events taking place. Here I'd like to record my thanks – and admiration. I'd also like to thank Alan Johnson, Colin Barker, John Molyneux and Lindsay German, who read and commented on the draft at various stages of completion.

2   Unison is Britain's largest trade union with approximately 1.3 million members. It represents both 'white' and 'blue' collar workers in the public services:

local government, the health services, voluntary organisations and a range of (privatised) health and welfare providers (www.Unison.org.uk).

3	The SWP (Socialist Workers Party) is a revolutionary socialist organisation operating in the classical Marxist tradition, the major theoreticians of which are Marx, Engels, Lenin, Trotsky, Luxemburg, Gramsci and (in the case of the SWP) the theorists of state capitalism. It has just over 10,000 members in Britain and is linked with various sister organisations across the globe within the International Socialist Tendency (www.swp.org.uk).

4	'Dole' is a colloquialism for unemployment benefits.

5	Shop stewards are locally elected office, departmental or section union representatives. They are not union employees but work beside their members, generally on the same pay and conditions of service as them.

6	That is, a full-time employee of the SWP.

7	The shop stewards and activists from Sefton were interviewed after the dispute had finished at the end of 1996.

8	Between 1996 and 1999 I carried out a number of interviews with SWP members; the responses given here are a small sample of this much larger set of interviews. First names only are given to maintain some degree of anonymity – essential at the time of writing as Unison, for example, is in the midst of a significant witch-hunt of SWP members within its ranks.

8

Juggling multiple futures: personal and collective project-formation among Brazilian youth leaders[1]

Ann Mische

Introduction

Leaders in social movements face a delicate balancing act as they invest both in the collective goals and projects of their organisations and in their own personal life projects and ambitions. For youth activists at a formative moment in the life course, the tension between these can be especially acute as they find themselves amidst quickly expanding possibilities for identity, commitment and recognition. Joining a movement almost by definition means engaging in something bigger than oneself, becoming a part of a collectivity whose projects to some degree surpass one's own. Yet for youth who move up from the ranks to emerge as 'leaders', the movement can be as much about personal mobility and achievement as it is about social change, whether this personal 'movement' is explicitly recognised or normatively suppressed.

The experience of movement leadership thus involves a dual expansion of future horizons for young activists. On the one hand, societal futures as narrated by their organisations 'open up', so to speak; what before had seemed an almost impenetrable mass of looming uncertainty (variously tinged by hope, cynicism or despair) now takes on tangible, far-reaching contours. The 'world that we want' is painted in vivid hues while the time between 'now' and 'then' becomes filled with tasks, tactics, strategies, and intermediate achievements. On the other hand, their own personal futures are also opening up, as youth activists move through adolescence into adulthood. The energy invested in the projects of a movement is also energy invested in oneself. The timeframes of 'oneself' are of course different from the timeframes of the movement; moreover, youth activists are often engaged in several different kinds of participation at once, each with its own calendar of projects, milestones and demands. Juggling these multiple temporal and social horizons in the midst of intense personal development becomes an important part of learning how to lead.

In this chapter, I examine how the formation of personal and collective projects among youth leaders is influenced by their multiple affiliations across different kinds of organisational contexts. I first argue for the relevance of the concept of 'projectivity' for the study of social movements and movement leadership. I apply this concept to the study of projective narratives among Brazilian youth activists in the mid-1990s, many of whom belonged to multiple organisations and thus faced considerable challenges in fusing different dimensions of the collective projects of their organisations with their own developing life horizons. I argue that the manner in which young people in different organisational settings learn to balance these multiple affiliations (and associated projects) results in distinct styles of personal and collective project-formation, which influences both the internal life of the groups and the longer-term futures of the individual activists. To understand this process, I examine the affiliations and projects of youth leaders in three different organisations: the Youth Pastoral for Popular Movements, the National Student Union, and the National Forum of Course Executives. This analysis allows me to explore the different kinds of strategies, tensions and interpretive resolutions involved in developing a sense of a personal future in the midst of multiple (and often conflicting) forms of social engagement.

Leaders, movements and projected futures

In much of the social movement literature, leaders are treated as political 'entrepreneurs', serving as intermediaries between potential recruits and the purposes, tasks and organisational structures of a movement. Often such entrepreneurs are depicted as responsible for the 'framing processes' by which movement goals are articulated in relationship to broader social meanings that appeal to recruits as well as to potential allies and partners (Snow *et al.* 1986; Snow and Benford 1988, 1992). Recently, the literature on social movement framing has come under criticism for being overly instrumental and inattentive to dialogic processes within movements and between movements and opponents (Goodwin and Jasper 1999; Steinberg 1998, 1999a). Yet there is something extremely suggestive about the notion of leaders as entrepreneurs that is worth exploring from a more interpretive perspective. The idea of entrepreneurship signals the 'in between' character of social movement leadership, which can operate on various levels: in between the recruits and the social movement organisation; in between the organisation and its allies, targets and publics; and often in between the multiple organisations to which the leader might belong (Rosenthal *et al.* 1985; Fernandez and McAdam 1988). Leaders are, to varying degrees, responsible for constructing meaning out of this betweeness, whether such meaning is best conceived of as frames, as narratives, or (as I join the dialogists in preferring) as conversations. Moreover, an often neglected dimension of the notion of political entrepreneurship is that such leaders are not only acting on behalf of their organisations, but also, like most media-tors, reaping some personal benefits for themselves, even if these come in the non-material form of status, recognition, and/or a sense of personal efficacy.

How, then, can we best study the interpretive work of social movement leaders located in multiple positions of mediation, as well as its impact on the life of a movement? One fruitful way is to conceive of this work as the articulation not merely of frames, but also of *projects*. A frame implies a pre-existing goal that needs to be appropriately packaged in order to be attrac-tive to prospective participants; hence the much-criticised instrumentalist overtones of the literature on collective action frames. A project, on the other hand, implies a more or less open-ended horizon of possibility, cultur-ally structured through existing narratives and yet implying orientation, mission, even vocation, in a self-conscious engagement of a changeable future. As Snow and Benford (1988) point out, the notion of frame align-ment does include future orientation by carrying with it a *prognostic* as well as a diagnostic dimension. And yet, the concept of 'frames' remains basically static; we gain a bit more motion by speaking of 'framing processes', but are still far from the complex socio-temporal constructions implied by the notion of projects, or projectivity.

To understand the projective dimension of social movement leadership, we must look more closely at the concept of 'project' as a tool for social analysis. With roots in Heideggerian existentialism and the social phenom-enology of Albert Schutz (1967), the idea of projectivity captures an essen-tial aspect of human agency (Emirbayer and Mische 1998); however, it has never been widely used in American sociology, due in part to the historical division between structural-functionalism and the abstract voluntarism of rational choice. The forward-looking thrust of the concept allows us to theo-rise how individuals and groups make use of the 'future imaginary' to for-mulate actions within historically evolving situations (Castoriadis 1987; Desroche 1979). Such projects always involve a narrative construction of projected future time, envisioned with varying degrees of clarity, detail, or temporal reach. And because of the intersubjective nature of human rela-tions, the process of project-formation also entails the capacity to interpret and coordinate one's actions in accordance with the motives and projects of other actors.

We can usefully distinguish between the personal or 'life' projects of par-ticular activists, and the collective projects articulated by the organisations and movements to which they belong. An individual's projects can include what we might call 'life goals' or objectives, related to institutionalised tra-jectories of family, career or lifestyle; they may also include what Rom Harre (1984) calls 'projects of personhood', which in Western culture tend to be aimed at cultivating a sense of ourselves as autonomous actors with unique, relatively consistent, and socially recognisable personal 'identities.' Such identities are in turn a key component of the reflexive theorising by which people organise their perceptions, emotions and actions in the social world. Collective projects, on the other hand, can be defined as public narratives of proposed interventions by groups or collectivities. Such narratives clearly have a projective dimension, in that they 'embed identities in time and place' (Somers 1992); they give a sense of where a society and an organisation have come from, while also delimiting where actors think, hope, or fear they may be going. The elaboration of projective narratives usually involves a process of synthesis on the part of actors, as they attempt to reconcile their own developing projects-in-formation with identities and narratives that are being projected at them from wider social and political arenas.

Social movement leaders learn to serve as the articulators of such projects in continual conversations with fellow activists and potential recruits, as well as with allies, opponents and the media. In fact, one could argue that a major part of what activists do is, precisely, talk. They talk about the problems with the existing society as well as the nature and shape of the alternative society that they believe they are working for; they debate issues of tactic and strategy; they plan events, negotiate logistics, and distribute responsibilities. And somewhere in there, either foregrounded in official movement settings or backgrounded to informal bar, car, or (sometimes) bed talk, they talk about their personal experiences, what the movement 'means' to them, and what they hope to take out of it for their own still uncertain life futures. Movements vary in the degree to which the personal dimension of movement activism is explicitly thematised. Some movements, like the Catholic youth group in my study, make personal growth a core part of their mission, while other groups, like the student movement and political parties, tend to subordinate personal development to collective projects (although personal projects enter through the backdoor in the form of leadership ambitions). Young activists caught up in the heat and pressure of movement leadership are often not very preoccupied with plotting out their personal futures beyond the short-term movement calendar; and yet they are also aware that various institutional clocks are ticking away, involving their education, families, jobs, or career paths, whether these are envisioned as taking place inside or outside the movement.

Multiple affiliations and styles of project-formation

These articulations, both personal and collective, are often complicated by the fact that young activists belong to more than one organisation at once. In the Brazilian case, for example, nearly all student activists I studied also belonged to political parties and/or factions; many had previous or continuing experience in church, community, or professional organisations; many of them had also accumulated multiple positions in internal coordinating bodies nested within these distinct movement sectors. This not only kept them very busy; it also provided them with the challenging task of balancing multiple sets of collective projects. These cross-cutting commitments created both stress and reinforcement for the youth leaders, as they attempted to carve out their own personal futures in the face of multiple forms of social involvements.

I argue that the ways in which activists juggle their multiple commitments have important consequences for the styles of project-formation that emerge within different organisational contexts. This argument is based upon Breiger's (1974) discussion of the duality of persons and groups: persons are carriers of the various groups they belong to, just as groups are the carriers of their individual members. We can extend this Simmelian observation to the current context by noting that while groups induce leadership (through recruitment, formation, appointment and/or election procedures), those leaders bring with them into a given leadership position all of the other groups and projects with which they are associated. These associations can either be explicit, as when a student leader is chosen to take part in a student coordinating body *as a formal representative* of some other group (e.g. a political party, church group, labour union, or black student organisation). They can also be implicit (as with many factional ties), or sometimes purposefully submerged; for example, religious orientations rarely received an open hearing within student settings. The important point here is that in addition to being a leader in a given group, an activist is also the conjunction of all of his or her other commitments outside the group, which must be balanced or coordinated in some way.

Each individual leader can therefore be characterised as having a particular array of affiliations, with an associated set of projects, commitments and demands. I will show below that these arrays vary systematically across groups, leading to what we can call 'affiliation profiles' at a group level. While I do not have space in this chapter to discuss the origins of (or reasons for) particular profiles, what concerns us here is that these patterns have several repercussions for leadership: (1) they provoke particular forms of *interpretive synthesis* on the part of young people as they attempt to reconcile personal and collective projects; (2) these syntheses are often supported by internal processes of leadership development within an organisational context, which in turn leads to the emergence of *styles of project-formation* at a group level that are associated with particular organisations; and (3) these styles in turn impact back upon internal dynamics within organisations as well as upon the longer-term futures of the leaders themselves.

I am using the term 'style' in a restricted sense here to refer not to the whole array of characteristics that contribute to the exercise of leadership in an organisational setting, but rather more specifically to the manner in which individual leaders tend to link their various personal and collective commitments. That is, the focus is on what it means for an activist to 'be a leader' in a holistic sense, in the context of his or her personal life horizons as well as multiple social involvements. Leaders are people who are also leading their lives; here I am especially interested in youth leaders who are beginning to survey their impending futures. My argument is that particular conjunctions of multiple commitments (by which I mean a combination of membership and project) create the need for certain kinds of efforts at coordination and synthesis – whether through stacking, integration, segmentation, or some other means, as we shall see below. By supporting such syntheses, organisational settings help to generate different processes of project-formation among young activists.

Juggling multiple commitments: the Brazilian case

In order to gain a more systematic understanding of the effects of multiple affiliations upon student politics, I collected questionnaires from youth leaders detailing their participation histories across different organisational sectors, along with their time management strategies, their social networks, and their personal and social projects.[2] Here I analyse the questionnaires collected from youth at the meetings of three different organisations: the regional assembly of the Youth Pastoral for Popular Movements (PJMP), the national directorate meeting of the National Student Union (UNE), and a planning meeting of the National Forum of Course Executives (Forum). The basic profiles of the organisations are sketched briefly below:

PJMP: started in 1978 by youth involved in Catholic base communities as a branch of the Catholic Youth Pastoral specifically aimed at the experiences and needs of youth from the 'popular' sectors: that is, the poor, marginalised and excluded, especially in the urban peripheries. Drawing from liberation theology, PJMP organised local, regional and national events for youth activists aimed at fostering reflection and growth in both religious and political domains, while also supporting the participation of activists in community-based popular movements.

UNE: one of Brazil's most historic student organisations, founded in 1937 and an important player in the anti-fascist struggles (1940s), the defence of the national petroleum industry (1950s), and the struggle against the dictatorship (1960s), after which the movement was brutally crushed. Following democratisation, UNE regained public prominence in the 1992 impeachment movement. Led by students linked to parties and factions of the left, UNE engaged in national lobbying efforts on issues such as university reform and opposition to privatisation.

Forum: initiated in 1993 as a gathering of course-based student organisations (e.g. groups specific to students of medicine, agronomy, communications, engineering, history, architecture, etc.). These 'course executives' saw themselves as an alternative to the highly partisan dynamic of the 'general' student movement (coordinated by UNE), elaborating proposals for curriculum reform and social involvement in the students' areas of expertise rather than focusing on broader issues of national politics.

All three organisations were national in scope, with national governing bodies as well as various intermediate organising bodies at regional and local levels. The meetings of UNE and the PJMP had 25–30 youth; the Forum had 40–50 (I was able to collect questionnaires from 21, 27, and 32 youth, respectively). These were mostly mid-to-upper-level leaders who were serving as representatives of other organisations (or local 'instances' of a given organisation). The PJMP youth were representing 'base groups' in their local communities; the UNE directors were representing their political party or party factions, as well as sometimes their regional student organisations; and the Forum leaders were representing their specific course-based organisations (e.g. agronomy, law, communications, etc.) based in different parts of Brazil. Moreover, almost all of the youth belonged to some other kinds of organisations beyond the one hosting the event.

The three organisations were also embedded in broader social movement 'sectors' (e.g. religious, partisan, student movement, professional, community, and/or NGO). Usually organisations could be identified as belonging most clearly to one particular sector (e.g. religious in the case of PJMP, and the student movement in the case of UNE and the Forum), although they also overlapped with other organisational sectors both in terms of their projects and through the multiple affiliations of their members. Viewed in the aggregate, the intra-sectoral and cross-sectoral affiliations of activists belonging to a given organisation constitute what I am calling the 'affiliation profile' of that organisation. Table 8.1 presents the affiliations profiles of all three groups, showing the numbers of affiliations *within* each sector that the group leaders have had in their careers, as well as the distributions across sectors. The average overall number of affiliations for the PJMP leaders was 6.3, with 3.3 of these within the religious sector; the UNE leaders averaged 9.5 affiliations each, with 4.9 within the student movement sector; and the Forum leaders averaged 7.8 affiliations, 4.6 of which were within the student movement.[3]

We can note a number of interesting patterns in terms of the distribution of affiliations across these different sectors. These differences fall into three main categories: (1) intra-sectoral activity, referring to the accumulation and diversification of involvements *within* the primary sector of each organisation (religious or student movement); (2) partisan affiliation, referring to membership in a political party; and (3) additional involvements, referring to participation in other kinds of group activities, ranging from cultural activity to participation in research institutes, NGOs, labour unions or pre-professional activity.

Table 8.1: Activist affiliations per social movement sector

	No. of involvements per sector			Total youth involved in sector (%)	
	5+ (%)	3–4 (%)	1–2 (%)		
PJMP (N=27)					
Student	0	4	37	11	(41)
Partisan	0	0	67	18	(67)
Religious	15	52	33	27	(100)
Popular	0	15	37	14	(52)
Cultural	0	0	37	10	(37)
NGO	0	0	7	2	(7)
Prof/Labour	0	0	19	5	(19)
Business	0	0	0	0	(0)
Research	0	0	4	1	(4)
Government	0	0	0	0	(0)
UNE (N=21)					
Student	62	29	10	21	(100)
Partisan	5	29	62	20	(95)
Religious	0	5	19	5	(24)
Popular	5	5	5	3	(14)
Cultural	0	5	43	10	(48)
NGO	0	0	19	4	(19)
Prof/Labour	0	0	19	4	(19)
Business	0	0	0	0	(0)
Research	0	0	19	4	(19)
Government	0	0	5	1	(5)
FORUM (N=32)					
Student	53	41	6	32	(100)
Partisan	0	0	53	17	(53)
Religious	0	3	25	9	(28)
Popular	0	3	47	16	(50)
Cultural	0	3	50	17	(53)
NGO	0	0	19	6	(19)
Prof/Labour	0	0	9	3	(9)
Business	0	0	0	0	(0)
Research	0	0	25	8	(25)
Government	0	0	0	0	(0)

Note: These entries represent the numbers of activists in each group who have the designated quantity of distinct involvements in each area of participation.

Intra-sectoral activity
- More than two-thirds of the PJMP leaders had three or more affiliations *within* the religious sector. This means that in addition to participating in PJMP, they also participated in their Catholic parishes or base communities (through activities ranging from organising liturgy to catechism instruction), as well as in various leadership bodies within the youth pastoral itself.
- Intra-sectoral activity was even more intense for the UNE and Forum youth, most of whom had three or more forms of involvement within the student movement. These ranged from local course-based associations to university-wide bodies to regional or national organisations. Note that a majority of the leaders in both groups had *five or more* student involvements (62 per cent for UNE and 53 per cent for the Forum).

Partisan affiliation
- Two-thirds of the PJMP youth had partisan affiliations, all of which were in the Workers' Party (PT).
- All of the UNE leaders except one were affiliated with political parties. These included a range of left-leaning parties, led by the Communist Party (PCdoB), with the Workers' Party (PT) a strong minority voice.
- One-third of the UNE leaders also had multiple intra-partisan involvements (e.g. faction membership, youth branch leadership, local directorates), highlighting the strongly partisan nature of the traditional student movement.
- In contrast, only a little over half of the Forum leaders had partisan affiliations. Most of those affiliations were in the Workers' Party, although there were a few others as well; the Communist Party was completely absent.

Additional involvements
- A very large percentage of youth from all of the groups (around 50 per cent of UNE and Forum youth and nearly 40 per cent of those from PJMP) participated in some sort of cultural activity, which most often included theatre, music, dance, and/or alternative newspapers; this perhaps indicates an important path by which many youth first became interested in politics.
- About half of the leaders from both the PJMP and Forum also participated in 'popular' social movements, which included both urban and rural community-based movements among the poorer populations; in contrast, only 14 per cent of UNE leaders participated in popular movements.
- About 40 per cent of the PJMP youth also participated in the student movement in their high schools or universities; a few others also were involved in professional/labour and/or research activity.

- The Forum leaders tended to have a broader range of non-student involvements than the UNE youth, especially in the areas of popular movements and research activity, although also edging them out in religious membership and cultural activity.
- While almost 20 per cent of both UNE and Forum members were involved in NGOs, a larger percentage of UNE leaders were involved with labour or professional organisations, perhaps indicating the more strongly organisational nature of the militancy of UNE leaders.

These distinct patterns of affiliation did not just reflect individual decisions, but were also associated with different sorts of internal dynamics within the three groups. There are three main comparisons to be drawn here, related to diversification, partisanship and organisational structure. First, the data show that while youth from all three of the groups had multiple intra- and cross-sectoral involvements, these were especially intense for the student leaders in UNE and the Forum. Becoming a leader (at least at the national level reflected here) meant dealing with many different kinds of participation, both at nested levels within the student movement as well as branching out into other non-student forms of participation. In contrast, the affiliations of the Catholic youth leaders in PJMP tended to be fewer in number and closer to their home base in local community politics, including church-based activism as well as community-based popular movements, cultural production and partisan activity.

Second, we can see three different strategies for combining partisan affiliations with other forms of participation, which I refer to as stacking, integration and segmentation. Partisan dynamics were strongest among the UNE leaders, setting the tone for an extremely conflictual and dispute-oriented internal climate. Since nearly all the youth belonged to competing parties that were disputing leadership at local, regional and national levels, partisan alignments were superimposed or '*stacked*' upon all forms of student representation. Student leaders thus had to become skilled at playing the partisan game at all times, while continuously mapping the factional affiliations of others. While the PJMP youth also tended to belong to a political party, they were much more homogeneous in their partisan loyalties. Support for the campaigns and activities of the Workers' Party was something most of the PJMP leaders could take for granted, and could be *integrated* into their other participation with relative ease. Although they periodically became involved in explicit partisan activity during election campaigns, this was not a central dynamic driving internal discussions. Partisan politics was even less evident among the course-based student leaders of the Forum, and in fact was a taboo subject at Forum meetings, which set a high value on the group's official non-partisanship. The half of the Forum leaders with partisan affiliations tended to identify with the Workers' Party, further diminishing the possibility for internal partisan dispute; however, these partisan affiliations had to be strictly *segmented* from their course-based participation.

Finally, outside of their core involvements, both the PJMP and Forum youth tended to gravitate toward support for loosely structured popular movements, while the leaders of UNE were drawn to forms of participation with a stronger organisational infrastructure. This reflects stylistic affinity as well as opportunities for integration with their religious or student participation. For the Catholic youth, this had to do with the fact that community-based popular movements were often closely associated with the Church (at least its liberation theology guises), and so youth group participation fed easily into community-based political activity (e.g. local movements for education, health, housing, sanitation, land, etc.). For the Forum youth, popular movements provided them with the opportunity to use their specialised professional skills in a sort of consulting capacity, for example when agronomy students provided advice for the land reform movement or medical students supported struggles for local health clinics or law students offered legal aid in the slums. In contrast, the leaders of UNE were drawn to forms of participation with a stronger organisational infrastructure, such as parties, unions or NGOs, perhaps reflecting a stronger cadre mentality of these leaders, who were trained in the control and administration of organisational apparatuses.

Projective narratives: combining personal and collective futures

As the youth leaders juggled these various involvements, they were also juggling the collective projects that these different forms of participation entailed. There was considerable overlap among the projects of all three of the organisations, especially in terms of long-term, societal goals. All of the groups wanted to create a just and egalitarian society, build citizenship, and oppose the 'neo-liberal plan', as represented locally by recent efforts at privatisation and deregulation by the government of Fernando Enrique Cardoso. The Catholic Youth Pastoral framed this in religious-transcendent terms, in terms of the construction of the 'Kingdom of God' on earth, while the National Student Union used the historical-dialectical frame of the fight against capitalist imperialism. The Forum of Course Executives steered away from dramatic triumphalism of either kind, perhaps because its leaders were aware of a greater heterogeneity among its participants in terms of political and professional orientation; for this reason it highlighted the goal of 'building citizenship' more strongly than any of the other groups, as a goal that could be pursued from multiple professional fields and perspectives.

In the medium-term and short-term goals, there was considerably more diversity, given the specific missions and contexts of the organisations. While all of the groups were interested in strengthening communication and integration among their respective 'base' groups (whether these were Catholic youth groups, student organisations, or course executives), PJMP was strongly oriented toward the personal, spiritual and political formation of its leadership, while UNE was more concerned with political mobilisation and participation in national political venues. The Forum was less interested in direct action than UNE, seeing itself as a more intermediate setting for exchange, discussion and elaboration of proposals regarding the university arena and specific professional areas of social intervention.

These differences in the collective projects formulated by the organisations came into play as the young people articulated their own projects for their developing lives. Section A of Table 8.2 presents a breakdown of the types of objectives listed by the youth on their questionnaires in response to an open-ended question about their dreams and objectives for the future. I have coded their responses into four categories: *professional, family/affective, organisational* and *social*. The table reports the number of youth from each organisation who referred to at least one item in that category (many youth listed items from multiple categories). Professional goals often included finishing their secondary or university course, being trained and working in their professional area, or pursuing an advanced degree. Family or affective goals included statements related to close personal relationships, such as 'to have a happy family' or 'to find someone who understands me'. Organisational goals were those related specifically to a given organisation to which they belonged, such as 'to participate actively in the party' or 'to have a successful term in UNE' or 'to be able to contribute to the expansion of PJMP', while social goals were more general statements of social intent, such as 'to see a more just and democratic Brazil' or 'to engage even more in the struggle of the people'.

While all of the youth expressed a strong desire to integrate social and organisational projects as part of their personal futures, the questionnaires reveal differences in the relative salience of these projects across the three groups. These patterns echo some of the differences between the groups noted earlier in the discussion of multiple affiliations. The main patterns can be summarised as follows:

Professional and family/affective
- A very high percentage of leaders from all three of the groups mentioned *professional* goals as important to them, with UNE leaders mentioning these at a somewhat higher rate (90 per cent) than the others (about 75 per cent each).
- PJMP leaders mentioned *family/affective* projects much more frequently (48 per cent) than youth of either UNE or the Forum (about 10 per cent each), showing the greater concern within PJMP for the personal and emotional development of its members.

Organisational and social
- The percentage of UNE leaders mentioning *organisational* goals was much higher (43 per cent) than that either of PJMP (30 per cent) or Forum (16 per cent), probably signalling again the more strongly developed 'cadre' mentality of these highly partisan national student leaders.
- While a strong percentage of youth from all three groups mentioned *social* goals, Forum youth mentioned *social* goals (59 per cent) with a much higher frequency than *organisational* goals (only 16 per cent), with a significantly lower mention of organisational goals than leaders in either of the other two groups. This signals that most of the leaders of course-based organisations saw themselves as conducting their social intervention via their professional careers, rather than through their participation in particular organisations (whether partisan or professional).

Table 8.2: Personal projects and life situations

	PJMP N=27 (%)	UNE N=21 (%)	Forum N=32 (%)	Total N=80 (%)
A. PROJECTS/GOALS				
Professional	20 (74)	19 (90)	24 (75)	63 (79)
Family/affective	13 (48)	2 (10)	3 (9)	18 (23)
Organisational	8 (30)	9 (43)	5 (16)	22 (28)
Social	12 (44)	13 (62)	19 (59)	44 (55)
B. ROMANCE/FAMILY				
Married	2 (7)	1 (5)	0 (0)	3 (4)
Steady romance	6 (22)	9 (43)	6 (19)	21 (26)
Casual romance	2 (7)	6 (29)	2 (6)	10 (13)
Not involved	14 (52)	5 (24)	19 (59)	38 (48)
C. DIFFICULTIES				
Time/no. of involvements	10 (37)	12 (57)	17 (53)	39 (49)
Money/job	15 (56)	8 (38)	9 (28)	32 (40)
Family/affective	10 (37)	2 (10)	10 (31)	22 (28)
University/education	4 (15)	4 (19)	11 (34)	19 (24)
Infrastructure/support	2 (7)	3 (14)	4 (13)	9 (11)
Brazilian/world situation	4 (15)	4 (19)	0 (0)	8 (10)
Movement structure/ group participation	4 (14)	0 (0)	2 (6)	6 (8)
Discipline/personal issues	1 (4)	0 (0)	1 (3)	2 (3)

Note: Entries refer to the number (and percentage) of activists in each group who referred to at least one item in each category (many youth made references to multiple categories). Questions in sections A and C were open-ended, while the question in section B had fixed options.

While these patterns show the overall differentiation across groups, what was striking in all of the groups was the leaders' frequent attempts to combine several of these different types of projects at once. Many of the youth gave synthetic statements that tried to fuse personal and collective projects in meaningful ways. For example, a woman from the PJMP declared that her goal was 'to act more actively in social movements, principally those linked to education and children. To find a job by which I can sustain myself, find my other half, marry and have children.' Another wanted 'to be able to continue studying to know more and be able to pass on my knowledge to those who are fighting for transformation that makes life more beautiful and pleasurable, where there is no more oppression'. Note here the attempt to link education directly with social movement activity, and to orient both of those toward improving the conditions of personal and/or family life.

Many of the student activists in both UNE and the Forum also saw their education and professional careers as a pathway to continued social and political commitment. One of the UNE directors hoped 'to be a social researcher in the area of anthropology and psychology or to be a political advisor for social or institutional movements'. A fellow director wanted to 'to provide technical contribution to society in the area of economics', declaring that 'my life objectives are linked to contribution to the process of transformation of society. The relation is very close as I don't think about being an economist without political engagement.' The Forum youth were even more insistent on this point, especially since social engagement via professional careers was a core projective narrative of the movement of course executives. A leader of the medical students' association hoped 'to be a doctor oriented to the more humanist and social side, having a critical vision of reality'. Likewise, a leader in the executive of physical education students wrote that 'after finishing my course in physical education, I intend to do a course in social science, followed a masters degree in the area of education … [studying] the social role of physical education. In truth, my main objective is the construction of a new world, not only in the future but beginning today.'

Switching hats: the problem of coordination

The juggling of these multiple social and political involvements was not without its difficulties. Most activists experienced a variety of personal and social costs as they attempted to coordinate different forms of participation. These difficulties ranged from tensions with romantic and family life to lack of time and financial resources as well as interferences with work, studies and career development. Some struggled to set personal priorities, while others found their priorities pretty much determined by the emergent demands of the multiple worlds in which they were involved.

Romance and family

One area in which these costs manifested themselves was in the romantic sphere. As Section B of Table 8.2 shows, nearly half of the activists reported not being involved in any romantic relationships, and many of them poignantly described the difficulties involved in trying to carry on a relationship on top of their political involvements. The difficulties often included finding time for their family life and romantic relationships, as well as lack of understanding from family and romantic partners for their way of life. As one Forum leader complained, 'It is very complicated, for [my boyfriend] does not participate in the movement, in spite of being a student, and he conspires with my family to cut me off from my political life'.

This varied by group; surprisingly, the UNE youth fared better than either those of PJMP or the Forum, despite the intensity of their high-level activism. A sizeable number of the UNE leaders (43 per cent) reported being involved in steady romantic relationships, while another 29 per cent reported involvement in casual relationships, in both cases far more than those in other groups. This could be due either to their high status as national leaders or to their greater tendency to form relationships within the movement. Note that in Section C of Table 8.2, the PJMP and Forum youth both reported considerable difficulty with family and affective relationships; 37 per cent and 28 per cent mentioned these as difficulties, respectively, as opposed to only 10 per cent of UNE leaders.

Often the strategy for dealing with these conflicts involved choosing a partner from within the movement. This tended to ease some of the tension, but did not eliminate it; as one PJMP leader said, 'as my wife is also a militant in PJMP this facilitates our participation, even so we are alert so that we don't get in the way of each other'. The difficulty of finding relaxed relationship-building time was evident even in apparently strong relationships, as a woman in the Forum noted: 'I have an excellent relationship with my boyfriend, as he is also a militant in the executive of our course, with this there is comprehension when some problem arises in relation to this question. But we have problems in relation to recreation.'

Time and money

Among the other difficulties in coordinating the different aspects of their lives, a significant number from all three of the groups reported problems with lack of time and/or too many involvements. This clearly interfered with their affective lives, but also had additional complications, affecting studies and jobs as well as increasing their general level of stress. One Forum leader wrote that his biggest difficulty was 'to have fun! … the nature of my political and academic involvement gives me little time for activities that are more pleasurable.' This problem seemed most acute for the UNE youth (57 per cent), followed closely by those in the Forum (53 per cent), who as we saw earlier had an average of 8–9 involvements each. It was less acute, but still prominent, for those of PJMP (37 per cent).

The PJMP youth, on the other hand, reported more problems with money and jobs than those in the other groups (56 per cent), followed by the UNE youth (38 per cent) and then by the Forum (28 per cent). Although youth leaders from all groups were scrambling for funds, this pattern reflects the lower socio-economic position (and corresponding financial concerns) of the PJMP leaders in comparison to the university students involved in the other two groups. Among these, the UNE youth were generally more removed from the world of work than the professionally oriented Forum youth. They were more likely to depend upon (often shaky) funding they could scrape together from the world of the militancy itself (political parties, unions, the student movement), as opposed to internships or pre-professional employment (teaching, research, etc.) that many of the Forum youth pursued.

The Forum leaders, on the other hand, were much more likely than the other group leaders to complain that their activism was interfering with their education and their university courses. This does not mean that the UNE youth were more successful as students; in fact most of them had suspended their matriculation in order to devote themselves full-time to their tasks as UNE directors, which perhaps made the issue less salient for them. On the other hand, since the activism of the Forum youth was so closely linked to their professional formation, the drain on time for their studies was especially frustrating to them.

Strategies of prioritisation
The youth leaders pursued various strategies for prioritising and conciliating the various demands on their time. For some of them, it was a clear question of sacrificing their personal needs to the emergent demands of the organisation; as one UNE youth said, he prioritised his activities 'in accord with political necessities. These needs constantly conflict with personal interests, which are administered day to day.' For many of them, there was little personal planning or preference involved in ordering those priorities, which were mainly reactions to the urgently pressing demands of their activism, leading them to prioritise 'through commitment and immediate necessity'. For many of the UNE directors, especially, the experience was one of considerable lack of control over their agendas and their organisation of time; as one of the newly elected leaders described it, 'the conflict is exactly that of prioritisation. In politics the moment is like the wind, and things, let's say, "they're blowing in the wind" [in English], so then the personal damage is extremely high because it doesn't depend on your individual priority; the priorities of politics carry their own logic and their own steamroller over us. That's the price!'

Other youth were more proactive in attempting to exercise personal control over the administration of these emergent demands in relation to their personal set of priorities: as one youth who was both an UNE director and a participant in the Forum described it, he organised his time 'in accordance with the calendar/demand and in relation to strategic priorities. The problems are that the agendas are always full on all sides and the demands are suffocating. If I don't plan and organise (chronogram) my activities, they are not accomplished.' The PJMP youth were most explicit in discussing their efforts to prioritise their participation; I found out that in fact this had been an important theme discussed in their meetings, as they tried to preserve the personal/spiritual side of the pastoral against incipient burnout many of them were experiencing: 'in the face of diverse activities, not only of a pastoral order but also academic and others, I try to live in fact by certain priorities, participating in the best form possible, prioritising the most urgent ones'.

A few of the youth leaders expressed the view that the ordering of priorities was a highly flexible, context-bound process, for which it was difficult to find any steady, all-encompassing rule. For some of them, this resulted in a sort of immediatism, an extreme short-term perspective on temporal organisation: 'at every moment I analyse the order of priorities', said one UNE youth. Others were able to contextualise their current involvement in a longer-term framework, looking forward to a day in which their lives would not be so heavily dominated by political engagement: as another UNE leader said, 'today without a doubt my principle activity is political, this doesn't mean that tomorrow it will be. You need to prioritise activities in accordance with your stage of life.'

Interpretive resolution: the challenge of synthesis

Despite these difficulties, most of the young people in all three of the organisations were very clear that the linking of personal and social projects was a good thing overall and that their political participation had made a positive contribution to their lives. In fact, the vast majority of the youth seemed to consider this link between personal and collective projects as an essential or *constitutive* part of their self-understanding. As one UNE director said, 'political and social participation gives me a great base for my future perspectives ... certainly it will be fundamental for my personal projects'. Or another: 'They complement each other. The latter are associated with the former.' A youth in the PJMP echoed this theme: 'They are interrelated, as one depends on the other to be realised ... It doesn't get in the way, as it causes me to be able to learn more and I have somewhere to apply it. It makes me grow and is so enriching.'

In all of these cases, the challenge faced by the youth was that of synthesis: how to conceptualise the link between their political participation and their personal lives in such a way as to bolster a sense of agency in both directions. It is in this sense that Harre's (1984) notion of 'identity projects' becomes relevant; not only were they learning from their activism about what they wanted to do (both socially and politically), but they were also learning on a kind of meta-level about 'who they were' (or would be) while they were doing it. This creates a kind of agentic synergy that works in a much more global, multi-dimensional way than would be implied by the particular projects to which they were linking their day-to-day choices and actions.

Many of the youth talked about how much they had benefited personally, politically and intellectually from their activism, despite the tensions. According to a UNE leader, 'IT HELPS!!! For it makes me grow personally and politically, and it gets in the way, relatively and temporarily, in completing my education and finding fixed work.' In most cases, this growth was not seen in narrow ideological terms, but in a more holistic manner that spread outside of the boundaries of their specific participation into other areas of their lives. Interestingly, the PJMP and Forum youth tended to speak in a more sustained and often eloquent way than the UNE leaders about the influence of participation on their personal lives, perhaps because the personal dimension was more salient than it was in the intensely politicised milieu of UNE's national leadership. Discussions within both PJMP and the course executives of the Forum explicitly thematised the link to the personal development of their participants. Among the PJMP youth, this sort of 'projective overflow' was clearly evident, linking political ideals to movement, family and spiritual life: 'PJMP today is in all the discussions that I have, inside as well as outside the church, I see myself with PJMP in the intermediate means or mechanisms in which I participate, and also in my life as a youth from the popular environment and a citizen preoccupied with life. And in family and sentimental life I bring my knowledge as a militant Christian committed to the popular struggle.'

The youth leaders from the Forum were equally insistent on the multi-layered quality of this influence, although they tended to highlight the effects their participation had had on their professional vocations as well as their political consciousness. As the medical student cited earlier said, 'politically it amplified my knowledge. In academics I now have a more critical vision of medical instruction. Professionally, I am more concerned with the social responsibility of the university, or rather, of the doctor with society ... I believe that for me it was very significant in making me grow.' Another Forum leader described how this extended into a broader civic consciousness as well as to a sense of personal agency: 'In comparison with other people around me, I see that I understand better what happens in the country, I vote with my own conscience and I demand my rights. [My] academic formation has been broader, giving me a more critical vision. In relation to life (professional/personal), being a subject agent, in almost all of the situations of life.'

A few of the youth, mostly members of UNE or the PJMP, described the contribution to their personal lives not as a result of the influence of political participation on them, but rather on their own (and their organisations') influence on society. By creating 'a better Brazil', they were thereby working to improve their own personal life opportunities (albeit in the long run). As one UNE leader said, 'it contributes [to my personal projects], as it is helping to resolve the political problems of the country'. Another noted that the history-making he was involved in had personal repercussions: 'you can't achieve social ascension without living your time and your own history'. Among the PJMP leaders, this point was especially salient due to their personal feeling of economic and political marginalisation: 'The relation is one of construction and transformation of society, since in accordance with the social changes that are happening it becomes easier to achieve my personal projects ... It contributes to the degree that the participation serves as an instrument of social transformation.'

Implications for leadership

The foregoing discussion indicates the opportunities as well as the tensions young leaders experience in their attempts to link personal and collective projects in a complex, multi-layered organisational context. We have seen how different organisations tend to facilitate or channel this linkage in particular ways. I would argue that these different styles of fusing personal and collective futures have important implications for leadership, both in terms of the internal dynamics of social movement organisations and in terms of the future careers of the youth activists as they move into their adult lives. While all three of the organisations tended to be all-encompassing in their demands on time, energy and resources, they varied in the relative emphasis they encouraged their leaders to place on the social, organisational, affective and professional dimensions of their projected futures. In this final section I pull together the observations made earlier about affiliations, projects, and interpretive synthesis in order to describe the distinct styles of project-formation that emerge in each of the three organisational contexts.

To return to my opening argument, processes of project-formation within organisations are not determined either by the individuals or by the organisations themselves, but rather are influenced by the array of affiliations – and therefore projects – that individual leaders bring with them into the organisational context. As we have seen, these affiliations are not distributed randomly, but tend to cluster in characteristic ways, composing affiliation profiles for each group. At an individual level, these multiple commitments result in a set of challenges for coordination and synthesis, provoking the need for some sort of interpretive resolution as the youth attempt to juggle collective and personal projects. Organisations assist in this process by providing both explicit guidance and implicit examples, leading to the emergence of characteristic styles of project-formation associated with particular groups. Activism in all of the three groups led to a strong link between personal and collective (or as they tended to call them, 'social') projects; however, the emphasis was different in each case. For PJMP youth, the social-affective link was most salient; UNE leaders stressed the social-organisational aspect of participation; while for the Forum leaders, the social-professional dimension came to the fore.

In the Catholic Youth Pastoral, the main focus was on the affective and social dimensions of the youths' participation, although organisational projects were also important, via participation in 'intermediary organisations' (partisan, student, labour, community). While the youth worried about their professional futures, these were not explicitly thematised within the organisation, perhaps because the access of most of the youth to higher education and thus to professional careers was precarious at best. However, PJMP was clearly concerned to integrate its projects for political and social transformation with the affective and spiritual development of its members. As a priest adviser to PJMP told me, 'we don't just want a man or a woman who is politicised. Our preoccupation is that the person earns well, in this capitalist context, has a dignified life, a good house, tranquillity, good health, has children, the normal process of existence.' The youth leaders, correspondingly, articulated a concern to develop these personal dimensions of themselves along with their commitment to social change. However, they acknowledged how frustrating this integration could be, especially given their scanty financial resources and the dangers of exhausting overextension in their multiple militancies: 'sometimes we're so busy, we forget our own lives; work, family, school, everything'.

In order to help its leaders with this difficult task of projective integration, the Youth Pastoral had developed a collective pedagogy of group and self evaluation (the methodology of 'SEE, JUDGE, ACT' coming out of Catholic Action) that sought personal reflection at the same time as group integration; this pedagogy was often accompanied by music, theatre, and group-building exercises. Since many of these youth also participanted in community movements and political parties, this reflective-integrative ethos infused their reflection about politics beyond what might have been officially sanctioned by the Catholic Church. One of the founders of PJMP in São Paulo told me that his goal (and that of PJMP) was 'to bring ethical, theological values into the party, the unions, the hierarchy of the church, based on profound human values, the essence of the human being'. Historically, the Catholic Youth Pastoral has been a source of leadership for community movements as well as for the ranks of the Workers' Party; however, to some extent its goals were more modest, seeking to develop the 'new man' and 'new women' conceived locally and as holistically as possible given the pressing demands of the militancy.

The UNE leaders, in contrast, expressed much less concern with the affective dimension (even though they reported a higher level of actual romantic involvement). The main emphasis was on the social and organisational dimensions of their projects, with professional concerns present, but again operating in a minor key. Many of the youth saw their layers of partisan, student, and other social movement activism as part of a seamless whole, although one in which the personal side was usually subordinated. As one UNE director said, 'it's all the same militancy. With militancy in the student movement, in UNE, in the PSTU [his party] ... it's one militancy as a whole. There is a single, dialectical relationship ... The militancy is a way of life, a way of relating with the world, with people, of how to interpret reality, our Brazil.'

While all of the UNE leaders identified as students, and therefore aspired to complete their academic careers, many of them were also steeped in a partisan organisational culture that prized oratory, dispute, and skill at backstage negotiation rather than personal growth or group integration. The extremely competitive, hierarchical structure fuelled leadership ambitions, even while these were officially frowned upon as an object of personal pursuit. Most of the UNE youth saw their personal futures 'after the student movement' in terms of a continuation of this militancy in other organisational contexts, with continuity supplied by the political parties. Directorship in UNE has historically been a jumping-off point for a career in institutionalised party politics, so some of the leaders looked toward possible candidacies at local or regional levels. Others talked about getting involved in labour or professional activism or partisan-supported research; several, interestingly, saw themselves engaged in theory development, which they felt was urgently needed on the left given the 'crisis of socialism'. As one of the UNE directors from the Workers' Party told me, he was eager to go back to school and finish his degree in social science after leaving UNE: 'I want to study a lot. Because I think that the great drama of the left today, the great challenge the left confronts if it want to be an effective force, is to have a strategic alternative for society. Because today it doesn't have that.'

For the youth leaders in the Forum of Course Executives, the link between professional and social projects took centre stage, with both affective and organisational goals clearly subordinated. The leaders of the course-based associations did not necessarily see their future commitments as being channelled through formal organisational contexts, although they were equally emphatic about their desire to make a social contribution. Most of them saw themselves primarily as 'future professionals' rather than as militants *per se*; hence they felt that their primary contribution would be made *as* lawyers, agronomists, engineers, doctors, journalists, teachers, or architects, rather then *as* political party members or even members of a particular civic organisation.

While in fact over half of the Forum leaders did belong to political parties, and thus shared many aspects of their basic world-view with both UNE and PJMP members, this partisan affiliation was de-centred to varying degrees in the internal dynamics of the movement. Some leaders of the course executives were stridently anti-partisan, while others were more deeply immersed in partisan politics, but all agreed that partisan squabbles needed to be suppressed in the context of the Forum in order to proceed with the primarily elaborative (rather than principally mobilising) work of the course executives. In the interest of creating a climate that favoured joint elaboration and exchange of ideas, they often engaged in group-building exercises reminiscent of the Catholic groups, which further helped to defuse factional conflict. Unlike the UNE members, they didn't feel that they needed to 'go back' to school after their student leadership positions in order to contribute to the elaboration of 'alternative projects for society'; rather such projects were conceived in terms of their specific professional areas, to which they could start contributing now, *as students*, rather than concentrate solely on the more 'general' questions of national and international politics on which the UNE youth tended to focus.

I am not making an argument here for which styles of project-formation are 'better' or 'more effective' than the others. I am simply arguing that the way social movement leaders combine personal and collective projects amidst the heat of competing demands and commitments *makes a difference*, both for the life of the movement and for the longer-term futures of the activists. Each approach sketched above must be understood as a product of a particular socio-cultural milieu: the PJMP came out of the Catholic Church's response to precarious social and economic conditions of the urban periphery, UNE came out of a long historical tradition of leftist organising, and the Forum came out of what might be considered a new cohort of socially minded middle-class university students who were sceptical of traditional leftist organisational forms but nevertheless wanted to express their commitment to a more just future through their professional careers. None of them meets an ideal of perfectly balanced and integrated activism in which personal, political and professional factors get equal weight, and each involves often severe costs and trade-offs for the youth leaders involved. But in all cases, the intense crucible that constitutes the activist experience results in a reformulation of future imaginings among the young leaders, with deeply personal implications that are often as strong as (or stronger than) the collective projects advocated by the organisations themselves.

Notes

1   I would like to thank David Gibson, Harrison White and the editors for their helpful comments on this chapter, as well as my research assistants Diane Bates, Sandra Baptista and Tom Degloma for their help in compiling the database on which this analysis is based. This chapter is based on ethnographic and documentary research carried out in São Paulo between 1993 and 1997 with funding from the Latin American and the Caribbean Program of the Social Science Research Council as well as from the Fulbright–Hays Doctoral Dissertation Abroad program. Data analysis was funded by a grant from the National Science Foundation (SES-9909168).

2 During my fieldwork in Brazil (1993–97), I accompanied eight different youth organisations, including student, religious, pre-professional, anti-discrimination and business organisations. I also accompanied the youth branches of several political parties, including the Workers' Party (PT), the Communist Party of Brazil (PCdoB), and the Brazilian Social Democratic Party (PSDB). In addition to observations at meetings and events, I collected taped interviews with over 70 activists as well as 350 questionnaires, only 80 of which are analysed here.

3 While not all of these involvements may have been active at the time they completed the questionnaires (these are reports of participation histories, not just current involvements), activists tended to carry these past involvements into new leadership positions with them as a source of networking and articulation, increasing the complexity and reach of negotiations for these national leaders, as well as the drain on time and energy.

9

Leaderless cultures: the problem of authority in a radical environmental group[1]

Jonathan Purkis

> This incredible challenge before us: how do we respond without becoming those people we are trying to destroy? How do we avoid that great pitfall of revolutionaries, to become what you revolt against? How do you fight tyranny without becoming tyrants? ... I don't know. (Dave Foreman – co-founder of US Earth First! – 1992: 32)

Introduction

The aim of this chapter is to offer an anarchist perspective on the notion of leadership in contemporary political and social movements, using the theory and practice of the 1990s radical environmental network Earth First! (EF!) as a case study. My claim is that we must see EF! as part of a long anti-authoritarian tradition, which has persistently questioned the notion that leadership and hierarchical structures are somehow natural to human societies. Indeed, the notion that 'leadership' is synonymous with 'hierarchy' forms a central tension within the discussion and is most visible in terms of EF!'s attempts to free itself from hierarchical methods of organising. As an anti-authoritarian – arguably anarchist – movement, EF! tries to practically realise a different philosophy of organisation that is based around consensus decision-making, cooperation and collective responsibility rather than representation, hierarchy and leadership. The struggle which one EF! group – that of Manchester during the period 1992–94 – had with maintaining its anti-authoritarian ideals is the subject of this chapter.

The argument is organised as follows. First, I will introduce and contextualise the emergence of EF! in the UK and outline its aims, organisational principles and attitudes to leadership. This leads into a discussion about the appeal of anarchism to activists and their views on the reasons for the existence of the environmental crisis, which lays particular emphasis on the issue of political organisation. Second, I concentrate on the operation of the Manchester group and identify the points where the activists' political practice was different from their theoretical ideal. The third section examines these disparities more specifically in terms of the use of power within the group and suggests why certain activists were able to exercise it through their use of 'cultural capital'. The fourth section considers how EF! activists sought to remedy these and other disparities which were occurring in the group. Last, I consider these disparities in the light of a number of theories of power not usually found in social movement literature, in particular the work of Michel Foucault and social ecologist Murray Bookchin. It is the latter's work which I suggest can most illuminate the kind of processes in which EF! is engaging.

This chapter draws on ethnographic data which formed the basis of my doctoral thesis as well as a number of publications (Purkis 1996a, 1996b). Although the data is very time and space specific and highly qualitative, I believe it to be not untypical of the experiences of other EF! groups in the 1990s and indeed similar anarchistic movements in the radical environmental milieu. All names of activists have been changed.

Earth First! and the anarchist ideal

Move over Greenpeace

EF! emerged in 1980 in the south-western states of America out of a radical conservationist rather than New Left tradition. Formed by half a dozen activists who had worked in organisations such as Greenpeace, Friends of the Earth and the Sierra Club, EF! was principally concerned with oil, road and logging industries' development of wilderness areas throughout the region, and the compromises which the existing environmental groups were making on the issues. As one of the EF! founders, Dave Foreman, noted, 'the environmental groups were becoming indistinguishable from the corporations they were supposedly fighting' and there was a need to 'spark ... a fundamentalist revival within the environmental movement' (Bookchin and Foreman 1991: 38).

The revival consisted of a network of small loosely affiliated autonomous groups who vowed to physically defend wilderness areas and who carried out their activities without bureaucracy, lobbyists, membership lists or official spokespeople. The kind of direct action carried out by USEF! groups has involved 'locking on' to earth-moving or tree-cutting machinery, tree sitting, and 'unsurveying' of roads, as well as older methods of civil disobedience such as human blockades, occupations and banner hanging. On a number of occasions these direct methods resulted in successful campaign outcomes (Scarce 1990: 71). Although the North American groups can be seen to have something of a different kind of protest aesthetics from those which emerged in the UK in 1991 – being much more nature-oriented in their iconography for instance (Taylor 1991) – many of the founding principles are similar and many of the slogans, literature and attitudes have had considerable diffusion in the UK.

EF! in the UK was initially concentrated around the south-east of England but quickly spread north and west to comprise between 50 and 60 groups during 1993, a number which has subsequently remained fairly stable. Like their American counterparts, most of the founding activists had had experience of other environmental groups, something clearly expressed in one of their early documents, *What is Earth First!?*: 'EF! arose from the belief that conventional green campaigns are not enough to prevent the destruction of the planet ... EF! believes that the greatest force for change is when individuals stand up to be counted and are prepared to put themselves and their bodies in the way' (1993: 1). Although the campaigns which EF! undertook were not new – opposition to the Tory government's £23 billion 'Roads to Prosperity' programme, the tropical timber trade, building on 'green field' sites, Third World debt, an end to the production of CFCs (chloroflouro-carbons) in Britain, opposing destruction of peat moors, and carrying out solidarity actions with indigenous peoples' fighting superdam projects in India – it was the manner in which they undertook them which surprised and even alarmed existing environmentalists. Rather than lobbying for change or expecting representation through Parliament, EF! activists believed in having an impact on government and business by directly attempting to stop destructive developments. Using many of the civil disobedience techniques practised by their American counterparts, they systematically targeted all aspects of the business in question. So, in the case of opposing a road scheme, all of the following would be targeted: contractors' offices, quarries, shareholders' meetings, funding organisations, security firms and even the houses of government ministers. Since the 'movement' was a network of effectively autonomous groups which did not need official permission to undertake activities, EF! could not be sued or have its funds sequestrated. Following the slogan 'No compromise in the defence of Mother Earth', EF! actions expressed an urgency about the need for an imminent end to the ecological devastation and frequently managed successfully to disrupt business (and occasionally Parliament) in a colourful, theatrical and irreverent manner.

In terms of its own self-definition, EF! has had little in the way of official policies and manifestos, keeping its bureaucracy to an absolute minimum. The 'Aims and Objectives' of EF!, drawn up at the first national gathering in 1991, still stand. They are as follows:

- To defend the environment.
- To confront and expose those destroying the environment.
- To realise a human lifestyle that exists in balance and harmony with the natural world that has respect for all life.

Similarly, its 'Methods' are:

- Empowering individuals and groups to take direct and focused action against those destroying the environment.
- Networking information and contacts between action groups to facilitate the growth of a movement and encourage group autonomy.
- By raising funds for direct action campaigns and networking costs.
  (Earth First! 1992: 3)

In addition, EF! mandates its local groups to organise their own campaigns, is committed to non-violence (although damage to property is the individual's own responsibility) and recognises diversity of opinion within the movement. EF! activists favour consensus rather than representative models of decision-making, and even in the midst of political actions, EF!ers refuse to speak on other people's behalf.

In the production of their literature, such as the bi-monthly newsletter *Earth First! Action Update*, editorial responsibility is rotated, with different groups taking over after every few issues, something which is common to other radical green or anarchist types of organisation (Atton 1999). Similarly, in less 'official' EF! publications, such as *Do or Die (Voices from Earth First!)*, diverse and sometimes controversial opinions are always printed (providing they are deemed not to be racist, sexist or homophobic).

In interview, EF! activists in Manchester were extremely clear about the importance of organising non-hierarchically. This can be illustrated by answers to one of the interview questions: *How important do you think that things such as structure and decision-making are in the work you do?*

Calum: I suppose structure is important in that EF! doesn't have a rigid structure like Friends of the Earth which makes it more different. It can be more radical as it doesn't have a list of members. It's designed for doing radical activities as opposed to lobbying.

Christine: You have to have a certain structure, but not a rigid structure ... Moving chairs. Everyone takes responsibility for the structure.

Dave: Structure ... I feel is unfortunately necessary but if more people were committed to the issue of structure, then we could have a more democratic structure ... it slips into hierarchy.

Louis: Structure and decision-making are extremely important. If you do something as an individual it has an effect on others.

Owen: Obviously they are important ... ends and means – you can't separate them. At the end of the day it's what you do which is important ... but I've not got enough experience to know how you get there.

Neil: Decisions and structure are absolutely central in what we do but half the time we're not aware of what we're doing.

Tamara: Very important. It seems to be the key to things to me ... it very much defines what their personal politics are ... the way people do it.

A number of issues are raised here: the means and ends of an action, personal politics and taking responsibility for the group as well as one's own actions, and the need to avoid hierarchical structures but still organise effectively. Any exercising of authority or 'leadership' – even temporarily – therefore appears to be 'bad'.

Indeed, in some respects the attitudes of EF! activists apparently mirror the classic anarchist perspective on leadership, which is based on a distinctive view of power and human nature. As Morland (1997) argues, anarchism has basically proffered a twin view of human nature as possessing both contextualist (sociability) and universalistic (egoist) characteristics. This interpretation of human history sees societies and political groups as being equally capable of cooperation or exploitation depending on the mode of organisation within them (rather than the material conditions as such). Any attempt to establish social or political hierarchy at the expense of cooperation results in a slide towards tyranny, a sentiment most famously expressed by Michael Bakunin: 'Take the most sincere democrat and put him on the throne; if he does not step down promptly, he will surely become a scoundrel' (see Dolgoff 1973: 91).

This, it should be said, is not the same as rejecting 'authority' as in the authoritative knowledge of – as Bakunin also suggested – the architect or the engineer. The classical anarchists were opposed to the use of expertise to oppress, regulate and oversee. Bakunin's remark that 'I bow before the authority of special men [*sic*] because it is imposed on me by my own reason' (1983: 313) is one which could translate to any contemporary context. The difference between authoritative and authoritarian is an important one and something to which I shall return.

Since I have just suggested that EF!'s attitude to authoritarian structures mirrors the classical anarchist one, it seems important to clarify a number of issues, in particular the relative awareness of the 'official' history of anarchism amongst activists and indeed why anarchist theory and practice might appeal. The following section constitutes a necessary deviation in order to understand the kind of political ideas which activists 'bring with them' to radical environmental protest, before we look at the dynamics of the group itself.

The appeal of anarchism

One of the most striking aspects about the politics of some of the 'new' social movements of the 1960s, such as the women's, peace, civil rights and environmental movements, was (at least during their early years) a commitment to non-hierarchical and anti-authoritarian structures and strategies. Although the re-emergence of interest in anarchism in the post-war era has been well documented – in the New Left, the American counter-culture, the 'Events' of May '68 (Apter and Joll 1971; Ehrlich *et al.* 1979) – the application of anarchist praxis to environmental politics has been only quite recent

(Welsh and McLeish 1996; Hart 1997). In part this has been a problem of periodisation and an over-preoccupation with nineteenth-century classical anarchism, with many contemporary commentators considering what Moore (1997: 157) calls the 'first wave' of anarchism (judged to have 'finished' with the failure of the Spanish Revolution in 1939) to *be* anarchism.

It seems an important methodological point, then, to note the tendency to equate 'anarchist movements' only with groups and networks who appear to be self-identified practitioners of anarchism rather than groups of people who are practising anarchism but who do not necessarily identify themselves as doing this (at least not explicitly). The failure of commentators to make such a differentiation may well have an influence on how future activists perceive themselves in relation to other movements.

Within EF!, acknowledgement of the 'official' theory and practice of anarchism has been mixed, at local and 'national' levels. Certainly there is enough evidence of an awareness of anarchist history, through references in EF! literature to 'classic' anarchist figures such as Emma Goldman, Pierre Joseph Proudhon and Buenaventura Durutti, as well as formal connections with the Industrial Workers of the World, the long-lived anarcha-syndicalist 'union' better known as 'the Wobblies'. Similarly, the influence of radical 1960s art practitioners the Situationist International – who combined anarchism, Surrealism and the work of Georg Lukács – has also been noticeable within contemporary radical environmentalism. In Britain, practical alliances have taken place with anarchist groups, occasionally with Class War, but more importantly with *Green Anarchist,* an idiosyncratic anti-technological paper/collective, which has existed since the mid-1980s (see Atton 1999).

More important, however, than identifying which aspects of anarchist history are known to EF! activists, is trying to establish the sociological contexts which motivate people to choose one type of political organisation over another. We can, I think, determine five areas of influence.

First, the decline in deference to politicians and political systems has become chronic, with increasing numbers of young people spurning the opportunity to vote or believing that existing institutions can create meaningful solutions to social and environmental problems (Mulgan 1994). In part this is the legacy of the 1980s and the major pieces of social welfare and law and order changes which widened the gap between rich and poor, limited the options of socially marginal people, and clamped down heavily on anybody who opposed, or was alien to, the new free-market hegemony.

Second, the existing opportunities for opposition to an ecologically destructive capitalist system are seen to be ineffective. This applies both to the traditional left, which is sometimes perceived by radical environmentalists as being too hierarchical and overly concerned with production struggles in the West, as well as the major environmental non-governmental organisations, which are seen to embody corporate values. The rightward move of

Friends of the Earth (in particular) and Greenpeace from 1988 onwards, to lobby rather than confront the suddenly eco-friendly Thatcher government, can be seen as critical to understanding the emergence of EF! (see Wall 1999).

Third, a combination of both of these factors has assisted in the growth of a do-it-yourself (DIY) political culture with the emphasis on self-organisation, the promotion of alternative ecological lifestyles, trading systems and cooperative living. A number of authors have couched this in terms of a new counter-culture akin to that of the late 1960s (McKay 1996).

Fourth, there has been the impact of activists with both peace movement and women's liberation experience, from whom radical environmentalists have learned the philosophies and language of non-violent direct action and consensus decision-making (although not necessarily any firm answers). Anecdotal evidence suggests it is here that knowledge of 'official' anarchist history is passed on.

Fifth, the role of popular culture cannot be underestimated, in particular the impact of the high-profile politics of bands such as *Chumbawamba* and *The Levellers*, who have attached themselves to various causes and evoked long counter-cultural and anti-authoritarian traditions in their music, as well as using the word 'anarchist' in their literature.

These factors, then, in various combination, can be seen to 'frame' the political psyche of the potential EF! activist and help us to understand why particular forms of organisation might be favoured. Certainly, within Manchester, many of the new EF! activists decided to join the group ahead of Friends of the Earth because of its flexibility at organising, readiness to break the law, and participatory decision-making, even if some of the demands were ultimately the same (such as ending the trade in mahogany). So, with these issues in mind, I will now provide an account of the actual running of the group.

The Manchester experience

When this research began in late 1992, Manchester EF! (MEF!) activists held their monthly meetings in each other's houses, although these moved to the nearby University Student's Union the following autumn. A typical meeting would be attended by an average of 12 people, half of whom constituted the 'core group' (i.e. the most regular attenders, and often most influential – see below). The meeting would start somewhat haphazardly, with teas, coffees and herbal teas passed round in a relaxed mood. Someone, usually one of the core group, would spread the mail which the group had received out on the floor, and start the meeting with a remark such as: 'these are the things we should discuss / do something about'. It was rare for a facilitator to be nominated, and it was more likely that the person who had 'opened' the meeting was assumed to have adopted that role (which is different from chairperson in so much that a facilitator has no special powers, is not a fixed post and actively tries to ensure the maximum participation of those present).

Group minute-taking was rare and it was more likely that activists would make their own notes on the basis of which activities they had agreed to take part in. Whilst there *was* an element of people taking responsibility for what they had agreed to do, the lack of group minutes to refer to from one meeting to another certainly reduced the effectiveness of how activities were carried out. The informality of these meetings was striking, sometimes including interruptions such as telephone calls to (or from) other 'northern' groups and off-the-point remarks, which often went unchecked.

The group's awareness of its decision-making processes was varied. One of the core group – Owen – had joked that group decisions were made on the basis of 'a great deal of aimless discussion and banter', which seemed an accurate description of the meetings, although the number of people contributing to discussions in a meeting could be less than a third of those present. Thus Carl's suggestion that decisions were made on a 'nod or murmur' basis was as true as Christine's perception that it was done by 'consensus' where 'everyone compromises until we all agree'. Sometimes decisions were arrived at through so-called 'go-rounds' where everybody was required to make a contribution; sometimes they were not.

How this translated into taking part in demonstrations (or 'actions') was equally unpredictable but did not necessarily lead to ineffectual outcomes. Here, the group had to balance up the ideal of every activist having complete freedom to do what they wanted – with potentially negative consequences for the group – and collective needs. EF! both nationally and locally had no provision for this type of situation except a 'get-out-clause' that everyone was responsible for their own actions and that EF! could not be responsible for anything an individual decided to do. However, this idealism of complete responsibility for one's own actions tended to be tempered with a general pragmatism among the more experienced or long-serving members. Subsequently, when a particularly difficult demonstration was planned it was often the case that one of the core group volunteered for the most potentially dangerous tasks, on the grounds of either safety or 'arrestibility'. Conversely, the unwillingness on the part of the core members to act with a degree of 'authoritativeness' and even sketch out contingency plans for imminent actions meant that sometimes spontaneous decisions taken in the heat of the moment could be the 'wrong ones'.

The role of the core group – 'prime movers' was their appellation – was therefore somewhat paradoxical. In conventional political terms, they were the leadership, but as far away from ballots and nominations as one could imagine. More of an accidental clique than an executive body, not as closed as a cell or a cadre, it often seemed to want to dissolve itself through extending the number of people responsible for particular tasks. The core group's defining feature appeared to be the level of commitment to the organising of EF! activities, with the other activists being constantly reminded that more people were needed for such purposes.

This led to something of a self-fulfilling prophecy. More peripheral activists were encouraged, yet the core group did not have the time to devote to them, or, in some cases, did not completely trust those who were somewhat 'hot-headed' in outlook. Periodically frustration would creep in, and core group members would feel obliged to take control of the situation and do all of the work anyway, thus leading to accusations of being domineering.

On a national level, many of these types of processes were repeated. There were clearly 'prime movers', some of whom had set the UKEF! network up in the first place, and others who became very prominent after high-profile events such as opposition to the M3 extension at Twyford Down in Hampshire during 1992/93. The level of accountability of these people was quite high given the extremely long and participatory nature of the EF! 'Gatherings', which happened three times a year, lasted three days and tended to include a large action as well as policy discussion.

However, at both national and local levels, this did not mean that there were not occasions when trust broke down or people who considered themselves to be part of EF! felt excluded.

'Accidental' uses of power

I have already suggested that members of the EF! core group in Manchester were able to exercise some control in situations where too much individual freedom could have serious consequences for the group. I want to suggest that these and other occasional uses of power, particularly by key members of the core group, can be explained in part by their 'cultural capital' (Bourdieu 1984) and in part by definitions of who had the 'right' to specific pieces of information. In the first instance, cultural capital can be understood as the collective amount of acquired knowledge, skills and aesthetic outlook which allows groups or individuals to produce themselves as a viable social force. Like economic capital, it too has its structured inequalities. In the second instance, I want to illustrate the way in which EF! operations can sometimes be understood in terms of Bert Klandermans's (1992) notion of the Multi-Organisational Field (MOF).

However, in order to understand any applications of power within the group, we also need to recognise the very particular circumstances of the group itself. The turnover of activists in EF! was very high, even within the core group, something which we can attribute to a large student composition and activists who, generally speaking, had little to tie them to Manchester specifically. It did mean, however, that those more enduring residents of the city would have a far better knowledge of the local political culture, its useful contacts and resources. There was also a likelihood that these activists would be the ones who had access to the group's Box number, which was a key source of campaign information and could allow those who had access to it to reflect ahead of time on potentially difficult decisions which the group might have to make. One such decision was how the group was to spend a donation of £5,000.

The issue was debated over the space of several meetings in spring 1993, but it quickly became apparent that the core group members were keen to make a substantial purchase rather than spending the money gradually. The two options were either to rent and equip themselves with an office (as a number of other EF! groups had recently done) or to purchase a van to increase access to protest sites.

There was already some evidence that two of the core group – Phil and Owen – were unhappy about the amount of organising which they were doing from their own homes, with repercussions on housemates' telephone bills and having filing cabinets in their living rooms. However, the donation arrived at the time when MEF! were making regular visits to the M3 extension protest site at Twyford Down and many of the activists were particularly inspired to keep on participating in actions there. What seemed significant about the discussion which ensued was that those arguing for a minibus were neither key organisers nor core group. When a decision had to be reached by the group, Phil invited his housemate Steve, who held a sabbatical post at the University Student's Union, to attend the meeting. Steve told the meeting the news that EF! could get cheap office space in the Student's Union building, as well as having special use of the Union minibuses, which seemed to bury the vehicle idea in one fell swoop. This was clearly a defining moment in MEF!'s development, which later gave the group much more practical flexibility.

The decision regarding the office outlined above was precisely the kind of incident which occasionally led to suggestions that the 'no leaders' principle within EF! was just rhetoric, and although Phil described himself as the 'convenor' of MEF! there was little doubt that he was perceived by other political groups in Manchester as the leader. This seemed to be reinforced by the cultural capital which he had at his disposal: home access to a fax machine and electronic services, personal friendships with several of the original half dozen members of UKEF!, and employment with a 'sympathetic' organisation. His stable position in Manchester ensured that, regardless of what other activists were doing, he always seemed slightly ahead of them, thus reinforcing the self-fulfilling prophecy described in the previous section.

That the unequal distribution of cultural capital might explain the power relations within EF! was reinforced by the fact that sometimes the definitions as to who was considered an EF! activist and who was part of a wider network of activists could itself reflect particular interests, despite the fact that anyone could in theory be an EF! activist. For instance, the boundaries of EF! often seemed drawn around the geographical specifics of two areas of

the city – Rusholme and Longsight – or were based around strong social and
cultural networks (as opposed to proven political commitment or expertise).
This, in very subtle ways, allowed the group to be selective about how information was distributed throughout the various social and political milieux
in Manchester. An example of this was the way in which certain people were
not entrusted with 'secretive' information pertaining to a series of actions
planned to disrupt an international conference in the city during the early
autumn of 1993. An important point here was the fact that 'trusted' activists
were the ones who had no major links to other organisations in the city,
whereas those that did (particularly if they related to Friends of the Earth)
tended to find out details somewhat later. On occasion, this closing of ranks
was very deliberate, but more often than not it was entirely innocent and not
part of any unofficial 'policy'. There were also one or two personal clashes
between individuals in the core group and other activists on the Manchester
'green scene' – linked to the emergence of EF! in the city – which tended to
exacerbate such situations.

If we consider Klandermans's (1993) suggestion that most social movement organisations exist within a general activist 'field' where groups are
much more interdependent and overlapping than many theorists acknowledge, we can see a useful parallel. He suggests that these Multi Organisational Fields are not static, but fluctuate depending on the local political
climate and the different interests of the relevant social movements. So,
whilst MEF! activists were clearly more radical than other environmental
and development groups in the city, they were prepared to share resources
and people. However, when sensitive information or action planning was
required, certain avenues of activism might be 'closed down' and more
peripheral activists find themselves slightly excluded. In such situations, it
was better to be in no group than another group!

This type of process could also be exercised by the whole group rather
than just a number of core members, if it was felt that the collective identity
of EF! was being undermined. For instance, if a newish activist made misleading or outrageous suggestions, a more experienced one might follow it
up with an even more elaborate activist fantasy scenario, thereby signalling
that it was not a legitimate suggestion.

So, whilst there did seem to be a taking of responsibility for the whole
group by many of the EF! activists in difficult situations such as this, not
everybody felt quite so confident about challenging the experience of the
core group on other matters. Even though the structure of EF! made it difficult to consolidate a power base, there was sometimes a sense that – to recall
the earlier remark by Bakunin – activists were not recognising the difference
between authoritative and authoritarian. As Coover *et al.* (1978: 47) note,
this is not unusual in radical groups and there is a need to concentrate on
'leadership' as a composite of learnable skills, a set of functions rather than
as a personal trait or the exercising of power *per se*. In this light, the posses-

sion of cultural capital by some of the core group, whilst giving an activist 'the edge', did not inherently translate into *abuse of power*, but it posed enough of a potential problem for activists to want to minimise the chance of it occuring.

The next section documents some of the strategies which EF! used to increase the number of activists taking responsibility for the organisation of campaigns, as a way of preventing the core group (or individuals within it) from becoming an identifiable leadership (in the normal sense of the word). This discussion will provide the basis for theorising these group practices in the final section of the chapter.

Searching for solutions

Many of the aforementioned difficulties and contradictions of organisation received attention within EF! at both national and local levels with 'skill sharing' weekends beginning during the second half of 1993. There was a sense nationally that more organisation was needed within and between EF! groups, more people should get involved in the decision-making processes, and, increasingly, the issue of male dominance within the movement should be addressed.

These developments coincided with a number of events in Manchester: the securing of the aforementioned EF! office, and the temporary departure of core member Phil for a period of three months. The new office, located in the basement of the University Student's Union building and only a few seconds away from Oxford Road, was very accessible and quickly became fully operational. Its location and useful holding capacity increased the activist attendance rate by nearly 100 per cent.

The temporary departure of key core group member Phil and a turnover in core group personnel was seen by many of the remaining 'prime movers' (as well as Phil himself) as an opportunity to alter the structure of the group and to empower others, rather than seeking a 'replacement' for Phil. New organisational strategies were developed: spreading campaign workload; computer training sessions for producing the *Earth First! Action Update*; running workshops on media skills with the assistance of 'sympathetic' broadcasters; and perhaps most importantly, organising an introductory meeting for newly arrived students within Manchester. This was a significant date on the EF! calendar and the group was eager to make up for the previous year's meeting – held in an activist's house – which had been generally regarded as a failure. The outcome of the 1993 meeting was a range of initiatives – including smaller 'splinter' campaigns – which it was hoped would also encourage participation from otherwise peripheral activists.

The new optimism also led to meetings on a fortnightly rather than monthly basis, a renewed interest in the (often gendered) dynamics within them, and developing activist strategies based on affinity groups (where small close-knit groups carry out specific activities for which they alone are responsible). This was one of the aspects of EF!'s evolution where it was possible to see the influence of the peace movement, both in terms of past or present activists running the workshops, through to the kind of literature upon which the sessions were based (such as Coover *et al.*'s [1978] *Resource Manual for a Living Revolution* and the classic debate between Freeman [1984] and Levine [1984] about the 'tyranny of structurelessness' in movement organisations). The importance of addressing male domination in EF! has been an important issue for the movement from its first 'Gatherings' (see Earth First! 1992) and remains so today (*Do or Die* 7, n.d.).

In Manchester some of the credit for this acceleration of awareness ironically went to a number of literally more peripheral EF! activists – based in the Chorlton part of the city – who had been amongst those who had felt excluded by some of the processes listed in the previous section. They organised a Manchester-wide 'training day' for political activists generally, which was attended by about ten men and women from EF! The impact of this and other local or regional ventures was often very noticeable for a period of some weeks, but the positive benefits seemed to wear off quickly. This was most apparent in terms of the facilitation of meetings.

Meetings in the new office space sometimes exceeded 30 participants and (bad acoustics aside) facilitation was always going to be difficult in comparison to the earlier (smaller) meetings in activists' houses. So, despite enthusiasm and recent training, some facilitators were not able to run the meetings with any degree of authoritativeness and the amount of 'drift' on agenda items was sometimes quite considerable. Similarly, consensus decision-making was difficult to achieve and sometimes very little of it seemed to be actually taking place.

The longer that these attempts to improve group working practices went on, the more activists seemed keen to 'buy' in skills to assist in the process. This was largely because the group's do-it-yourself philosophy could not fully cope with all of the implications of such activities. First, some EF! activists felt that this was time taken away from planning direct action. There was already a fear of bureaucracy in the air, articulated around the 'office vs minibus' debate, and the meetings were getting progressively longer. Second, in addition to all of the extra work it would require of the group, there were also more interpersonal issues at stake. The group skills which EF! wanted guidance on were precisely the kind which involved touching on thorny issues such as group dynamics, male dominance and how to run big meetings using consensus decision-making. All of these required some degree of emotional engagement which might lead to tensions between existing members, particularly if the skill sharing workshop was being run by somebody with either a vested interest in improving the group or who was seen to embody a number of the problems within it. A number of activists had already in interview suggested that they found organising their cooperative house meetings difficult. In such circumstances it was hardly surprising that the group looked to more peripheral experts.

In this respect MEF! was able to evolve in new ways by drawing upon the skills of the Multi-Organisational Field in Manchester, using its contacts in the media and the more experienced activists who could assist the process of group self-development. By using people from outside the group, a number of potential flashpoint areas were, at least partially, ameliorated: those activists who wanted *less* meetings did not have to attend and couldn't complain that group energies were being misdirected; and the people who felt excluded could feel more included, because their contributions were suddenly valued. The use of the Multi-Organisational Field also helped to avoid the classic social movement situation whereby a group in crisis can spend so much energy on analysing its own methods of working that it 'organises itself to death' (Benford and Hunt 1992: 44).

However, it was only a partially successful group evolution. The awareness of the need to experiment with more participatory structures and decision-making processes certainly evolved during the period described. More people did participate, engage in media work, attempt to facilitate meetings and raise questions of male dominance. There was clearly a recognition of the problem of the tyranny of the loudest voice or most media-friendly member of the group. On the other hand, despite the often enthusiastic response of EF! activists to the new developments, a number of factors affected the percolation of the ideas into everyday activities. The first was the sheer turnover of people: it was hard to maintain certain practices when half a meeting might be unaware of the particular procedure in question (such as the 'goldfish bowl' technique, where activists watch each other summarising each other's suggestions to ensure consensus). Second, often EF! activists were afraid of being too prescriptive, thus leading to a situation whereby nobody took the initiative. Finally, expecting a culture change in the space of weeks – given that there was little in the way of literature distributed to new or old activists – was unrealistic for any organisation, let alone one which is constantly trying to deconstruct itself. How we theorise these processes of self-deconstruction is the subject of the next section.

Theorising leaderlessness

That activists in possession of significant cultural capital might pose problems for the organisational philosophy of EF! is, as I have suggested, something which is broadly acknowledged by the movement. Moreover, the above discussion demonstrates the extent to which MEF! activists attempted to alleviate problems of power imbalance within the group. Given that potential EF! leaders sought to empower other activists and deconstruct their own position poses a problem for theorising 'leaderlessness' along the lines of individual cultural capital alone. In this final section I want to con-

sider a more structured theoretical approach, using the work of Michel
Foucault and Murray Bookchin, both of whom move beyond economic and
materialistic analyses of power. To simplify, Bookchin is basically an ecological Enlightenment humanist, and Foucault is a dabbler in post-structuralism
and the micro-politics of power. Both are interested in how relations of
power become naturalised by historical processes.

For Foucault, power is not something which can be 'owned', or indeed
observed in the positivist sense; rather it is a relationship between people
which is produced at an everyday social level and runs through the capillar-
ies of the 'social body'. By this he means that power is everywhere rather
than being exacted from a single source, and both organises and normalises
social practices through specific discourses at particular times. This is also
the case with resistance, so whilst on the one hand saying that where there is
power there is also resistance, he also claims that acts of resistance cannot
stand outside of that power relationship. Foucault, like Louis Althusser, is
working with a sense of the ideological which is inescapable – it defines our
being. For Foucault, then, resistance is part of the ideology. He uses the concept of *agonism* to describe this phenomenon: two forces eternally circling
each other, defined by each other and, to all intents and purposes, cancelling
each other out (Foucault 1982: 221).

This is valuable because it bears strong similarity to the anarchist critique
of power which 'forbids' the establishment of any structures which even
temporarily mirror the ones which are being opposed in the first instance.
Thus, the brave and sometimes tortuous attempts within EF! to abolish
power relations appear to make sense, given that they recognise (and to
some extent attempt to stand outside of) this agonistic process. That they
also 'fail' is also understandable within these terms, but they do actually
perceive themselves as actors wrestling *with* this paradox. They recognise
the difficulty of overcoming years of identification and definition with structures which are very different from their goals. This applies to individual
leadership roles just as much as it does to political structures which have
'official posts' and electoral procedures.

This is the first of the two major problems with uncritically embracing
Foucault: that he brackets out the possibility of escaping power. The second
concerns the matter of historical memory and the importance of developing
political strategies which challenge power based on past experiences.
Foucault's work on power concerns itself with how different discourses – of
sex, madness, punishment and others – construct people in highly specific
historical circumstances. As with other post-structuralists, he resists notions
of dialectics and teleology (on the grounds of dogmatism), which presents a
problem for explaining how those who try to 'escape' power might be linked
to similar historical movements.

Here, I believe, the work of Murray Bookchin and the philosophy of
social ecology is of value. Although controversial (see Light 1998),

Bookchin's work has been profoundly influential on radical environmentalists and is broad enough in scope to locate 'the problem of authority' in
terms of an ecological sense of dialectics and teleology.

   Social ecology updates the kind of classical anarchism epitomised by Peter
Kropotkin's *Mutual Aid* (1939), yet places a different emphasis on the evolution of human societies. Murray Bookchin's *The Ecology of Freedom* (1982)
offers an anti-authoritarian explanation for the current environmental crisis
by finding parallels between human domination of both fellow humans and
nature. In short, he claims that in order for the domination of nature to
occur, it has to be premised on the domination of humans (a reversal of
Adorno and Horkheimer's position in *The Dialectic of Enlightenment* – see
Eckersley 1992). He traces the evolution of hierarchical societies back to the
transition from the organic societies[2] of the preliterate Neolithic period to
the ancient civilisations of Mesopotamia and the Mediterranean basin, identifying many of the (well documented) material shifts of this period – new
agricultural technologies, development of larger centres of habitation – but
also an accompanying series of psychological shifts which 'naturalised' hierarchical ways of organising and thinking. He calls these 'epistemologies of
rule', by which he means the manner in which the 'naturalness' of domination has come to be inscribed in particular systems of knowledge over many
centuries.

   In a sense this is Bookchin's concept of the Fall, when the integrated and
(largely) non-hierarchical relationships (see Kovel 1998 for a critique of this)
break down and human societies begin to coalesce around practical and
intellectual systems of domination. So, for Bookchin, given that this process
is a counter-liberatory evolutionary 'mistake', we can see evidence of it in all
of the grand narratives, be they Platonism, Christianity, Liberalism, Marxism and even latter-day Darwinism/socio-biology. Bookchin's point is that
these privilege certain types of relationships and structures as given and un-
changeable – hierarchical ones – and the consequence of this has been to
limit the possibilities for intellectual and physical freedom. Domination is
inscribed in the very assumptions of the theories, and thinking outside the
parameters of authoritarian structures or concepts is difficult.

   Bookchin is no mystic, however; he firmly believes in the use of reason
and logic to conceptualise the complementary pattern of human and non-
human ecosystems. He is seeking a necessary reintegration of these two (now
separate) worlds and there are, he believes, moments when glimpses of this
have happened. Using a theory of 'natural dialectics', whereby societies are
understood in terms of their social and ecological balance, Bookchin looks
for a counter-history where no social systems dominate either each other or
'natural' ecosystems and there is evidence of the evolution of notions of freedom, or what he calls 'the actualisation of [one's] potential'. These manifest
themselves in particular ways: the dualistic processes dominating the society
break down; and there are social and political experiments where non-

hierarchical methods of thinking and organising take place. These are often associated with millenarian movements (from the Anabaptists and the Brethren of the Free Spirit in the fourteenth century to the English Revolution in the seventeenth), but more recently with the 'official' history of anarchism and all manner of interventions in culture and society, right up to the Situationists and May '68.

The implication of Bookchin's work is that it is how one organises which is central to contemporary radical environmental practice. It *matters* that some people fighting environmental problems do organise in hierarchical fashion. From an EF! point of view all forms of hierarchy and those theories which support them are part of the problem. They, like Bookchin, look for historical evidence of moments of social freedom that support the notion that they are part of a revolutionary (and evolutionary) project. Frequently, the 'problem of authority' was the fear of doing the wrong thing, and in effect by not acting at the time, the familiarity of somebody taking the lead was an easier choice.

Yet at the same time we can see moments when EF! attempts to deconstruct its own structures and make room for more flexible and participatory politics were befitting of its and Bookchin's ideals. The EF! activists' wish to equate the means of their actions with the ends, to take responsibility for their actions and to recognise the existence of power at the most microsociological level, demonstrates that for some moments they were able to stand outside of the 'epistemology of rule' of hierarchy as natural and to actualise their own potential.

This is where EF! activists prove Foucault to be wrong, as they can quite clearly be seen to be part of a political evolutionary process, locating themselves in terms of other historical moments and movements. EF! has learned to adapt to its political environment in a way that earlier movements did not do. EF! has resisted going any further down the feared bureaucratic road than in the establishment of offices, resource centres and bank accounts for some of its literature. Friends of the Earth and Greenpeace (see Hunter 1980) became institutionalised and only sustained the ideas of 'leaderlessness' for a short time in the early 1970s.

Conclusion

In this chapter I have tried to step outside some of the assumptions of social movement theorists to date and to understand the disparities within an EF! group in a critical light. This has been a study in both anarchist theory and practice.

In contemporary radical environmentalism, leaderlessness is seen as a strength, and part of an overall philosophy of self-organisation and individual and collective empowerment. Yet the realisation of these goals – part of a desire for radical transformation of society – is not without its problems.

The group studied here – Manchester EF! – was in a constant process of wrestling with its organisational and decision-making practices, struggling to find the time to explore fully its own potential. The constant sense of vigilance and reflexivity at its own practices made it difficult for strong cadres or leaders to emerge, even though some activists possessed more cultural capital than others. As a movement EF! has managed to retain its anti-authoritarian roots and achieved many of its objectives without adopting the authoritarian structures of older environmental groups such as Friends of the Earth or Greenpeace. This was down to a number of factors, principally a desire amongst activists to deconstruct their own processes and prevent themselves slipping into more dominant patterns of organisation, by empowering others to act and learn new practical and interpersonal skills.

If in UK politics the kind of formations described above are to become increasingly prevalent, then there will be even more assaults on the kind of 'epistemologies of rule' which Bookchin describes (even though not necessarily in the same ecological terms) and the opening up of new ways of thinking. The next few decades might well reveal a further disintegration of the political forms which have been found wanting in the complexities of late twentieth-century life. If the history of anti-authoritarian movements can tell us anything, it is that there are always new people 'discovering' such ideas and that there is always the possibility that at some future historical juncture they will have their day.

Notes

1   Thanks to the editors for valuable constructive criticism, Nicole Matthews for comments on Foucault, and Chayley Collis for keeping my feet on the ground.
2   Bookchin is not using the word 'organic' as it is often used in theoretical contexts – conceived as though it was an organism, rather a society which is a '*spontaneously formed, noncoercive, and egalitarian* ...' (1982: 5). It should be said, however, that social ecologists are careful not to glorify the past or fetishise existing primitive cultures and are interested in what we can learn from them in terms of their attitudes to nature and to each other, particularly their tolerance of difference, their preferring 'wise' rather than 'authority' figures, and the concept of usufruct.

10

A model of crowd prototypes and crowd leadership

Steve Reicher, John Drury, Nick Hopkins and Clifford Stott

The emptiness of rhetoric

Anyone interested in how to sway the masses has to contend with a chorus so loud and so united that it threatens to drown out any discordant note. That unity is all the more impressive for being built out of highly diverse voices who, nonetheless, manage to sing from the same song-sheet. Within the academic world, perhaps the most famous of these voices is Gustave Le Bon. Certainly Le Bon is the most influential crowd psychologist. But, as Moscovici (1981) notes, his work *The Crowd: A Study of the Popular Mind* did not just serve as an explanation of mass phenomena, it was part and parcel of the making of twentieth-century mass politics. Indeed, far from being a conventional academic text, the book serves more as a practical primer for those wishing to win crowds back to the side of the social order.

Le Bon's advice is terse and clear. Anyone who wishes to influence crowds should dispense with argument and reason. The golden rules are to keep things simple, to assert one's claims as unimpeachable truths and to hammer these claims home through constant repetition.

The list of those influenced by Le Bon is long and varied and reads, in part, like a roll call of the great dictators of the twentieth century. Mussolini declared that *The Crowd* was a work to which he regularly referred, even stating that he had used some of Le Bon's prescriptions in building the Italian fascist state. Hitler may not have made such an open acknowledgment, but if imitation – or even plagiarism – is flattery, then he can certainly be numbered amongst Le Bon's acolytes, as the following passage suggests:

> the receptivity of the great masses is very limited, their intelligence is small, but their power of forgetting is enormous. In consequence of these facts, all effective propaganda must be limited to a very few points and must harp on these in slogans until the last member of the public understands what you want him to understand by your slogan. As soon as you sacrifice this slogan and try to be many-sided, the effect will piddle away, for the crowd can neither digest nor retain the material offered. (Hitler 1980: 165)

Perhaps such disdain for the masses is unsurprising coming from such fascist sources. So consider another voice – this time of a different era and a very different politics from those above. In 1984, a conversation analyst, Max Atkinson, produced an influential book entitled *Our Masters' Voices*, analysing the stylistic devices designed to elicit applause from an audience – literally 'claptrap'. These included the use of three-part lists, of contrastive pairs, of alliteration and – particularly – of combinations amongst these devices. Such devices can clearly be found in the rhetoric of famous orators and they clearly coincide with audience applause. But Atkinson's argument went further. It implied that style alone is sufficient to get people clapping. This implication was made explicit by the political scientist David Butler in his introduction to the book: '[Atkinson] can show how forms of words, balance of sentences, rhythms of speech can induce an audience to applaud, *almost irrespective of the intellectual content of what is being said*' (Atkinson 1984: xii, emphasis added).

Atkinson's book gained publicity, if not notoriety, from a television documentary broadcast to coincide with its publication. The programme took a working-class political neophyte from a South London housing estate and trained her up, using Atkinson's techniques, to deliver a speech at the 1984 Social Democratic Party conference. The speech was delivered as part of debate on a somewhat technical party document which attempted to apply the theories of John Rawls to policies on social justice. It was certainly a stark contrast in terms of both style and humour to what had gone before. In a key passage the speaker promised to 'come clean'. Pausing only to express the hope that it wasn't an expellable offence, she then admitted that she wasn't a *Guardian* reader (loud laughter).[1] She went on to stress that even if all the *Guardian* readers in all the constituencies in the country voted SDP, and only them, the party would still lose its deposit in each and every seat. A nice three-part list topped off with a contrastive pair. Tumultuous applause. So prolonged was the applause during the speech that the speaker ran out of time before she had finished. When the chair of the session tried to cut her off, the audience bayed for an extension.

Undoubtedly, the speech was a success and the form of delivery had much to do with that success. However, it is worth dwelling for a moment on the *content* of the argument. The SDP, a breakaway from the Labour Party, posed itself as also breaking away from the class polarisation between Labour and Conservative. Indeed it aspired to represent a cross-class alliance and thereby bring a new stratum of people into politics. The speech pointed out that the practice did not live up to this aspiration. The party – as represented by those present at the conference and the way they conducted debates – was a tiny middle-class fraction. By contrast the speaker in her person, in her working-class accent, in her use of common speech and in what she said exemplified the cross-class alliance that the party was meant to be. In other words there was a homology between the individual, the style and the substance. That homology resulted in a performance that, in all its dimensions, exemplified the party's collective identity. To abstract form from content is not only one-sided. It also misses the way in which form and content must be seen in combination and how that combination works in relationship to audience identity. This is a point which we will consider in much greater depth later.

In addition to the academic argument we have a second voice – that of the mass media which supports this notion that mass rhetoric exists in an intellectual vacuum. We turn to a second example, again from the 1984 conference season. A *Newsnight*[2] report during the Labour Party conference concentrated on Arthur Scargill, leader of the National Union of Miners which was then in the midst of a year-long strike. At the centre of the report was Scargill's speech to the conference. A few of his words were heard before a voice-over cut in to declare that the speech pushed every button designed to bring a response. Then, accompanying images of massed audience applause, the voice declared that the response was 'almost Pavlovian'. It is worth hearing Scargill's words in somewhat more detail. One passage which received sustained applause went as follows:

> I reject the right of any employer to turn around and destroy the jobs of miners or any other workers. We should not stand aside when faced with the fact that communities may be laid desolate as a result of the economic philosophy of either this government, or an employer, or both. As we go into the eighth month of this dispute, there is one thing coming through loud and clear: the miners' union is winning this fight and it is not only winning for miners, but for you and for the entire labour and trade union movement. (*Applause and cheers*). (Labour Party 1984: 34, emphasis in the original)

At one level, this could seem to support Atkinson's claims. The applause occurs after another three-part list combined with a contrastive pair. However, it is evident that these forms work in conjunction with rich and complex argument and that this argument centres on the nature of the social categories and social relationships which constitute the phenomenon at hand. The miners' strike is constituted in class terms, the audience is appealed to as a working-class category and the miners are portrayed as carrying the burden of a struggle on behalf of that class. The words may be sparse, but with the elegance of a skilled draughtsman, a few lines sketch out a rich picture. Support is sought and received by a speaker who defines the identity of his audience and characterises his actions in terms of their collective interest.

This chapter, then, will challenge the consensual portrait of leadership and political rhetoric as a matter of using the appropriate techniques to draw unthinking approbation. We will argue instead that leadership rhetoric relates to the way in which social categories are defined and to speakers' ability to define themselves and their projects in relation to those category definitions. But first, we need to consider and challenge the suppositions about crowd psychology which, explicitly or implicitly, underlie received wisdoms about leadership. Here, too, we will find the issue of identity to be quite central.

Crowds, psychology and the roots of social influence

The notion that mass rhetoric must be kept as simple as possible rests on the assumption that members of masses are incapable of thinking or making rational judgements. This idea is so widespread and of such long lineage that it would be quite misleading to ascribe it to any one person or to any one era. Riewald (1949) provides a 400-page compilation of comments, including some from biologists, sociologists, psychologists, historians, politicians, poets and writers, nearly all of whom echo with more or less wit and savagery the words which Schiller puts into the mouth of one of his characters:

> The majority? What is the majority? The majority is non-sense; reason has only ever been the prerogative of small numbers. One must weigh voices, not count them. The state would inevitably perish, sooner or later, if the majority triumphed and unreason ruled. (quoted in Riewald 1949: 338, translation by the authors)

Two ideas implicit in this quotation are central to understanding the birth of a 'scientific' crowd psychology and the work of Gustave Le Bon in particular (Barrows 1981; Nye 1975). The first is that fear of the crowd is elided with a general fear of the masses. The second is that this fear is that of an elite which is concerned for the stability of the state.

Crowd psychology arose in the late nineteenth century and reflected the overarching social question posed by the growth of an industrial society: how could the social order be preserved in the face of the new urban masses (cf. Giner 1976)? Or, to expand on the ideological shorthand embedded in this question, how could the bourgeoisie maintain their dominance over a class that was so large, so concentrated and, in their separate neighbourhoods, so suddenly freed from the direct surveillance that characterised previous peasant existence? If the masses were of concern as an ever-imminent threat, the crowd – as the mass in action – was the object of particularly acute fears. This was nowhere more true than in France, which had seen the temporary victory of the masses during the Commune of 1871 and where the Third Republic, which emerged from the ashes of the Commune, remained beset by mass agitation.

Le Bon shared these concerns and wrote of crowds as an outsider with obvious political hostility. He argued that when people are 'submerged' in the crowd they lose their sense of self and gain a sense of invincible power through numbers alone. Since the individual self is the sole seat of rational judgement, crowd members no longer have any basis for evaluating what to do. They are subject to 'contagion' in that they automatically follow any idea or, more particularly (because their intellectual functioning is so diminished), any emotion suggested to them. These suggestions emanate principally from the 'racial unconscious' – a primitive and collective substrate underlying our conscious minds which is revealed when our selfhood is stripped away. Crowd behaviour reflects the atavistic nature of this unconscious: crowd members are barbarians, they are only powerful for destruction, above all they are mindless (Le Bon 1947).

While there are many levels on which Le Bon's crowd psychology can be criticised (cf. McClelland 1989; McPhail 1991; Milgram and Toch 1969; Reicher 1982, 1987, 1996a; Reicher and Potter 1985), all problems can be traced to a great disappearing trick. While Le Bon's concern was the class conflict of his day, all that appears in his theory is the crowd as if acting in a vacuum. The context is invisible. The role of the state and its agents in the production of conflict has been written out. The crowd alone is present for questioning. Its actions, which gain meaning from the struggles in which they are embedded, are therefore rendered meaningless. In one fell swoop, mass action is rendered irrational, the state is excused all responsibility for conflict and the agents of repression are given a free hand. After all, if the crowd is inherently violent and beyond reason one cannot negotiate with it. One can only use a big stick.

If, at least from an elitist perspective, such theory provides a substantial ideological payoff, there is an equally substantial explanatory cost. Once crowds are removed from their context, it becomes difficult to explain contextual variations in crowd action. Certainly crowds can be violent, but many crowds are non-violent and members can show remarkable forbearance even in the face of considerable provocation. Martin Luther King's descriptions of early civil rights demonstrations are a case in point (King 1964). It becomes even more difficult to explain how patterns of crowd action reflect larger patterns of belief. Yet historical studies have shown that even where there is violence and destruction, the targets and forms of action chosen by crowd members reflect their collective beliefs. Following her study of religious riot in sixteenth-century France – riots of great brutality in which people were killed, bodies mutilated, holy objects desecrated – Natalie Zemon Davies concludes:

> religious violence is intense because it connects intimately with the fundamental values and self-definition of a community. The violence is explained not in terms of how crazy, hungry or sexually frustrated the violent people are (though they may sometimes have such characteristics), but in terms of the goals of their actions and in terms of the roles and patterns of behaviour allowed by their culture. (1978: 90)

Reddy draws a very similar conclusion from a study of grain riots in the city of Rouen over two centuries: 'the targets of these crowds glitter in the eye of history as signs of the labourers' conception of society' (1977: 84).

The psychological task is to explain how culture can come to inform, shape and limit the behaviours of individual crowd members. To fulfil this task, the first necessity is to address Le Bon's underlying psychological assumptions which – albeit in more muted and more acceptable terms – continue to exert a wide intellectual influence to this day (Brown 1988; Reicher *et al.* 1995). For Le Bon, *personal identity* is the sole basis of judgement and the sole criterion of rational action. Insofar as this self is idiosyncratic, there is no social basis for the control of individual action in any conditions. Insofar as this self is extinguished in the crowd, then there is no basis at all for the control of individual action in collective conditions. That is, the link between the social and the self as well as the link between the self and action is broken in Le Bonian psychology. His conception of identity serves to block any connection between social and individual levels of explanation in the crowd – or indeed in any circumstances.

We have already encountered a very different notion of identity, both in our analyses of political rhetoric and in historical analyses of crowd events. In these cases, identity has related to the nature of social categories rather than the attributes of particular persons and it has been used to position individuals within the social world rather than divide them off from it. The implication is that, by reconceptualising identity, it can be turned from a blockage into the pivot between the individual and the social. This is precisely what has been provided within social psychology by the social identity tradition – first developed by Henri Tajfel and his colleagues (Tajfel 1978, 1982; Tajfel and Turner 1986) and then extended by self-categorisation theorists (Turner *et al.* 1987; Turner *et al.* 1994).

Within this tradition, identity is seen as a complex structure which can be defined at different levels of abstraction. Most notably we can define ourselves in terms of what renders us unique compared to other individuals ('I' vs. 'you') or in terms of what makes our social category unique compared to other social categories ('we' vs. 'they'). In fact we all belong to a variety of social categories which will be salient in different circumstances – the same individual may define herself as a Catholic in church, as British on holiday abroad and as a worker in a union meeting. The cognitive act of self-definition as a category member forms the psychological basis for group behaviour. When individuals define themselves in terms of any given category, they act in terms of the values, understandings and beliefs which define that category rather than the idiosyncratic beliefs which mark them off from other individuals. The key point is that such social identities are both profoundly important to the individual and irreducible in meaning to that individual. People care about being British, they will countenance killing and even dying for their nation, but what it means to be British is a historically evolving cultural product. So when we act in terms of this – or indeed any other – social category, our behaviour is defined by reference to collective culture. The idea of social identity therefore provides the pivot we have been looking for.

The social identity tradition relates to the behaviour of groups in general, including crowds. Whereas Le Bon believed people lose identity and hence lose control in the mass, the social identity tradition suggests there is a shift from personal to social identity and hence a shift in the bases of behavioural control. People act in terms of the definitions associated with the relevant social category. But in the midst of a riot it is impractical for people to stop, discuss and vote on how they as (say) anti-fascists should respond to the police cordon separating them from a fascist march. Instead, crowd members employ a process of induction whereby norms are inferred from the behaviour of typical group members (Reicher 1982, 1984, 1987). As a result, crowd behaviour may be under-determined and it may be labile, but that lability will have limits. While a range of suggestions may be compatible with the superordinate category identity, behaviours or suggestions which are clearly dissonant with that identity will not be emulated.

Such a suggestion makes sense of the historically observed patterning of crowd action and is also supported by contemporary data. Reicher (1984) shows how the 'riot' of April 1980 in the St Pauls area of Bristol had clear limits in terms of targets and geography and that these reflected the collective sense of community articulated by participants. For them, whether black or white, being from St Pauls was defined in terms of a black experience. They were exploited by a nexus of financial institutions, their poverty was exemplified by the shops taking advantage of low rents to sell luxury goods to outsiders, and they were kept in check by police oppression. Accordingly, attacks against the police, against the financial institutions such as the local bank and against externally owned shops instantly received collective support. When attacks were directed at other targets they were either ignored or actively repressed. People literally took control of the streets of St Pauls until over a thousand police moved back in to take control. But the 'riot' did not move outside the neighbourhood, however tempting the targets nearby.

Armed with a new understanding of crowd psychology, we are now in a position to revisit the questions of crowd leadership and of mass rhetoric. If crowd members are seeking to determine how they should behave as category members, then the issue of influence comes down to the process of how categories are defined and how proposals come to be construed as either consonant or dissonant with such definitions. Equally, the issue of leadership comes down to the question of how individuals come to be seen as defining these matters of category identity.

Entrepreneurs of identity

In recent years, social identity theorists have begun to consider the issue of leadership. Their simple and powerful point is that leadership exists in a group context and therefore needs to be understood in relation to group processes (Hogg 1996). As Haslam (2001) puts it, effective leaders are those who relate to followers as members of a common category. They are then in a position to represent the interests, values and aspirations of the group and thereby to gain influence over all category members.

Haslam cites evidence that when such things as leadership selection or a highly differentiated reward structure serve to disrupt the common categorisation between leader and follower, they diminish both leader effectiveness and the effectiveness of the group as a whole. He also shows that leaders are effective to the extent that they are seen as supporting the specific norms and values which characterise the relevant group identity. This echoes findings by Hogg and his colleagues (Fielding and Hogg 1997; Hains *et al.* 1997; Hogg 1996). However, Haslam goes one step further and argues that, to the extent that group position changes as a function of context, so different leadership qualities will prove effective. Thus, in situations of inter-group conflict, leaders who show favouritism towards those who exemplify group norms are both preferred and exert more influence. However, in intra-group contexts, leaders who are more even-handed amongst group members receive more support.

These various experimental studies support the argument that leadership in collective settings is not a matter of demonstrating generic qualities or else using universal techniques. Rather it must be related to the specific identities of the specific categories in the specific context. The advantage of the experimental methodology used in these studies is that it allows subjects to be provided with a set definition of both the leader and the category and hence a clear manipulation of whether the two are matched or not. This allows for powerful quantitative demonstrations of effects. At the same time, reliance on such methods also has a downside. If the definitions of category identity, of the leader and of the leader's proposals are always taken as givens, there is a danger of representing the leadership process as passive, as lacking agency, as if people simply stand around until the movement of circumstance happens to determine a match between a particular person and a particular category, thereby delivering the mantle of leadership for a passing moment. This would miss the process whereby leaders actively seek to construe themselves, their proposals and the categorical identity of their audience such that they represent the interests, values and aspirations of this audience. It would miss the very stuff of mass politics.

Let us be clear what is at stake here. If the psychological basis for collective action lies in a set of people acting in terms of a common category membership, then the matter of how categories are defined acquires societal as well as individual significance. Those who control category definitions are particularly effective in influencing collective action. Or, to put it the other way round, the way to shape mass mobilisation is through the construction of social categories. So, while it might seem reasonable to suppose that

something, like identity, which has such substantial and material consequences would be equally solid in itself, the opposite is true. It is precisely
because social identity has such powerful implications that it becomes a
focus of contention. Those who wish to mobilise people to different ends
will seek to provide different categories through which people should see
their world, themselves and their actions in the world (Reicher and Hopkins
1996a, 1996b; Reicher *et al.* 1997a, 1997b). In a phrase, leaders can be
described as entrepreneurs of identity in a world of fierce competition (cf.
Besson 1990). Their effectiveness depends upon their ability to construe
themselves, along with those they wish to mobilise, as part of a common
category and to so constitute their voice and their proposals that they appear
as the embodiment of category identity.

This entrepreneurial process can be broken down into three constituent
elements, all of which must be attended to by the successful entrepreneur.
First of all, it is necessary to define the boundaries of the relevant identity
such that it includes all those whose support is sought. Categories which
exclude a proportion of those one seeks to mobilise inevitably limit one's
appeal. Second, it is necessary to define those for whom support is sought
(the individual leader, the organisation) such that they are undoubtedly part
of the group. To be able to act as a representative depends upon being seen as
representative. Third, it is necessary to define the content of the relevant
identity and the nature of one's proposals such that the two are consonant.
These proposals will gain normative status to the extent that they are seen as
the practical manifestation of the aspirations, values and interests of the category. Above all, however, it is necessary to work on these various constructive dimensions – the boundaries, prototypes and content of the category –
such that they form a coherent and seamless whole.

In 1989, David Alton MP sponsored a bill in the British Parliament which
sought to limit abortion rights. As part of the campaign he spoke to a medical audience at Ninewells Hospital Dundee. The medical constituency is
obviously of crucial importance in the abortion controversy. However, a traditional anti-abortion position, based on metaphysical and doctrinaire religious argument, is unlikely to appeal to this constituency. Not only is it
likely to be perceived as 'unscientific' but it can also be easily characterised
as uncaring and dogmatic. Such a position is at odds with a medical identity
and hence medics are likely to see themselves in an out-group relationship to
anti-abortionists. If Alton was to have any chance of success, he needed to
reconstitute the categories. For now, consider the way in which Alton characterised the issue of boundaries.

The issue, he argued, needs to be put in a wider context:

> living in society today is like living in a greedy grab bag, where people are
> encouraged to take bigger, faster, better and more grand, whatever they can
> for themselves and never mind the consequences. It is my right to pollute the

countryside, my right to do this, my right to do that, regardless of the consequence to others. That to me is a selfish society and I belief that the way we
treat the vulnerable, powerless, unborn child epitomises our own contemporary selfishness. (cited in Reicher and Hopkins 1996a: 303)

Thus the abortion debate is not about the religious versus the secular, the
doctrinaire against the scientific or the dogmatic against the liberal. Rather it
is about the caring versus the uncaring. Doctors and nurses – the archetypal
caring professions – are thereby repositioned at the very core of the category
which takes an anti-abortion position. With boundaries redrawn to constitute medics within the same category as anti-abortionists, their support can
be canvassed for the anti-abortion campaign (cf. Reicher and Hopkins
1996b).

Consider, now, a very different campaign – that of the Gulf War. We want
to show how boundaries are redefined as a function of different projects of
mobilisation. On 20 August 1990, shortly after Iraqi forces had moved into
Kuwait, the American President, George Bush, declared that 'we need the
oil. It's nice to talk about standing up for freedom but Kuwait and Saudi
Arabia are not exactly democracies.' By 16 October, the President was complaining that: 'some people never get the word. The fight isn't about oil, the
fight is about naked aggression.' In his speech to the United Nations on 1
October, Bush had been more explicit about the source of aggression and
therefore about who was fighting whom: 'our quarrel is not with the people
of Iraq. We do not wish for them to suffer. The world's quarrel is with the
dictator who ordered that invasion' (Reicher 1991).

Why this shift? Early on in the war, at the instigation of the Royal House
of Saud, US strategy increasingly focused on mobilising an international task
force to repel the Iraqis from Kuwait (Hiro 1992). The task force needed to
be based in Saudi Arabia and for that to be politically possible it was essential that it be seen as a global instrument, incorporating Arab and Muslim
forces in particular, and not a tool of Western policy. Hence the original
rhetoric which defined the conflict in terms of a Western 'we' who are
dependent upon oil versus an Arab 'they' who produce oil served to exclude
crucial elements of the coalition. How can one win allies who are rhetori-
cally constituted as enemies? The rhetoric had to change so as to constitute a
more global in-group – the whole world – against an out-group that comprised one single individual: Saddam Hussein. Even as Iraq was pulverised
with some 80,000 tons of bombs and its leader, in his reinforced bunker, was
probably the least likely person to be hurt by the bombing, politicians and
media headlines continued to stress that they were only attacking Saddam
(Reicher 1991).

Of course different mobilisation projects do not necessarily mean different choice of categories and category boundaries. There will be times when
the same speaker may wish to mobilise the same constituency to different

ends or when different speakers may appeal to the same constituency. In that case one may find similar definitions of categories and their boundaries from these different sources even when they ostensibly disagree. Over a number of years we have been studying the rhetoric of Scottish politicians and activists (Hopkins and Reicher 1997a, 1997b; Reicher and Hopkins 2001; Reicher *et al.* 1997a). Of the major parties, only the Scottish National Party tends to be called 'nationalist', and it is the only party which, in conventional terms, would be described as promoting 'identity politics'. However, all the politicians we studied characterised their policies as reflecting Scottish identity and advancing Scottish interests. Whether in favour of Scottish independence, of the devolution of some powers to a Scottish parliament within the United Kingdom, or resolutely opposed to any Scottish parliament, they all – to invoke a phrase we encountered repeatedly – deferred to no one in their Scottishness. Where they differed was in the meanings and interests they ascribed to the nation and hence the policies that would realise those interests. We have space here for just one contrast. Consider the following two extracts, one from a Labour politician and the other from a Conservative spokesperson:

> I think the Scots are far more at ease with the idea of the public sector or the state interfering. The Scottish tradition is far more egalitarian; there is very little private health in Scotland for example, very little private education. There is a much wider reliance on the state in Scotland and people don't get uncomfortable with the idea of things being under public ownership which seems to be the case much more in England.

> Socialism believes that a bureaucracy that can do it better than anybody, bureaucracy does better than teachers ... you know, health authorities do it better than doctors ... but the spirit of independence, the independence of spirit is a very important characteristic in Scotland and that sort of thing gradually mulches it down and withers it ...

For the one, then, Scots are natural supporters of the welfare state and, being different from the English in this regard, need their own government to promote their interests. For the other, Scots are natural opponents of welfarism which destroys their identity. In both cases, though, the content of identity is such that it can only be realised by party policy. What remains constant, then, is not the content of identity but rather the relationship of consonance between the way in which identity is given substance and the policies being proposed.

In the same way, all the politicians we studied sought to portray themselves as typically Scottish, even if their versions of Scottishness, and hence of themselves, showed considerable variation. Of particular popularity, even amongst Unionist Conservatives, was the symbolism of the kilt. When Conservative MP Bill Walker introduced a bill to Parliament which would limit the possibility of Scottish devolution, he began by establishing his credentials: 'I stand before you, Madam Speaker, wearing the dress of Highland Scotland'. He was interrupted by Nicholas Fairbairn, a fellow Scottish Tory MP and long-time rival, who sought to puncture his effect by questioning his sartorial authenticity: 'On a point of order, Madam Speaker. My hon Friend the Member for Tayside North suggested that he was in highland dress. He is in nothing of the kind. He misleads the House and I have reason to believe that he is wearing little red pants under his kilt.' A 'true' Scot, of course, goes without.

These few illustrations must suffice. At every turn we have found that speakers appeal to their audience on the basis of identity. Even when they challenge one set of categories they do so in the name of another. These category arguments take place on many levels, with disputes about what the categories are, how inclusive they are, what content is ascribed to them and who best represents them. All this raises an obvious question: if everyone is at it, what decides which version prevails?

Speakers devote considerable effort to represent their contingent versions of identity as an uncontestable account of who and what we are. There are various techniques through which they seek to bring about such a transformation: national character can be linked to aspects of the natural landscape – Scots as hard and independent because of the rugged terrain and hard weather, or Scots as communal and mutually supporting due to living in small isolated communities. National identity can also be derived from commonplace sayings, from the writings of national icons or from other generally valued cultural resources. However, perhaps the most common technique is to invoke history. By showing traits as staying constant across time they can be argued to exist outside of time and hence appear as eternal and essential aspects of identity. But of course, as present projects change, so history must change to provide the appropriate lessons. That is why national history (or indeed the history of any category) 'is a history of rewriting its history' (Holy 1996: 118).

Rhetorical skills are undoubtedly important. However, are they enough? To use Billig's term, could the sufficiently artful orator get the crowd to do anything using 'witcraft' alone (Billig 1996)? Have we criticised traditional theory for its view of collective malleability only to reach the same conclusion under a new guise? Eyerman and Jamison (1991), whose account of social movements and the role of 'movement intellectuals' in creating both their own roles and the very movements in which they participate has much in common with our arguments, provide one way out. They suggest that the ring is held by the media, whose power to recognise or to ignore the various competing arguments does much to decide which will prevail and which will fail. Obviously, being accepted depends upon being heard. However, we would suggest a further level of analysis which is crucial to whether particular constructions of identity are accepted even amongst those who are exposed to them.

Our central argument has been that self-categories relate to the organisation of social action. So far, we have emphasised how rhetoricians seek to organise action by characterising people's position in a set of social categories. But the link between categorisation and action works in both directions: just as categorisation shapes the limits of collective action, so limitations on action shape the plausibility of category constructions. To understand how category constructions are accepted or discarded we must therefore examine more than how leaders are able to instigate action. We must also examine how group members encounter resistance to their actions from others in the social field. In other words, we need to study leadership and influence in the detail of interactions between social groups. This takes us back once more to studies of crowd events.

Social influence and leadership in inter-group contexts

In a number of recent studies, we have argued that crowd events are characteristically inter-group encounters – notably between crowds and the forces of authority. In order to understand what goes on within the crowd it is important to analyse the developing interactions between crowd and, say, the police. This is particularly important in explaining the psychological and social changes that occur. The first of these studies (Reicher 1996b) – concerning the so-called 'Battle of Westminster' which began as a demonstration in London on the issue of student finance but ended with prolonged fighting between police and students – arose out of a question of changing influence. How was it that, at the start of the event, most demonstrators shunned those radicals who were urging confrontation with the authorities, but at the end, they not only heeded those radicals but, if anything, castigated them for selling their papers rather than getting fully stuck into the action?

Most students went on the demonstration believing that, if only they could get Parliament to listen to their case, they had a chance of achieving their aims. Indeed, the event had been originally intended as a lobby of Parliament and many of those present had arranged to see their MPs. These students saw themselves as responsible citizens exercising the democratic right to protest. Part way through the march some students broke away from the agreed route march and went towards Westminster Bridge, at the other side of which sat the House of Parliament. In the ensuing confusion, some 5,000 students congregated on the approach to the bridge.

The police viewed the demonstration as a whole as a potential problem. This was exemplified by a number of radical groups in the crowd, but all the students were seen as potentially dangerous. Police concerns were clearly exacerbated when the breakaway approached Westminster Bridge and threatened to breach a law against demonstrations within a mile of Parliament when it is in session. The police therefore blocked the Bridge, refused to let anyone across and tried to force the students back. Even students who showed their letters of appointment with MPs were pushed away and the students as a whole were treated roughly. In response the students pushed back and a period of escalating confrontation culminated in a charge by mounted police.

In more formal terms, when the students viewed themselves in terms of one set of social relationships, as citizens, the police appeared a neutral group existing to guarantee the democratic system, while radicals threatened to undermine their cause by acting in illegitimate ways. However, the police saw the students as existing in a different set of relationships: they were in opposition to the social system and prone to illegitimate action. What is more, the police had the organisational and technological power to act upon the crowd in terms of these perceptions. They treated the students as oppositional, blocking their route, denying their demands to approach Parliament, physically forcing them back and dispersing them. Placed in this new set of relations, the 'responsible' students redefined their identity. Being treated as oppositional they came to see themselves as oppositional. The police, hitherto seen as neutral, came to be construed as an illegitimate out-group denying students their rights. Radicals, hitherto seen as an out-group, came to be seen as fellow oppositionalists. A previously fractured crowd was united through the police action; gaining the power of unity (the weight of numbers and the expectation of mutual support), students and radicals were able to challenge the police and attempt to enact their perceptions of proper action.

This is a dynamic we have found in a number of very different crowd events, including football-related 'disorder' (Stott and Reicher 1998; Stott *et al.* 2001), Poll Tax demonstrations (Drury and Reicher 1999; Stott and Drury 2000) and environmentalist protests (Drury and Reicher 2000). Under conditions where there is an asymmetry between the categorical perceptions of the crowd and the out-group and where the out-group has the initial power to enact its perceptions, then, for crowd members, acting on the basis of one understanding of their social position can lead them into a new social position. In effect this means a change of social identity since, as we conceive of it, identity describes an understanding of where one stands in a system of social relations along with the actions that are proper and possible within such a position (cf. Drury and Reicher 2000; Reicher 1996c; Stott and Drury 2000). Social identity describes one's position in a set of categorical relations. This new position entails a new set of values and understandings, providing a new basis from which actions are held to be legitimate or illegitimate. Second, it also leads to a change in one's relation to others (who is included as in-group and who is excluded as out-group) and hence a change in who will be prepared to act together. Third, there will be a change in who is seen as a typical group member and hence who will be a source of influence. The extent of these shifts can be illustrated from our study of an anti-roads protest in Wanstead, north-east London (Drury 1996). What began, for many, simply as a matter of trying to save the trees on the local green changed radically after protestors were met by a massive police operation. One protestor, drawing on the news, exclaimed that: 'it was just like us, what Shell is doing to Nigeria; protestors there are being cut up'. Wanstead residents and the Ogoni tribe might previously have seemed worlds apart, but they came together as part of a common oppositional category.

Our analyses have shown other changes linked with shifting social positions and shifting identities during crowd events. These include changes in power relations and senses of empowerment (Drury and Reicher 1999; Stott and Drury 1999) and changing notions of what constitutes successful action (Drury 1996). However, for present purposes, it is the three dimensions of change we have referred to above that are of interest. It should be apparent that these correspond to the domains of identity construction we have outlined in the previous sections: the category content, the category boundaries and the category prototypes. In all its aspects, then, social identity is both used to shape action and (re)shaped in the process of action. So, while the leaders may affect one aspect of this process by mobilising one party to intergroup events, their autonomy and effectiveness are still limited by the counter-mobilisations of others.

We are now in a position to understand the changing pattern of influence in the 'Battle of Westminster' and also to make some more general points about leadership in the crowd. In terms of the original student identity, the radicals are an out-group, their support for confrontation makes them atypical of student identity and indeed is dissonant with in-group self-definitions. Hence they achieve no influence. While, in traditional terms, they may be seen as 'agitators', there is no evidence here for the idea that such 'agitators' are guaranteed success due to the gullibility of the crowd. However, it is the assumption that agitators may move the crowd to violence, as acted upon by the police, which creates a new student identity wherein the radicals are part of the in-group, their oppositional stance makes them prototypical of the in-group and the confrontation they advocate is consonant with the new identity. In these conditions they move from pariahs to prophets and acquire leadership status. In other words, the police fear of 'agitators' is a self-fulfilling prophecy.

More generally, we argue that effective leadership depends not only on constructing a set of social categories through which a collectivity can be mobilised, but also on ensuring that these categories match the organisation of the social world. In the cases we have just considered, this is achieved indirectly. Due to the initial relations of power, radicals do not directly create a social world in the image of their words, they achieve influence through out-groups creating contexts in which their rhetoric and actions make sense.

Where power relations are different, it is possible to be more direct in assuring a homology between rhetoric and the organisation of practice. Perhaps the best example of this can be found in Hitler's mass rhetoric, thus bringing us to where we started. Take a simple exchange between Hitler and his audience, repeated many times, especially amidst his Nuremburg rally speeches:

Hitler: 'Deutschland'
Answer: 'Sieg Heil'

At first sight, such ritualised rhetoric might seem all but devoid of content and to exemplify Hitler's dictum to keep it simple and to rely on repetitive slogans. However, the exchange, for all its simplicity, incorporates many central dimensions of the Nazi world-view: politics as based entirely on the national community; a view of this community as hierarchically organised; a leadership principle in which the Führer and his party embody the interests of the people. Thus Hitler starts by naming the national community and the audience responds with a salute of loyalty to the Nazi Party and to Hitler himself. These relationships were not limited to words alone but to the whole display of which speech formed part. Hitler would often march with the crowd only to emerge alone in order to give his address (Mosse 1991). He would deliver the speech in militant and aggressive rhythms, putting violent emphasis on key terms (Mosse 1991; Stern 1984). He would be standing out above the crowd, often bathed in light as they watched in darkness. In its every aspect, the performance constitutes a dynamic totality. In every aspect of its organisation, the relationship of audience to Führer is reinforced. Although an individual, he is transmuted into an almost mystical symbol of the German *Volksgemeinschaft*.

   In contrast to Hitler's advice, his rhetorical practice was far from devoid of content. The simplicity of his rhetoric was not a sign of emptiness, but was possible only because of a set of category constructions that were so well known they needed very little in order to be invoked. These categories were familiar not only from the frequency with which they were spoken but also from the way in which they were lived. It is the perfect match between the structure of categories in rhetoric, the practical structure of the rhetorical event and the organisation of everyday life which is crucial. Each element sustained the other and ensured that Hitler's version of the social world remained predominant.

Conclusion: beyond the practice of domination

Perhaps the real lesson to be learnt from Hitler, Le Bon and the others comes not from what they wrote, nor from what they did, but in the contrast between the two. By denying in theory the categorical bases of rhetorical practice, it becomes easier to take particular categories as givens, to mythologise a certain way of organising the social world and thereby to limit choice to one form of present and one form of future. We must beware of such mythologies for they are profoundly anti-democratic in their denial of choice to their audience and are often used to lead them into the denial of choice (and worse) for others. As Miodrag Popovic argues in his study of myth in Serbian culture, it is only if '[we are] emancipated from blind slavery to whatever we have inherited since time immemorial, [that] we could be what we would like to be' (quoted in Anzulovic 1999: 8).

There is something depressingly wistful about these words, but at the same time Popovic can also be accused of undue optimism. Rhetorical domination does not exist in isolation and cannot be addressed on a purely rhetorical level. If the Serbian leadership sought to reify the notion of Serbs as heroic victims of Muslim duplicity, they likewise promoted repression against those who sought to live in more harmonious relations with Muslims or even sought to overcome ethnicity as a dimension of differentiation. If Hitler sought to reify a racialised and hierarchical notion of being German, he also repressed any attempts to disseminate an alternative vision of society and destroyed any attempts at living in alternative social relations. Peukert (1987) makes the point that Nazi anti-Semitism was not only a policy directed against Jewish people, but also a strategy to police the non-Jewish population by holding out the threat that any dissenting behaviour could lead them to be defined as 'community aliens' and undergo the terrible fate that attended such outsiders. This is a pattern repeated all too often. Whether under Hitler or Stalin, in Serbia or Rwanda, the demonisation of an out-group provides a means of maintaining hegemony over the in-group and a pretext for destroying dissidents.

An understanding of the multiple dimensions through which leaders deny choice is crucial if we are to formulate some guidelines for demystificatory leadership. In essence, our message is that, because rhetorical domination is bound up with practical domination, then one cannot begin to unravel the one without addressing the other. However, let us be a little more explicit about what we mean in both regards. On the rhetorical level, we are not suggesting that the demystificatory leader should eschew the invocation of social categories. Quite the opposite in fact. We have argued that collective action depends upon self-categories insofar as these categories specify who is part of the collective, how self and other should be defined, the values which should guide behaviour – in short, those various psychological constructs which render collective action possible. All rhetoric is either implicitly or explicitly based on self-categories. The only question is whether the categories are kept implicit or made explicit. Those who purport to eschew self-categories can only be concealing them.

Hence demystification depends upon making one's categorical choices explicit, upon making clear the grounds on which these choices are made and upon clarifying the practices to which these choices lead. Equally, we are not suggesting that leaders neglect history or environment or culture in order to define the content of categories, but rather that they make clear that they are making a choice and thereby allow their audience to see if they want to share that choice. As we found from our studies of Scottish politicians, many sought to reify identity by reifying certain moments as the key to Scottish identity – most notably the Battle of Bannockburn in 1314 which ensured the independence of the Scottish crown. Sometimes, though, other moments were offered and the basis of the selection was made available. One Labour MP, for instance, sought to draw inspiration from the 1820 Uprising due to the radical programme that it supported. He expressed a clear political choice as a guide to political vision rather than using historical myth to exclude political choice.

On the practical level, there is an obvious point to start with. The notion of demystificatory leadership will always remain empty unless one extends the discussion to include the means of dissemination (particularly access to and control of the media) and constraints on social activity. How can one have a fair debate about, say, the family, when all of our society is structured so as to promote particular types of relationship – from the content of school books through the structure of inheritance laws to the physical nature of our housing stock which makes living in anything but small units very difficult? In this sense those who wish to change social relations will always start at a disadvantage and will face a worrying paradox: if the structure of under-standing reflects the structure of practice, how can one ever get people to support and hence create forms of being which do not as yet exist? The answer, we would suggest, is that movements that seek to reconfigure our social world must themselves be that new world in microcosm.

Only if the means of political actions themselves embody the ends can they realise those ends. The failure to take heed of this could be said to be one of the great political tragedies of our past century. Perhaps in a new millennium we will discover that it is not enough for leaders to envision a new world. Rather they must ensure that the practices of their movements realise for members what members seek to realise for society at large.

Notes

1 The *Guardian* is a UK left/liberal daily broadsheet newspaper. Its circulation in 1984 was about 250,000 compared to 2–4 million for the popular tabloid newspapers
2 *Newsnight* is a UK in-depth news and current affairs programme broadcast by the BBC on weekday nights.

11

The cult of personality: reassessing leadership and suffrage movements in Britain and Ireland

Louise Ryan

> Movements today still largely correspond to the description provided of them by Gerlach and Hine (1970): they are segmented, reticular, polycephalous networks. The formal role of leadership within an organisational structure in recent movements has been at least partially delegitimised.... Within contemporary movements, power relationships have many facets which can only be partially grasped using an approach based on an analysis of personal qualities or group dynamics. (Melucci 1996: 344)

A question of leadership

In the quotation above, Melucci suggests that, within 'contemporary' movements, the formal role of leadership may have become 'delegitimised'. He goes on to say that the 'decisional role of an individual or collective body is simply no longer recognised as such' (1996: 345). Leadership has become diffuse: 'one member in the group fulfils the ideological role of the leadership, another expresses its creative component, and still another interprets its solidarist-organisational function' (1996: 346). The implication of Melucci's argument is not simply that the leadership of social movements is segmented and diffuse, but that this is recent, it has not always been the case. He implies that leadership roles and functions were more easily discernible in earlier, hierarchically structured movements. This dichotomous construction of contemporary or 'new' social movements and former or 'old' social movements has led, among other things, to polarised representations of movements' leadership and organisational structures. For example, there is an assumed split between formal, structured, hierarchical movements of the past and fluid, flexible, informal and non-hierarchical movements of the present (Offe 1985). But in the last decade there have been growing claims that the school of New Social Movements (NSMs) may have exaggerated the distinctions between so-called old and new movements (Ray 1993; Calhoun

1995). In addition, it has been argued that most social movement theories are gender-neutral, ignoring the particularities of feminist organisations and structures (Taylor 1999). The dichotomy of old and new movements misrepresents the continuities of women's campaigns across time periods (Offen 1992).

This chapter will engage with the 'old' versus 'new' social movement dichotomy by raising questions about the structure and leadership of women's suffrage movements in the past. The image of 'old' movements as hierarchical and formally structured relies in large part on specific representations of leadership. I argue that images of leadership have been influenced by a 'cult of personality' that has been constructed around particular individuals. This is particularly likely to occur in studies of historical movements. The records and documents of social movements tend to chronicle the activities and views of the 'leaders', rather than the 'rank and file'. When all the actors have died and no one is available for interview, such records may contribute to the simplification of the movement by exaggerating the importance of its 'leader'.

The chapter draws on case studies of two movements from the early twentieth century, beginning with the British suffragette movement and concluding with the Irish suffrage movement. Although both of these movements were engaged in the campaign for female enfranchisement in the early twentieth century, they represent very different examples of social movement structure and leadership.[1] In relation to the British suffragettes, a 'cult of personality' has been constructed around women like the Pankhursts (Kean 1994; Mayhall 1995). The militant organisation founded by Mrs Pankhurst, the Women's Social and Political Union (WSPU), has become synonymous with the entire campaign for female enfranchisement. Thus, analyses of individual leaders may lead to a concentration on particular social movement organisations that then come to be equated with the social movement as a whole. The second case study draws on my research on the Irish suffrage movement and explores how this movement can be retrospectively analysed in ways which challenge rather than reinforce the narrow focus on individual leaders. My analysis raises questions about the ways in which leadership can be understood. In drawing on contemporary social movements theories I seek to assess the extent to which the 'leadership' of the suffrage movement may demonstrate many of the charactistics usually ascribed only to NSMs and thus challenge the dominant perception of old movements. I suggest that the Irish suffrage movement was in many ways a loose network of scattered groups where deep divisions were temporarily put aside in the pursuit of a common goal. I argue that instead of a centralised, hierarchical leadership, the Irish movement had a fluid, multiplicity of leadership. To borrow the terms used by Melucci (1996), the organisational structure of the Irish movement can be seen as segmented (numerous cells in continual rise and decline), polycephalous (many leaders, each with a limited following) and reticular (multiple links between the different cells forming a loosely bound network).

Theorising social movements and the old/new dichotomy

In the 1980s and 1990s theorists such as Alberto Melucci, Alain Touraine and Claus Offe helped to define the conditions and limits of NSMs, and by so doing also distinguished what was 'new' about these movements. For example, Offe wrote that NSMs were marked by concerns about the body, nature, identity, culture and sexuality. Prominent among their values were autonomy and an opposition to control, regulation, manipulation and bureaucratisation:

> The NSMs consist of participants, campaigns, spokespeople, networks, voluntary helpers and donations. Typically in their internal mode of action, NSMs do not rely, in contrast to traditional forms of political organisation, on the organisational principle of differentiation, whether in a horizontal (insider vs outsider) or in the vertical dimension (leaders vs rank and file members). (Offe 1985: 829)

In contrast to the 'old paradigm', Offe adds that NSMs display a 'poor' and at best 'transient' demarcation between leaders and members. He argues that formal organisation and large-scale representative associations marked the internal modes of action of 'old' movements, while informality, spontaneity and a low degree of vertical and horizontal differentiation mark 'new' movements.

But Offe was by no means the first or the only theorist to establish such a rigid dichotomy between old and new movements around issues of structure and leadership. In his early and influential article 'The New Social Movements: a theoretical approach', Melucci claimed that NSMs were marked by direct participation and a rejection of representation. 'Hence, the importance of direct action and of direct participation, in other words of the spontaneous, anti-authoritarian, anti-hierarchical nature of the protests originating in these movements' (1980: 220). What emerges from these theories is a clear assumption that 'old' movements were, in contrast to NSMs, rigid in structure, with clear hierarchies of leadership. Although Melucci's work has been much criticised and he has been forced to defend many of his earlier arguments (Melucci 1995a), presumptions about leadership and organisational structure continue to inform images of contemporary social movements and, therefore, perceptions about how earlier movements were organised.

In theorising social movements since the 1960s, Della Porta and Diani (1999) provide a framework for analysing the structure and leadership hierarchy of social movements. In describing contemporary movements as having a decentralised structure, they also adopt the categories of Gerlach and

Hine (1970). Movements are represented as segmented, polycephalous and reticular, having a strong emphasis on participation and on internal solidarity. In addition, they have a particular type of leadership, charismatic rather than traditional or rational-legal. 'Leadership in social movements is *ad hoc*, short lived, relates to specific objectives and is concentrated in the limited area of the movements themselves' (Della Porta and Diani 1999: 142).

Calhoun has argued that NSMs have been theorised in very particular ways that seek to differentiate them from all social movements that have gone before: 'movements are committed to direct democracy and a nonhierarchical structure, substantially lacking in role differentiation, and resistant to involvement of professional movement staff' (1995: 191–2). However, in challenging the dichotomy between so-called old and new movements, he argues that the image of old movements as highly structured, hierarchical and with rigid leadership roles is at best exaggerated and at worst largely inaccurate. Such an image tends to be based upon a stereotype of the organised labour movement as a typical 'old' movement. Drawing on a wide range of historical studies, Calhoun claims that social movements in the nineteenth century displayed a diversity of organisational forms and structures. Several movements challenged institutionalised internal hierarchies and top-down structures of decision-making. He gives the example of the communal movements, radical religious communities and some socialist movements that all advocated democratic, participatory processes and were wary of the emergence of any leadership that was too autonomous from the members.

Calhoun's research makes a significant contribution to debates about the distinctiveness of NSMs. He has been particularly effective in questioning the rigid dichotomy outlined by such theorists as Offe and Melucci. In analysing the leadership and organisational structure of suffrage movements, I will draw on Calhoun's research and, like him, I will engage with some of the taken-for-granted assumptions about the characteristics of so-called old social movements. In addition, I will suggest that the formulation of leadership and movement structure employed by Melucci (1996) and Della Porta and Diani (1999) may prove useful in helping to provide a better and deeper understanding of the organisation of social movements *in the past*, as well as the present.

However, researching social movements from the past raises very specific problems, particularly in relation to studies of movement leadership. Ironically, it is Melucci who most clearly indicates this in his discussion of the difficulties of researching social movements' collective identity (1995b). This is ironic because in outlining the problems involved in studying and observing social movements, Melucci's work suggests the ease with which movements in the past may have been simplified or misunderstood. He argues that there is a tendency, when studying movements, to rely upon either the observation of demonstrations and protests or interviews with movement spokespeople. These methods provide a snap-shot of particular events and information rather than an insight into the internal dynamics of the movement. Displays organised for the mass media may tend to focus attention on key individuals or spokespersons rather than the formation of collective identity through internal processes of debate, disagreement, consensus and negotiations. Because Melucci is exploring these research problems in relation to contemporary social movements, he can attempt to overcome them by attending movement meetings, conducting group interviews with activists, observing processes of interaction between various activists, etc. But what interests me is that Melucci has not only helped to pin-point the difficulties in researching historical movements, but he has also, perhaps unwittingly, suggested why and how a narrow image of leadership and rigid hierarchical structures may have emerged in studies of 'old' movements in the past.

Women and social movements

According to Taylor, the study of social movements has remained remarkably 'gender-neutral':

> Despite considerable interest in women's movements, until recently political sociologists and sociologists of social movements rarely evoked gender as a force in the emergence and development of social movements. This is not surprising, since the field of social movements, especially compared with other areas of study, has been remarkably untouched by the gender scholarship produced in the social sciences over the past decade. (Taylor 1999: 8)

She argues that movement mobilisation, leadership patterns, strategies and ideologies are all gendered. The failure to analyse these gendered roles and processes has meant that important aspects of social movements have been ignored or simplified. In developing a theory that addresses the intersection of gender and movements, she draws upon 'recent theoretical formulations that combine the insights of classical collective behaviour theory, resource mobilisation theory, and new social movements theory' (Taylor 1999: 12). First, in examining political and cultural opportunities she explores how shifting gender differentiation and gender stratification contribute to the mobilisation and formation of collective identities. Second, she examines gendered mobilisation structures, arguing that mobilisation may be underpinned by inequalities embedded in the informal and formal organisational structures of the movement. Taylor draws on Joan Acker to argue that 'gender divisions and hierarchies are a subtext in the structure of all organisations' (1999: 18). Taylor suggests that some women's movements may set out to challenge these gendered structures and so create more diffuse, loose, local and fluid movements. In the third aspect of her theoretical framework, Taylor draws upon the school of NSMs to understand issues of identity formation. Similarly to Melucci (1995a, 1995b), Taylor suggests that people do not bring ready-made identities to a movement but that identities are formed through the collectivity. The processes through which those identities come to be gendered are very significant and cannot be ignored. Taylor concludes:

> The ignoring of a wide range of women's collective action by mainstream social movement scholars has led to a preoccupation with movements operating in the political and economic arenas rather than the cultural arenas, an emphasis on formal organisations and exclusion of more fluid and diffuse forms of association, the accentuation of cognitive factors and negation of emotions in social protest and a focus on institutional change strategies rather than identity politics. (1999: 26)

Taylor's analysis is particularly apt in relation to historical movements and may prove helpful in analyses of leadership. Her exploration of gendered movements not only brings a new dimension to the study of social movements, but also provides a framework within which 'old' social movements may be seen as more diverse and complex. Her work challenges the assumption that all old movements were, like the Labour movement, narrowly concerned with political and economic reform and formally structured with a clearly organised leadership. In my opinion a dichotomy that constructs NSMs as 'cultural' and old movements as 'political and economic' not only ignores the cultural dimension of earlier movements but also negates the continuities between movements across time. Movements such as the suffragists engaged with culture as well as politics and economics. To dismiss the movement as simply a political reform group underestimates not only the breadth of its interests, but also the diversity of its campaigns. An understanding of the range and complexity of the suffrage movement begins to raise questions about its organisational structure and leadership. As Taylor (1999) argues, women's movements, because of their range of interests and the nature of their campaigns, may deliberately develop a loose, fluid structure and more diffuse and localised forms of leadership.

But, while I am influenced by Taylor's arguments, I am wary of essentialist assumptions that women's approaches to mobilisation and leadership are intrinsically different from those of men. There is a danger here of constructing an essentialised dichotomy between 'masculine' movements and 'feminine' movements. Nevertheless, I agree with Taylor that gender dynamics do inform social movements and it is important to analyse how gender impinges upon their mobilisation and organisation. This raises questions about the extent to which women's movements may contest or perpetuate traditional, 'masculine' forms of leadership, authority and organisational structure. Thus, a gendered analysis is important in understanding suffrage movements, not just because the vast majority of members were female, but because such an analysis highlights the varied ways in which women's movements have been organised and structured.

Reassessing/reconstructing suffrage leaders

My work on suffrage movements attempts not only to illustrate the diversity and complexity of movement leadership, but also to highlight the particular difficulties in assessing collective action and identity frames in a historical context through several layers of representation. At first glance the campaign for female enfranchisement in the early decades of the twentieth century may appear to conform very closely to the type of old social movement discussed above. The apparently rigid structure and hierarchical leadership appear very different from contemporary women's movements. However, in this section I will analyse the processes through which images of suffragism have been constructed and the ways in which particular leaders have been singled out for special attention. The focus of attention on one particular organisation, the militant WSPU, illustrates the confusion between specific social movement organisations and social movements as a whole.

In analysing the construction of suffrage leadership, Kean (1994) begins by highlighting the role of Emmeline Pankhurst in the collective memory. Her portrait in the National Portrait Gallery and her statue in the grounds of the Houses of Parliament single her out as the most, if not the only, significant leader of the campaign for women's enfranchisement. The focus of attention on one leader of one organisation may well give a mistaken impression of how the overall movement actually worked. The process whereby Mrs Pankhurst came to be singled out as 'the leader' is interesting and may shed some light on the internal dynamics of the movement itself. A crucial period in the construction of suffrage history is the 1920s and 1930s when many of the former activists wrote accounts of the movement, and it is these accounts more than anything else that shaped how future generations regarded the movement, its leadership and its strategies (Kean 1994; Mayhall 1995). According to Kean, 'it is not history but the autobiographical (or biographical) genre which dominates the output of former suffrage feminists' (1994: 65). The many autobiographies by former militant 'suffragettes' tend to follow a rather similar narrative, telling tales of the first encounter with the suffrage movement, frequently involving a meeting with, or hearing the speech of, one of the Pankhurst family. From here the authors relate stories of conversion, initiation and the whole-hearted immersion in the cause. Several authors describe how they found their true selves through their membership of the movement: 'In post-suffrage writing we do see the glorification of the cause and of individual feminists. However, within such reflections of past glories of a triumphant movement there is also the concept of the movement as a mechanism for discovery of the self' (Kean 1994: 70). In terms of the framework outlined by Taylor (1999) above, it is clearly apparent that the suffrage movement facilitated gendered frames of collective identity and collective action. Collective action repertoires were informed by notions of womanhood that sought to challenge traditional perceptions of female passivity. Militant strategies negotiated gender in complex ways as smartly dressed young women behaved in a violent and 'unladylike' manner. Collective identity frames drew upon a strong sense of unity, solidarity and shared experiences. The old self was subsumed within the collective so that the new 'suffragette self' could emerge. Usually written by those fiercely loyal to the militant movement, suffragette autobiographies can be seen as reinforcing the image of Emmeline and Christabel Pankhurst as the primary leaders and strategists of the militant movement. There is rarely if ever any explicit criticism of the movement, its aims or its leaders (Kean 1994: 73). But the leaders emerge not merely as decision-makers and strategists but as charismatic figures who inspire complete devotion and loyalty in their followers. Obviously it is impossible to know whether this image represented the views of all suffragettes or merely those who wrote autobiographies.

But it is not just these autobiographies which constructed a particular image of the leadership. Laura Nym Mayhall (1995) has examined the role of the 'Suffragette Fellowship Collection'[2] in defining the 'Suffragette Spirit' and thus helping to keep alive in the popular imagination the image of militant suffragettes under the leadership of the indefatigable Pankhursts. Begun in the 1920s and 1930s, this was the self-conscious project of a group of former militants. Their unequivocal loyalty and devotion to Emmeline and Christabel ensured that these two women were enshrined in the collection as the absolute founders and leaders of the movement, thus eclipsing all other leading activists and organisers, including Annie Kenney, Mr and Mrs Pethick Lawrence and even the socialist Sylvia Pankhurst. In addition, the thousands of constitutional activists, who operated outside the narrow militancy of the WSPU, for example the National Union of Women's Suffrage Societies (NUWSS) and the Women's Freedom League, were completely excluded and rendered invisible. The Suffragette Fellowship has become particularly significant in recent decades because so many feminist researchers have drawn on these sources to reclaim suffrage history. In the researcher's quest for unity and completeness, these suffragette sources present us with ready-made answers (Kean 1998). However, as Kean suggests, we must be cautious about simply accepting these answers. Those involved in the process of recording suffrage history were amongst the most militant and extreme activists, they were also marked by a deep loyalty, indeed a devotion, to their 'leaders', and the images they have carefully constructed of the militant movement and its leaders must therefore be read with some caution.

In challenging the dominant representation of Emmeline and Christabel Pankhurst, Purvis (1996) analyses a wide range of historical texts. Focusing on many of the same sources explored by Kean and Mayhall above, Purvis argues that the Pankhursts have been misrepresented and their autocratic leadership styles have been exaggerated. Christabel Pankhurst, in particular, has been dismissed as 'cynical and cold at heart' with a 'fitful and impulsive ambition' and 'ruthless love of domination' (Purvis 1996: 267). In questioning the image of autocratic leadership, Purvis argues that for most of its existence the WSPU was a loose coalition, members opinions and actions varied enormously, and it is clear that several new tactics were tried out without the knowledge of Emmeline and Christabel. Purvis lists such examples as the smashing of windows at No. 10 Downing Street in 1908 and the first hunger-strike in 1909. 'The representation of rank and file members as cultural dopes who somehow mindlessly followed their autocratic leaders is, to say the least, troubling. In particular, it denies feminist women agency for their own actions' (1996: 271). Purvis concludes her article with a note of caution reminding us that 'the stories upon which we rely for knowledge about key feminist figures in the past have been socially constructed and culturally produced' (1996: 272).

Clearly, there is a growing debate about the 'true' role of Emmeline and Christabel Pankhurst and the extent to which they dominated and controlled a rigid, hierarchical organisation. The research cited above begins to suggest that representations of leadership need to be treated with some caution. While, in my view, there is insufficient evidence to challenge the overall impression of the Pankhursts as 'leaders' of the WSPU, there are various ways of interpreting their leadership. This raises questions about how we define leadership. Is a leader someone who formally occupies the key role of decision-maker, or is the leader a figurehead, a symbol who inspires devotion, or is leadership more complex and ambiguous? On the one hand, Mrs Pankhurst may be seen as the charismatic founder, a heroine who inspired thousands of women, while Christabel may be seen as the pragmatic strategist and publicist. On the other hand, Emmeline's and Christabel's leadership may not have depended on their formal roles as founder and coordinator of the organisation, but on the tremendous influence they exerted as high-profile symbols of the cause. In returning to Taylor's (1999) analysis, it is apparent that the WSPU provides an interesting example of the complexity of applying a gendered analysis to social movements. As a movement made up overwhelmingly of women, led by women, demanding women's enfranchisement, the WSPU illustrates that women's movements do not necessarily offer specifically 'feminine' models of leadership.

It is indicative of the continuing 'cult of personality' surrounding the Pankhursts that they remain synonymous not merely with the suffragette movement but with the entire suffrage movement. This is problematic for several reasons. First, it continues to prioritise militancy over constitutional tactics. Second, it masks the extent of class divisions within the suffrage movement as a whole. Third, it not only overshadows the other suffrage movement organisations within England, Scotland and Wales but also renders invisible the suffrage agitation in other locations. The next section of this chapter focuses on a case study of the suffrage campaign in Ireland, which, as a small, scattered and highly diverse movement, represents a very different example of organisational structure and leadership.

The Irish suffrage movement

My own research draws upon analyses of the Irish suffrage movement as a social movement that challenges many of the perceived notions of old, hierarchical, reform-oriented social movements. In attempting to study that movement I am mindful of Melucci's (1995b) remarks about the difficulties involved in studying any social movement. In trying to avoid the narrow focus on individual personalities and in aiming to achieve a deeper understanding of the complexities of the movement's structure, I will draw on a number of the theorists discussed above. In particular, I will employ the typology of social movements as polycephalous, segmented and reticular. Although it may seem somewhat anachronistic to apply a framework from the late twentieth century to a movement from the early twentieth century, I believe that such an experiment may serve to indicate some of the false dichotomies between the structure and make-up of old and new movements.

Although both the WSPU and the Irish suffrage movement were part of the same campaign for female enfranchisement from the British government at Westminster, they were operating in very different social, political and cultural contexts. Despite the fact that there was a good deal of contact and some close personal friendships across the two movements, tensions around colonialism and nationalism led to several disagreements, especially in relation to the autonomy of the Irish movement. Many in the British movement, particularly in the WSPU, did not appreciate the sensitivity of the Irish situation and were less than sympathetic to the nationalist campaign for independence from Britain (Ward 1995). The British and Irish suffrage movements also differed in other key ways. In Britain, suffrage movements such as the WSPU and the NUWSS were large, with tens of thousands of members, and achieved a high level of publicity. The Irish movement, by contrast, was significantly smaller with only a few thousand members. It was also much less militant; the vast majority of Irish suffragists were constitutional, opposing any form of militancy. In addition, it was considerably overshadowed by the large-scale nationalist movement and, therefore, never achieved a lasting place in the Irish popular imagination (Ryan 1996, 1997).

The existing research on the suffrage movement in Ireland has tended to concentrate on certain groups and individuals. In any field of research where history is being uncovered and written for the first time it is inevitable that particular individuals will prove more 'accessible' than others. Those who have left diaries, letters and autobiographies, or whose family had the foresight to leave their papers to a library or museum, will yield the most promising results for the historian. Thus women such as Hanna Sheehy Skeffington and Louie Bennett emerge from the mists of time not only as the leading suffragists but also as women who continued to play active and visible roles in Irish public life for many decades.[3] While there can be no doubt that these were courageous, hard-working, inspirational women, the tendency to focus on these particular individuals threatens to reinforce the 'cult of personality' which may lead to a narrow view of suffrage 'leaders' while rendering invisible the vast majority of suffrage activists. This approach may also perpetuate the old militancy versus constitutionalism dichotomy. As co-founder of the Irish Women's Franchise League (IWFL), Sheehy Skeffington represents militant tactics culminating in imprisonment and hunger-strike. Bennett, on the other hand, represents the constitutional tactics of the Irish Women's Suffrage Federation (IWSF). Because the British 'militant versus non-militant' framework is so powerful and so pervasive, it is all too easy to present the Irish suffragists in this format. This is inappropriate for several reasons: first, it underestimates the cultural and political specificity of the Irish movement, and second, it exaggerates the extent of militancy in the Irish case. In fact, militancy in Ireland was concentrated in Dublin and Belfast and involved small numbers of women. While receiving a certain degree of publicity, much of it negative, militant tactics were short-lived, only used between 1912 and 1914. Militancy never achieved the levels of violence carried out by British suffragettes and has been described as rather tame by comparison (Cullen Owens 1984). Third, the militant/constitutional dichotomy is inappropriate in the Irish case because it simplifies the more serious divisions within the movement, i.e. the split between nationalist suffragists who supported independence from Britain and unionist suffragists who vehemently opposed the establishment of an independent Ireland (Ward 1995).

Leadership

My discussion of the Irish suffrage movement focuses upon how one may study this historical social movement in a way that indicates the true complexities of its leadership and thus avoids the pitfalls of reconstructing a 'cult of personality'. In drawing on contemporary social movement theories I seek to assess the extent to which the structure, organisation and 'leadership' of the suffrage movement may demonstrate many of the charactistics usually ascribed only to NSMs and thus challenge the dominant perception of old movements. I will suggest that the Irish suffrage movement was in many ways a loose network of scattered groups where deep divisions were temporarily put aside in the pursuit of a common goal. In terms of organisational structure it can be seen as segmented, polycephalous and reticular.

These points are suggested in an article that was published in the Irish suffrage newspaper, the *Irish Citizen*, in April 1913. Entitled 'Tactics and a leader', the article was written by Mrs Coade, Honorary Secretary of the Newry Suffrage Society:

> We have Generals many, leaders of proved mettle and worth, but not one among them all who can command the whole of our women's forces, and lead us in solid union on to victory. Our sore and trying need is for a commander in chief. We present the sad spectacle of a disunited army. (19 April 1913)

As a militant, Mrs Coade uses very militarist language to describe the lack of leadership. It is indicative of the divisions within the movement that Coade as an Ulster Unionist should recommend that a British woman take overall charge of the suffrage movement. This met with a rapid reply from Rosamund Jacob, a Southern Nationalist suffragist who pointed out that the Irish and British movements were entirely separate (*Irish Citizen*, 3 May 1913). Nevertheless, Coade's comments are interesting and illustrate precisely the questions that I seek to explore in this section. The Irish suffrage movement was highly segmented with over 20 separate cells. It was polycephalous: each group had its own committee, and different individuals tended to take a lead on particular campaigns; in that sense leadership was localised and fairly fluid. In addition, the movement was reticular: the loose network formed by the various cells cooperated on various issues but did not come together to share any rigid rules or organised structures. While Mrs Coade views this as a weakness, a sign of disorder and disunity, I believe that it suggests many of the characteristics usually attributed to NSMs. This apparent 'disunity' raises many questions about the ways in which leadership operated within the movement. My analysis attempts to cast some light on this complex issue.

As discussed earlier, the study of movements – particularly historical movements – often fails to uncover their true dynamism, the lively discussions and debates that form the basis of collective identity processes. How can this problem be overcome? One way of analysing the debates, conflicts and disagreements between the various suffrage 'cells', as well as assessing the breadth of activity and multiplicity of leadership, is through the suffrage newspaper – the *Irish Citizen* (Ryan 1992, 1996). However, this is by no means a foolproof method. First, members of the IWFL edited this paper for much of its existence, and thus, while it was the only Irish suffrage paper and presented itself as a forum for all suffragists, editorials frequently indicate a pro-IWFL position. Second, as a propaganda vehicle intended for wide consumption, the paper attempted to present suffragists in the best possible light. Nonetheless, the tensions and disagreements between groups are very clear and easily discernible. Third, the paper cannot give voice to all the divergent views within the movement; only the most literate and articulate suffragists are likely to be included. While acknowledging this drawback, it is remarkable just how many suffragists are represented in the pages of the *Irish Citizen* over its eight-year history from 1912 to 1920.[4] In addition to the invaluable letter pages and activities noticeboard which provide an insight into the views and activities of all suffrage groups, regular articles were penned by men and women representing the broad spectrum of groups, local branches and supporters.

On Saturday 8 June 1912, the *Irish Citizen* editorial clearly outlined its aims and objectives: '(a) to form a means of communication between Irish Suffrage Societies and their members, (b) to provide a reliable source of publicity for suffrage activities in Ireland ... (c) to provide a means of cheap and effective propaganda'. In order to attain these ends the editors requested that '(a) all responsible officers of societies will send reports of meetings and notices of forthcoming events; (b) all suffragists should induce newsagents to display copies and posters; (c) those who have the power of expression will send us articles, notes and letters'.

In June 1912 the first mass meeting of Irish suffragists was held in Dublin to demand the inclusion of a female enfranchisement clause in the forthcoming Irish Home Rule bill to be brought before the British Parliament. The *Irish Citizen* devoted a great deal of coverage to this event and listed all participants. Nineteen suffrage societies and their various branches were represented. These groups demonstrate not only the spread of suffrage groups across the country from the north to the south, but also the splits and divisions within the movement. While many of the societies were affiliated to the umbrella group the IWSF, nonetheless they remained scattered and independent. The absence of any one clear leader is aptly demonstrated by the report in the *Irish Citizen* that 35 women sat on the platform. These women reflected the broad interests of the movement including trade unionism, education, cultural nationalism, militant republicanism and unionism, as well as militant and constitutional approaches to enfranchisement. In a sense many of these women can be described as 'leaders' of a sort; many were founders, secretaries or committee members of the various societies. The *Irish Citizen* gives no indication of any particular leader emerging from the meeting. Instead, these reports hint at the underlying tensions within the movement.

The segmentation of the Irish suffrage movement not only reflected the deep divisions within the movement but probably represented the only realistic strategy for containing these divisions. The reticularity of these loosely bound networks ensued that they were able to communicate and cooperate in the pursuit of their common goal. But it is the polycephalous nature of these scattered networks that is particularly pertinent here. How does leadership operate in this context? Clearly there was no one, overall leader, no one charismatic character who represented the entire movement. Therefore, is it accurate to say that there was no leadership in the Irish suffrage movement? Or is it more accurate to say that leadership existed in more diffuse, complex and transitory forms? From my research it appears that particular women emerged as spokespersons and took a leading role in specific campaigns and debates. In that sense, it seems appropriate to speak about a 'multiplicity of leaders'. In the absence of any one leader, the diffusion of leadership roles meant that the various skills and responsibilities of leadership were spread across a number of different individuals. These individuals each represented different interests and networks within the movement, hence the need for 35 women to sit on the platform at the 'Mass Meeting' in June 1912.

The tensions between the various networks came to a head on several occasions and the letter pages of the *Irish Citizen* testify to the disagreements between individuals and groups. When militancy began in the summer of 1912, after the Irish MPs had refused to back female enfranchisement, the other suffrage societies reacted quickly to express their disapproval of militancy. However, the most vocal condemnation of militancy followed the arrival of British suffragettes in Ireland. The IWSF immediately dissociated itself from the violent acts of militancy carried out in Dublin by three members of the WSPU: 'We wish to dissociate ourselves from the recent militant action in Dublin, and to reiterate our determination to pursue a non-militant and non-party policy in our demand for Woman Suffrage' (*Irish Citizen*, 3 August 1912). The Irish Women's Reform League (IWRL) offered a more complex view.[5] While echoing the views of the IWSF (to which they were affiliated), they added an addendum: 'At the same time we feel strongly that the entire responsibility for the present unrest and disorder among women lies at the door of the Liberal government which has it in its power to restore tranquility at once, not by coercion but by undertaking to deal honourably with the question of woman suffrage' (*Irish Citizen*, 3 August 1912). As the *Irish Citizen* was edited by members of the IWFL it had a strong bias towards militancy, giving over a great deal of coverage to Irish militants, their arrests, court appearances, imprisonments and subsequent hunger-strikes. Nevertheless, anti-militant letters and statements such as those above were regularly printed. For example, anti-militant and legal reform activist Marian E. Duggan LLB of the IWRL regularly wrote lengthy articles in the *Irish Citizen* not only criticising the efficacy of militancy but outlining alternative strategies (10 August, 7 September, 5 October, 26 October 1912). But it is important to emphasise, once again, that the militancy versus constitutionalism debate was not the sole preoccupation of the suffragists. The *Irish Citizen* indicates not only the ongoing processes of collective action frames – particularly the heated debates around tactics – but also processes of collective identity formation. As Taylor (1999) has suggested, early women's movements engaged with contentious issues around gender roles and identity, challenging the conventional boundaries of femininity. In my view the Irish suffrage movement engaged in similar and equally contentious processes (Ryan 1994a, 1995, 1996). Suffragists debated topics such as women's role in public life, employment, marriage, motherhood, housework, war, pacifism and nationalism.

One of the most potentially divisive aspects of identity focused not so much on gender but on national identity. The splits between those who defined themselves as Irish nationalists and British unionists traversed several suffrage societies (for example, the Munster Women's Franchise League included committed unionists and ardent nationalists). The pages of the *Irish Citizen* were frequently given over to heated debates about the relationship between female enfranchisement and Irish Home Rule. These tensions became progressively more irreconcilable as nationalism became more militant in the period surrounding the 1916 uprising.[6] However, prior to this period the women did manage to maintain very loose networks of cooperation centred around their shared collective identity as 'suffragists'.

The activities pages of the *Irish Citizen* provide a valuable insight into the work undertaken by the various societies and in so doing highlight the diversity of campaign work and the range of women who were associated with particular campaigns. Throughout 1912–13 one of the key issues, particularly for the IWSF, was 'white slavery'. Several lecture tours were organised with Irish and overseas speakers travelling to all the suffrage societies presenting talks to women-only audiences on the dangers of prostitution, particularly the procurement of young girls. On 26 October the IWRL reported that they had organised 'a most successful meeting' at the Mansion House, Dublin, drawing a crowd of 1,000 women. Militant groups – the IWFL and the Irish Women's Suffrage Society Belfast – also reported holding similar meetings (21 December 1912). The Munster Women's Franchise League (MWFL) held a meeting at Cork City Hall, attended by over 700 women, which was addressed by Susanne R. Day. A committee member of the MWFL, Day appears to have been one of the most energetic speakers, travelling throughout Ireland addressing various suffrage groups. For example, in April 1913 she addressed the IWRL in Dublin on the topic of 'the vote and wages'. This networking between groups was very common, particularly between the 20 or so societies affiliated to the umbrella IWSF.[7]

The activities pages of the *Irish Citizen* indicate the diversity of the movement but also the range of women who played a leading role in specific groups and particular campaigns. Several of these women were very experienced public orators who attracted large crowds and who may well have had charismatic personalities. But would it be accurate to describe them as leaders? This brings us back to the complex questions which have underpinned this chapter – what is leadership and how does it operate? Melucci argues against the notion of formal leadership: 'it is difficult to identify once and for all a set of stable leadership functions which would concentrate themselves into a single entity' (1996: 344). He goes on to say that 'short-term mobilisations require decision-making processes that are less formalised and representatives that are more temporary' (1996: 345). Of course, Melucci is applying this argument to an analysis of NSMs. But, in my opinion, his argument is equally applicable to the Irish suffrage movement. Although some suffragists like Mrs Coade may have bemoaned the absence of a 'commander in chief', it is doubtful if one formal leader could have emerged or that such a leader would have satisfied the various components of the movement. It is possible to speculate that the absence of a single, overall coordinator may have hampered the efficiency and organisation of the suffrage movement. But regardless of how democratic or charismatic she may have been, it seems extremely unlikely that one leader could have represented the very diverse interests and political affiliations of such a deeply fragmented movement. Under these circumstances, I believe that the flexible, transitory and diffuse leadership adopted by the Irish suffragists not only reflected the segmented and reticular nature of the movement, but was also the most practical option available to them. Considering the deep divisions within the movement as a whole, polycephalous leadership was probably the only way to facilitate temporary cooperation and unity.

Conclusion

This chapter analysed the question of movement leadership by examining three related issues. First, I engaged with the dichotomous construction of old versus new social movements. Drawing on the work of both Calhoun (1995) and Taylor (1999), I challenged the narrow assumptions about leadership and organisational structure of so-called 'old' movements. Second, I have raised questions about the difficulties of studying movements in the past; images of activists and leaders have become mediated through layers of representations. It is all too easy for movements to become reified, their internal dynamics and collective identity processes no longer visible to the modern researcher. In our search for neat, complete and comprehensible histories, 'the cult of personality' focuses our attention on the 'leading lights' of specific organisations and masks the wider complexities of leadership in the movement as a whole. Third, I have drawn upon the Irish suffrage movement to highlight the complex and messy dynamics of a historical social movement. Applying a typology of social movement leadership, I have suggested that the Irish suffragists share many characteristics with more recent movements: *ad hoc*, fluid and segmented formations, multiple, temporary leaders and reticular cooperation between scattered cells on particular issues and campaigns.

Like Calhoun (1995), my research suggests that movements in the past have used varied forms of leadership. This work challenges our perceptions and indicates the need to think about leadership in new ways. It is apparent that small, informal movements like the Irish suffragists developed *ad hoc*, diffuse and localised forms of leadership to suit their particular needs and circumstances. Hence, rather than attempting to uncover and restore 'the leaders' of historical movements, we need to reassess our understanding of what leadership means, the forms it takes and the ways it operated in very varied contexts.

Notes

1 Women in Britain and Ireland won enfranchisement in 1918, but voting rights were limited to women over the age of 30 years who also fulfilled property qualifications or were university graduates. Women in the Irish Free State won universal suffrage in 1922, while women in Britain won similar rights in 1928.

2 Housed at the Museum of London.

3 Both women have been the subjects of biographies (Fox 1938; Levenson and Natterstad 1986; Luddy 1995; Ward 1997a) and both have had articles written about their political activism (Hazelkorn 1988; Ward 1997b).

4 For the purposes of this chapter I will focus on the years 1912–13 when the Irish movement was particularly active.

5 The IWRL was set up in October 1911 as a Dublin-based group of the IWSF, initially with 20 members. In March 1913 it reported having 230 women and 12 men members. Its two main aims were to achieve enfranchisement for women and 'to help forward any reform movement which furthers the advancement of women'. It now claimed to be 'one of the leading suffrage societies in Ireland' (*Irish Citizen*, 22 March 1913). Very little research has been done on this group (see Ryan 1994b). Yet it appears to have been one of the more politically radical groups, tackling a wide array of issues including child sexual abuse, women's working conditions and legal reform.

6 In May 1916, the Irish Republican Brotherhood led a militant uprising in Dublin declaring Ireland to be a sovereign Republic. The British army quickly put down the uprising but the heroic martyrdom of the young revolutionaries captured the public imagination leading to a groundswell in support for nationalism in Ireland.

7 The MWFL began in Cork but also had branches in Limerick and Waterford. In February 1913 it reported having over 340 members across the province of Munster. Groups like the IWRL and MWFL were larger than many of the other suffrage societies; for example, the Lisburn Suffrage Society had only 77 women members (*Irish Citizen*, 1 February 1913). However, other groups were significantly larger in size. The IWFL reported having 695 members (over 100 of whom were men). The Irish Women's Suffrage and Local Government Association, which was originally set up in 1876 and continued into the early 1900s with only about 50 members, also reached a peak of approximately 600 members in the period 1912–14 (Ryan 1994a). It is difficult to be certain about the exact membership of the suffrage movement as a whole, but judging by the declared membership of each society it is likely that membership stood between 2,000 and 3,000.

12

Lenin and hegemony: the Soviets, the working class and the party in the Revolution of 1905

Alan Shandro

Introduction

Most thoughtful treatments of leadership understand it as a complex relationship between leader and led. If the literature on Lenin is to be relied upon, the pre-eminent practical leader of the Marxist working-class movement would have little of theoretical importance to contribute to an understanding of leadership. For the predominant tendency in this literature suggests that the distinctive conception of the vanguard party developed by Lenin merely reassigns revolutionary agency from the working class to a vanguard organisation led by intellectuals of bourgeois provenance. Lenin's project, in this sort of reading, was to identify an agent capable of substituting its revolutionary consciousness for the alleged incapacity of the working class for revolutionary activity. But by framing Lenin's position in terms of the categories of his opponents, this reading misidentifies it. Lenin's core thesis, that social-democratic consciousness must be introduced into the spontaneous working-class movement from without, might now be reformulated as the idea that the working-class movement cannot, without the organised intervention of Marxist theory in its struggle, generate revolutionary socialist consciousness (see Shandro 1995). I claim that the effect of his thesis was to reorganise the categories with which Marxists could approach the phenomena of leadership and to do so in a way that yields some conceptual purchase upon the complex dynamics of the relation between leaders and masses.

The vanguard and socialist consciousness

If the spontaneous working-class movement is equated with the economic base and social-democratic consciousness with the superstructure, then Lenin's thesis amounts to a voluntarist reversal of the Marxist primacy of the base; revolution is no longer grounded in a materialist analysis of class relations and becomes instead the expression of the will of the conscious

revolutionary intellectuals. These categories provide little conceptual space
in which to grasp the phenomena of leadership: revolution is accomplished
either by the working class *or* by the vanguard party; *either* the working
class spontaneously generates a consciousness of its revolutionary vocation
or the self-professed vanguard of revolutionary intellectuals substitutes itself
for this spontaneous process. Situated in this context, leadership could only
consist in imparting consciousness of a revolutionary vocation. Politics is
thus effectively equated with education and the essential political division
rests upon whether or not the educator respects the autonomy of the
learner.

Lenin's thesis, however, resists any simple identification of the distinction
between spontaneity and consciousness with that between base and superstructure. In the course of his argument, the conscious vanguard is called
upon both to foster the spontaneous working-class movement and to combat it. The apparent ambivalence of this stance is grounded in an assessment
of spontaneity itself as at once embryo of socialist consciousness and repository of bourgeois ideology, a contradiction Lenin states pointedly as follows:
'The working class spontaneously gravitates towards socialism; but the most
widespread (and continuously and diversely revived) bourgeois ideology
none the less spontaneously imposes itself upon the worker to a still greater
degree' (1961b: 386n). Marxist sense can be made of this claim only by
examining the dialectical process whereby the ideological dominance of the
bourgeoisie is established in struggle with the spontaneous socialist tendencies of the working class.

The terms of the problem (spontaneity/consciousness; bourgeois sponta-
neity/socialist spontaneity) must be set within a dynamic of struggle. This
requires two levels of analysis: at an initial level, abstraction is made from
the influence of ideology – that is, of 'consciousness' – upon the spontaneous
struggle of social forces, a struggle characterised in terms of the social relations of production. Since, at this level, the interests of the working class can
be shown to be in irreconcilable conflict with the fundamental social relations of the capitalist mode of production, the workers may be expected, by
virtue of these social relations, to gravitate spontaneously toward Marxist
theory for an explanation of their situation and orientation in their struggle.
But Lenin argues that the spontaneous movement is not only determined by
the socio-economic base of the class struggle. The claim

> that ideologists (i.e., politically conscious leaders) cannot divert the movement
> from the path determined by the interaction of environment and elements ...
> ignore[s] the simple truth that the conscious element *participates* in this inter-
> action and in the determination of the path. Catholic and monarchist labour
> unions in Europe are also an inevitable result of the interaction of environment
> and elements, but it was the consciousness of priests and Zubatovs and not
> that of socialists that participated in this direction. (Lenin 1961a: 316)

Reckoning with this 'simple truth', Lenin analyses the spontaneous movement as the movement of the working class, not simply as it is determined by
the relations of production, but also as it is subjected to the influence of the
ideological apparatuses of the bourgeoisie (institutional vehicles of ideas and
information, such as political parties, government offices, newspapers, and
churches, whose operation simply assumes or otherwise accepts the dominance of capitalist interests). Understood in these terms, the spontaneous
movement is that which confronts the socialist consciousness of the would-
be vanguard of the proletariat, within its field of action but beyond its control. Only at this second, more concrete level of analysis does Lenin locate
the dominance of bourgeois ideology; what is thus subject to this domination is not the working class as such but the spontaneous unfolding of its
movement, that is, the working-class movement considered in abstraction
from its revolutionary socialist vanguard, from those intellectuals and workers whose political activity is informed by Marxist theory and is, in this
sense, conscious.

There is no need, on these assumptions, to suppose that the dominance of
bourgeois ideology is perfect or that the workers are incapable of spontaneous resistance, political struggle or, indeed, innovation. The logic of spontaneous struggle generates a dynamic through which bourgeois ideology and
proletarian experience come to be partially constitutive of each other. The
limitation of the spontaneous struggle consists, not in an absolute incapacity
of the working-class movement to generate any particular form of political
activity, but in its inability, in the absence of Marxist theory, to establish a
position of strategic independence *vis-à-vis* its adversaries. Lenin's thesis of
consciousness from without can thus be restated as the following three
claims: first, the working-class movement cannot assert its strategic independence without attaining a recognition of the irreconcilability of its interests with the whole of the politico-social system organised around the
dominance of bourgeois interests; second, such recognition implies that
attempts to reconcile proletarian with bourgeois interests be assessed in the
context of the Marxist critique of capitalist political economy; hence, third,
this recognition cannot be brought to bear effectively upon the class struggle
in the absence of an organised leadership informed by Marxist theory. An
implication, not immediately drawn by Lenin, is that revolutionary consciousness must be open to the ability, not only of the bourgeois, but also of
the workers, to innovate spontaneously in the course of the struggle.

This set of assumptions, which sustains the thesis of consciousness from
without, is needed in order to conceive the political project of a Marxist
vanguard as a determinate intervention within a complex, uneven, contradictory logic of struggle for hegemony. But this is just what the circumstances of class struggle in tsarist Russia called upon the Russian Marxists to
do. While the extension of capitalist social relations eroded the feudal and
patriarchal foundations of absolutism, the unfettered growth of capitalism

and the prospects for proletarian socialism made a thoroughgoing democratic transformation of the institutions of tsarism and landlordism imperative. But the dependence of the Russian bourgeoisie upon the state and upon international finance rendered it an unlikely leader of a consistent democratic revolution; the precocious strength of the working-class movement made tempting a 'moderate' political settlement between bourgeois liberals and the more progressive landlords. A thoroughgoing bourgeois-democratic revolution seemed to depend upon the political initiative of the proletariat. But this would require, not a simple and straightforward polarisation along class lines, but the orchestration of a revolutionary-democratic alliance of diverse social and political forces. The struggle for leadership, for hegemony in the democratic revolution, was thus a struggle over the constitution and the political orientation of alternative systems of political alliances. Consciousness, as conceived by Lenin, had reflexively to grasp the complex and uneven process of the struggle for hegemony. In focusing upon the contradiction between the conscious vanguard and the spontaneous working-class movement, the thesis of consciousness from without enabled Lenin, paradoxically, to situate himself, as Marxist theorist and political actor, within the class struggle. It assumes a conceptualisation of class struggle in which both conscious vanguard and the spontaneous movements of the masses are capable of effective and sometimes of innovative action, although different, even contradictory modes of action are characteristic of each and a certain conjunction, even 'fusion', of the two is needed to sustain a hegemonic position in the process of revolutionary transformation. The claim that socialist consciousness must be imported into the spontaneous working-class movement from without does not signify the substitution of one collective actor for another but serves to open a conceptual space in which the relations between different actors, and hence the complex and contradictory relation between leaders and led, can be subjected to critical examination.

Through an examination of Lenin's response to the emergence of the Soviets in the revolution of 1905, I will trace out some of the contours of this space. In so doing, I will argue that sense can be made of Lenin's stance *vis-à-vis* the spontaneous working-class movement and the Soviets only in the context of the politico-strategic logic of the struggle for hegemony that sustains his thesis of consciousness from without. The shifts in Lenin's stance do not indicate an abandonment of this thesis but actually depend upon it. He situated the demands of leadership, distinctively, in relation to the logic of a political struggle for hegemony that implicated adversaries and allies as well as leaders and masses. In this respect, his strategic analyses produced a richer appreciation and a more effective grasp of the dynamics of the relation between leaders and led than did the principal alternative available to the Russian working-class movement, the one represented by Lenin's adversaries in the moderate wing of the Russian Social-Democratic Labour Party

(RSDLP), the Mensheviks. I will suggest, further, that Lenin's stance in the struggle for proletarian hegemony represents a more effective coming to grips with the diversity of revolutionary mass movements and the complexities of the leadership relation than does the influential 'post-Marxist' notion of 'counter-hegemony'.

Theory and the practice of revolution

The Russo-Japanese war of 1904–5 brought to the surface the tensions that pervaded the social and political structures of tsarist Russia. Taking a cue from liberal intellectuals campaigning to extend the bounds of free political speech, the priest Father Gapon led a procession of St Petersburg workers to present Tsar Nicholas himself with a petition to remedy their grievances. When the Tsar's troops responded by gunning down hundreds of the petitioners, the tsarist faith of even the most backward workers was shattered. A process of revolutionary struggle was unleashed, punctuated by waves of mass political strikes, mutiny in the armed forces, land seizures and persistent disorders in the countryside, and concessions by the authorities, followed by brutal repression. Revolution would shift the ground upon which politics moved in Russia and Lenin's political thought would move with it. But just how it moved is a matter of controversy. Lenin would formulate the relation between the spontaneous working-class movement and the conscious vanguard party in somewhat different terms from those he had used before the revolution. Struck by a shift in emphasis, tone and formulation, a number of writers have tried to counterpose, more or less systematically, a Lenin of the mass democratic revolution of 1905 to the pre-revolutionary party politician of *What Is To Be Done?* Foremost among them, Marcel Liebman has characterised this shift as 'Lenin's first revolt ... against Leninism' (1970: 73). Captivated by the spontaneity of the proletariat, Lenin, it is claimed, would now discard his previous distrust for the spontaneous working-class movement. His calls for a thoroughgoing democratisation of the RSDLP are supposed to belie his earlier 'elitist conception of the party' (Liebman 1975: 29). Reliance upon professional revolutionaries from the intelligentsia is said to give way to enthusiasm for the influx of revolutionary workers into the party as a tonic to relieve the bureaucratic lethargy of the committeemen. Whereas intervention on behalf of centralised control from above had seemed so essential in the underground, in the light of revolutionary reality Lenin would make himself the spokesman for creative initiative from below. The previous supposition that revolution 'must necessarily be the work of a vanguard group rather than a mass party' would now be replaced by a recognition of the Soviets, broad organisations of the power of the working masses, as vital centres of revolutionary activity (Liebman 1975: 29–31). Thus was 1905 'a revolution that shook a doctrine' (Liebman 1970).

Do Lenin's reformulations of 1905 amount to a theoretical reversal or do they merely represent an adaptation of the available analytical tools to altered circumstances? Liebman's approach, which abstracts spontaneity and consciousness, workers and intellectuals, democracy and centralism, party and class and so on from the context of Lenin's thinking on the strategic problems of the revolution, is not well designed to judge the issue. Thus abstracted, these concepts no longer occupy a determinate place in Lenin's Marxist project of grasping theoretically, so as to transform politically, the complex and shifting constellation of class forces; they figure, instead, as a set of essentially moral distinctions, each of whose terms represents a contrasting value, repeated shifting of emphasis between which merely serves to enact the drama of a soul torn between the demands of conflicting political moralities. But these terms may also be approached in light of Lenin's strategic orientation to political struggle, an orientation shaped by an appreciation that the identity of political forces, movements, institutions, policies, issues, ideas, etc. is not a simple reflex of the socio-economic class position of the actors, but responds as well to the conduct of the actors in the struggle and is therefore always subject to re-evaluation in relation to the logic and the development of the political (and ideological) struggle itself. I use the term 'politico-strategic logic of the struggle for hegemony' to designate this Leninist insight and I argue that without such an organising concept, it is not possible to account for the play, the dramatic shifts in emphasis, or the learning, the real theoretical movement, in Lenin's political thought.

'Undoubtedly', Lenin would write, 'the revolution will teach us and will teach the masses of the people. But the question that now confronts a militant political party is: shall we be able to teach the revolution anything?' (1962b: 18). Something new could be learned from the revolution and from the masses in the course of revolution only by grasping them in a conceptual framework capable of responding to conjunctural variations in the revolutionary process and consequently of formulating the appropriate questions. To express the same point somewhat paradoxically, it was only because he was ready to teach the revolution something that he was able to learn from it what he did. By incorporating the experience of the spontaneous revolutionary movements of the workers and peasants into his analyses of the politico-strategic logic of the struggle for hegemony, Lenin would work out a Marxist conception of proletarian hegemony in the bourgeois-democratic revolution. In so doing he would come to grasp his own Marxism reflexively as itself situated in the midst of the struggle for hegemony and thus to rectify his account of the relation of spontaneity and consciousness. He would do so, not by abandoning the thesis of consciousness from without, but precisely by pursuing its logic, the politico-strategic logic of the struggle for hegemony.

Lenin's response to the peasant movement of 1905 cannot be extensively considered here but perhaps the following incident can serve to indicate that

his response to the spontaneous working-class movement can be fully understood only in conjunction with it. The Inaugural Congress of the All-Russian
Peasant Union held in August 1905 proposed to send greetings to 'our
brothers the workers, who have for so long been spilling their blood in the
struggle for the people's freedom'. But when a Social-Democratic delegate
intervened in the discussion with the claim that 'without the factory workers
the peasants will achieve nothing', he was met with shouts from the floor
that 'on the contrary, without the peasants the workers can achieve nothing'
(see Perrie 1976: 110–11). Apparently, proletarian hegemony was not exercised just in being asserted, even where there was a measure of goodwill and
a recognition of common interests. The sophistication of Marxist socio-
economic analysis and political calculation would seem a thin thread, in
historical materialist terms, upon which to hang a claim to proletarian leadership in the bourgeois-democratic revolution; and even if the organisation
of the RSDLP had responded reliably to these calculations, it would still
have been in no position to bring their insight to bear in the villages. The
hegemony of the proletariat would have to be spread through a more exten-
sive and more deeply rooted network than the party. It would require,
therefore, a reappraisal of the spontaneous working-class movement, a reappraisal occasioned by the emergence of the Soviets.

The spontaneous movement and the Soviet

The most prominent exemplar of this institution, the St Petersburg Soviet of
Workers' Deputies, emerged at the height of the general strike of October.
The workers of the capital were acquainted with the idea of representatives
elected in the factory. Under a law of 1903 factory elders (*starosti*) could be
chosen by management from candidates nominated by the workers to negotiate their grievances; committees of deputies had been organised in a
number of factories since the January strike; and in the aftermath of Bloody
Sunday, the workers took part in two-stage elections for representatives to
the abortive Shidlovsky Commission, established by the government to in-
vestigate the causes of unrest among the factory workers (see Harcave 1965:
181–6; Anweiler 1974: 24–7, 32–7). In addition to this practical experience,
the workers had been exposed during the summer to Menshevik efforts to
popularise slogans in favour of a 'workers' congress' and 'revolutionary self-
government' (Anweiler 1974: 45–6).

As the strike wave reached St Petersburg, deputies were spontaneously
elected in a number of factories. When the Mensheviks initiated a workers'
committee to lead the general strike and, seeking to broaden its representation, agitated for the election of one deputy for each five hundred workers, it
was under the rubric of 'revolutionary self-government'. The Soviet of
Workers' Deputies thus came into being as a strike committee but one that
was already animated by a broader political vision (see Schwarz 1967: 168–

78). In response to the practical imperatives of the general strike, the Soviets began to act like a 'second government', ruling on matters of everyday life and issuing instructions to the post office, railroads, even policemen (see Anweiler 1974: 55–8). The momentum of the strike movement was such that the Tsar felt obliged, in order to bring the moderate opposition into the camp of order and pacify the situation, to concede civil liberties, a representative assembly with legislative powers, ministerial responsibility and universal suffrage. The revolutionary impetus of the working class was not broken. The Soviets continued to spread through urban Russia. In taking up the everyday concerns of the masses, they won the allegiance of broad strata of workers and attracted sympathy and support among the non-proletarian population of the cities. They renewed strike activity against state repression and martial law, for the eight-hour day and 'a people's government', and encroached more and more upon the prerogatives of the state. In accordance with the logic of an illegal confrontation with the tsarist state, they began to assume a new dimension as an agency of insurrection and an organ of revolutionary state power. Before the autocracy could restore its order and deploy its forces against the peasant risings in the countryside, it would have to put down workers' insurrections in Moscow and other cities (see Harcave 1965: 233–42; Trotsky 1973: 249–64).

By the time Lenin returned from exile in early November, the terms had already been defined in which the Russian Social-Democrats, both Mensheviks and the more intransigent Bolsheviks, debated the significance of the Soviet. Partially constitutive of the new institution were the Menshevik watchwords calling for 'revolutionary self-government' and a 'workers' congress'. They entered, through the early influence of the Mensheviks in organising the Soviet, into its self-conception. A plan for revolutionary self-government called upon workers' organisations to take the initiative in organising, parallel to the official Duma elections, an electoral process open to the masses. This would bring the pressure of public opinion to bear upon the official electors and the people's representatives could, at an auspicious moment, declare themselves a constituent assembly. Whether or not it reached this 'ideal objective', such a campaign would 'organise revolutionary self-government, which will smash the shackles of tsarist legality, and lay the foundation for the future triumph of the revolution' (cited in Lenin 1962c: 224; see Schwarz 1967: 168–71). The idea of a workers' congress, as presented by the Menshevik theorist P. B. Axelrod, was to embody proletarian self-activity. The congress would be comprised of delegates elected by assemblies of workers to 'adopt specific decisions concerning the immediate demands and plan of action of the working class'. It would debate the stance to be adopted toward 'the government's caricature of a representative assembly', the appropriate terms for agreements with liberal-democratic bodies, the summoning of a Constituent Assembly and the kinds of economic and political reforms to be advocated in elections to that body, and other such current public issues. Agitation around this idea, Axelrod wrote, could 'captivate tens of thousands of workers', a mass large enough in a period of revolution to 'endow the congress, its decisions and the organisation set up by it with tremendous authority, both among the less conscious masses of the proletariat and in the eyes of the liberal democrats'. Even if the congress did not come to fruition, by contributing to 'the political enlightenment of the working masses, strengthening their combative spirit and developing their ability and readiness to meet force with force in defence of their rightful demands', such agitation might occasion an uprising (Axelrod 1976: 65–7).

The Mensheviks hoped that such proposals, by providing a forum for working-class self-activity, might culminate in the formation of a mass party of labour. What was most fundamentally at stake in the institution of the Soviet was thus the relation between the working class and its political party rather than the more inclusive political agenda of the democratic revolution. Unable to grasp the new institutional form in different terms from those proposed by the Mensheviks, the Petersburg Bolsheviks reacted defensively. Fearful that the influence of an amorphous, non-socialist political organisation could undermine the political evolution of the workers toward social democracy, they greeted the formation of the Soviet with suspicion. Their leader, Bogdanov, favoured setting the Soviet an ultimatum: accept the programme and leadership of the RSDLP or the Bolsheviks would withdraw. In the end they stayed in the Soviet with a view to correcting spontaneous anti-social-democratic tendencies and expounding the ideas of the party. Perhaps mindful of Lenin's earlier warnings about the danger of non-partisan political organisations serving as conduits for bourgeois influence over the proletariat, they sought to distinguish the need for the Soviet as 'the executive organ for a specific proletarian action' from presumptuous 'attempts on its part to become the political leader of the working class' (cited in Schwarz 1967: 186, 187; see Lenin 1962a: 507–8). But by the time Lenin arrived, the Soviet had concluded the 'specific proletarian action' for which it had been formed and showed no sign of withdrawing from the field of political action.

Lenin's intervention

Read in terms of the debate between Mensheviks and Petersburg Bolsheviks over the Soviet, Lenin's intervention must seem unstable, ambivalent and ultimately incoherent. It is this appearance, I believe, that has occasioned the invention of Lenin's alleged 'revolt against Leninism'. I will argue on the contrary that by setting the Soviet in the context of the strategic logic of the struggle for hegemony, Lenin was able to conceive it as an apparatus for the exercise of proletarian hegemony and thereby to shift the terms of the debate. Once this shift is recognised, the case for his 'revolt against Leninism' simply collapses. Once the relation between the spontaneous working-class movement and the Marxist party is re-examined in light of it, the real movement in his thought can be established.

Lenin cautiously advanced his reading of the situation in a long letter, 'Our tasks and the Soviet of Workers' Deputies', submitted to the editorial board of the Bolshevik *Novaya Zhizn* but not published. Beginning as a strike committee, the Soviet had spontaneously assumed the features of a hub of revolutionary politics, capable of unifying 'all the genuinely revolutionary forces' and serving as the medium for an uprising against the state. It should be regarded, consequently, as 'the embryo of a *provisional revolutionary government*'. But considered in this light, the broad, non-partisan composition of the Soviet was no disadvantage. On the contrary, '[w]e have been speaking all the time of the need of a militant alliance of Social-Democrats and revolutionary bourgeois democrats. We have been speaking of it and the workers [in bringing forth the Soviet] have done it.' The question as to whether the Soviet or the party should lead the political struggle was ill-conceived: both the party and a reorganised Soviet were equally necessary. Indeed, the Soviet, considered 'as a revolutionary center providing political leadership, is not too broad an organisation but, on the contrary, a much too narrow one'. It must constitute a provisional revolutionary government and must 'enlist to this end the participation of new deputies not only from the workers, but ... from the sailors and soldiers, ... from the revolutionary peasantry, ... and from the revolutionary bourgeois intelligentsia' (1962e: 21–3).

This estimate of the Soviet was accompanied by a call for the reorganisation of the party in line with the new, albeit precarious, conditions of political liberty. While its secret apparatus would have to be preserved, the party must be opened up to social-democratic workers. Their initiative and inventiveness would have to be engaged in the task of devising new, legal and semi-legal forms of organisation, broader and less rigid than the old circles and more accessible to 'typical representatives of the masses'. Accordingly, the party must adopt democratic practices, including the election of rank-and-file delegates to the forthcoming Congress. The workers who join the party would be dependable socialists or amenable to socialist influence. 'The working class is instinctively, spontaneously Social-Democratic, and more than ten years of work put in by Social-Democracy has done a great deal to transform this spontaneity into consciousness.' The workers, better than intellectuals at putting principles into practice, must take the issue of party unity in hand (1962f: 34, 32).

The Soviet figured in Lenin's analysis not only as an organiser of the general strike but also as a non-partisan political organisation. Within days of this assessment, however, he would support the Bolshevik critique of '"non-partisan" class organisations' by declaring 'Down with non-partisanship! Non-partisanship has always and everywhere been a weapon and slogan of the bourgeoisie' (1962g: 61); and shortly thereafter he would pronounce the Soviet 'not a labour parliament and not an organ of proletarian self-government, nor an organ of self-government at all, but a fighting organisation for the achievement of definite aims' (1962h: 72). He had pronounced the Soviet just as necessary, in order to provide the movement with political leadership, as the party; he had indicated that the party was itself in need of revitalisation through the influx of 'typical representatives of the masses'. Yet he could, at the same time, issue a warning that the 'need for organisation which the workers are feeling so acutely will', without the intervention of the social democrats, 'find its expression in distorted, dangerous forms'. He could acknowledge that were the party inclined to demagogy or lacking a solid programme, tactical precepts and organisational experience, a sudden influx of untried and untested new members could threaten the dissolution of the conscious vanguard of the class into the politically amorphous masses (1962f: 29, 32). Though the workers were 'instinctively, spontaneously Social-Democratic', it was still necessary to reckon with 'hostility to Social-Democracy within the ranks of the proletariat', hostility that often assumed the form of non-partisanship. The transformation of the proletariat into a class was dependent upon 'the growth not only of its unity, but also of its political *consciousness*', and the transformation of 'this spontaneity into consciousness' was still envisaged in connection with the intervention of the Marxist vanguard in the spontaneous class struggle (1962g: 60).

Considered in abstraction from the logic of the struggle for hegemony, Lenin's response to the Soviet and to the spontaneous working-class movement that had called it into being would seem to collapse into a welter of conflicting formulations. His discourse can then be partitioned into elements reflective of the reality of the spontaneous class struggle and those marked by the resistance of the Bolshevik apparatus. This procedure, which reduces Lenin's discourse to a battleground for contending political forces, is most systematically deployed by the Menshevik historian Solomon Schwarz, but it is implicit in Liebman's interpretive apparatus of Leninist 'doctrinal rebellion'. It becomes superfluous, however, once Lenin's stance toward the Soviet is re-examined in the context of the struggle for hegemony.

The Soviet and the struggle for hegemony

The 'instinctively, spontaneously Social-Democratic' disposition Lenin ascribed to the working class in the immediate triumphant aftermath of the general strike did not consist in its pursuit of specifically socialist objectives. In an essay written to explain the prevalence of non-partisan ideology and institutions in the revolutionary movement, he characterised 'the striving of the workers towards socialism and their alliance with the Socialist Party ... [even] at the very earliest stages of the movement' as a consequence of 'the special position which the proletariat occupies in capitalist society'. He claims at the same time, however, that an examination of the petitions, demands and instructions emanating from factories, offices, regiments, parishes, and so on throughout Russia would show a preponderance of 'demands for elementary rights' rather than 'specifically class demands': 'purely socialist demands are still a matter of the future.... Even the proletariat is making the revolution, as it were, within the limits of the minimum programme and not of the maximum programme' (1962i: 76, 77). If the working-class movement was spontaneously social-democratic, it was so not in virtue of its consciousness but of its practice, not in virtue of what it thought but of what it did and how it acted. In order to grasp how this could be so, the practice of the spontaneous working-class movement must be situated in relation to the politico-strategic logic of the struggle for hegemony, specifically in relation to the struggle between the two possible paths of the bourgeois-democratic revolution, the landlord-bourgeois path and the proletarian-peasant path.

First, the general strike rendered unworkable the proposed Duma, thereby disrupting the compromise it represented between Tsar and bourgeoisie. The revolutionary struggle of the workers thus escaped the strategic hegemony of the liberal bourgeoisie spontaneously – by its fighting spirit, its tenacity and its 'plebian' methods – although not yet consciously and not, therefore, durably. In the aftermath of 'the first great victory of the urban revolution', it was incumbent upon the proletariat to:

> broaden and deepen the foundations of the revolution by extending it to the countryside.... Revolutionary war differs from other wars in that it draws its main reserves from the camp of its enemy's erstwhile allies, erstwhile supporters of tsarism, or people who blindly obeyed tsarism. The success of the all-Russian political strike will have a greater influence over the minds and hearts of the peasants than the confusing words of any possible manifestoes or laws. (Lenin 1962d: 433).

Not only did the spontaneous movement of the general strike open up the possibility of a decisive revolutionary transformation, in so doing it exemplified the exercise of hegemony materially through the production/imposition of *faits accomplis* and not only ideologically through the generation and transmission of consciousness, belief and conviction. It foreshadowed the hegemony of the proletariat as a reorganisation of the system of alliances of social and political forces, both destabilising the adversary's forces and mobilising an incipient revolutionary coalition. The working class was 'spontaneously Social-Democratic' to the extent that its spontaneous struggle was congruent with the strategic orientation of Russian Social-Democracy toward the hegemony of the proletariat in the bourgeois-democratic revolution.

Second, the Soviet thrown up in the course of the general strike provided an institutional form through which the alliance of revolutionary democrats could be concluded on a mass scale. Since the political independence of the proletariat from the influence of the liberal bourgeoisie required it to ally with other revolutionary democrats, especially with the peasantry, to effect the thoroughgoing destruction of the foundations of tsarism, the Soviet constituted the form in which the 'imprint of proletarian independence' could be placed upon the path of the revolution. Though it emerged from the working-class movement, Lenin did not treat the Soviet as a specifically proletarian class institution, a form of organisation exclusive to the workers. Indeed, what was decisive in his analysis was that, as a mode of organisation, the Soviet constituted an opening to the masses of workers and peasants, intellectuals and petty bourgeois, sailors and soldiers, a political terrain upon which a coalition of revolutionary democrats could take shape. As such and only as such did it represent an embryo of revolutionary-democratic state power.

This estimate of the Soviets was pointedly formulated in a Bolshevik resolution prepared for the April 1906 Unity Congress of the RSDLP and elaborated more fully in a lengthy pamphlet, *The Victory of the Cadets and the Tasks of the Workers' Party,* distributed to Congress delegates. According to the resolution, Soviets, arising 'spontaneously in the course of mass political strikes as non-party organisations of the broad masses of workers', are necessarily transformed, 'by absorbing the more revolutionary elements of the petty bourgeoisie, ... into organs of the general revolutionary struggle'; the significance of such rudimentary forms of revolutionary authority was completely dependent upon the efficacy of the movement toward insurrection (Lenin, 1962j: 156). In the context of this movement, however, the 'Soviets of Workers', Soldiers', Railwaymen's and Peasants' Deputies' really were new forms of revolutionary authority:

> These bodies were set up exclusively by the *revolutionary* sections of the people; they were formed irrespective of all laws and regulations, entirely in a revolutionary way, as a product of the native genius of the people, as a manifestation of the independent activity of the people which ... was ridding itself of its old police fetters. Lastly, they were indeed organs of *authority*, for all their rudimentary, spontaneous, amorphous and diffuse character, in composition and in activity.... In their social and political character, they were the rudiments of the dictatorship of the revolutionary elements of the people. (Lenin, 1962k: 243)

Established in struggle against the *ancien régime*, the authority of the Soviets and kindred institutions derived neither from the force of arms nor from the power of money nor from habits of obedience to entrenched institutions, but from 'the confidence of the vast masses' and the enlistment of 'all the masses' in the practice of government. The new authority did not shroud its operations in ritual, secrecy or professions of expertise: 'It concealed nothing, it had no secrets, no regulations, no formalities ... It was an authority open to all, ... sprang directly from the masses, and was a direct and immediate instrument of the popular masses, of their will.' Since the masses also included those who had been cowed by repression, degraded by ideology, habit or prejudice, or who simply inclined to philistine indifference, the revolutionary authority of the Soviets was not exercised by the whole people but by 'the revolutionary people'. The latter, however, patiently explain the reasons for their actions and 'willingly enlist the *whole* people not only in "administering" the state, but in governing it too, and indeed in organising the state' (1962k: 244–5, 247). The new authority thus constituted not only and not so much an embryonic state as an embryonic anti-state. This implication was not yet drawn but a certain dissolution of the opposition between society and the apparatus of politics, between the people and the organisation of state power, does emerge. The Soviet provided an institutional form in which the social, economic and cultural struggles of the masses, workers and peasants could be combined with the revolutionary struggle for political power, amplifying and reinforcing each other.

Self-government or revolutionary hegemony?

Properly understood, not only does Lenin's criticism of 'revolutionary self-government', the 'workers' congress' and the principle of non-partisanship not contradict his analysis of the Soviet in 1905–6, it follows logically from it. To invoke the theme of 'revolutionary self-government' in order to characterise the Soviets was to invoke the political orientation of those, the Mensheviks, who gave it currency. As Lenin saw it, they simply juxtaposed the exercise of 'revolutionary self-government' to cooperation in the rites of the tsarist government without strategic forethought as to the inevitability of counter-revolutionary repression. Thus conceived in abstraction from the logic of the struggle for hegemony, however, 'self-government' represented a denial of the need to organise the revolutionary insurrection or, at best, a refusal to take the initiative in organising it. In this context, it does not signal a call for the dictatorship of the revolutionary people but subordinates it to an experiment in political pedagogy. This was the target of Lenin's criticism.

The same holds *a fortiori* for such formulations as 'labour parliament' and 'workers' congress', which bear the additional disadvantage of identifying the Soviets as non-partisan organisations of the working class. Framed in this way, the Soviets would exclude the non-proletarian masses and depreciate the leadership of the Social-Democratic Party. The non-partisan structure of the Soviet was essential, in Lenin's analysis, precisely because it provided a political arena in which a coalition of the proletarian, petty-bourgeois and peasant masses could take shape. Non-partisanship was indeed a bourgeois principle, but inasmuch as the revolutionary process called for an alliance of the workers with bourgeois democrats, this was not a drawback but an asset. In order to preserve the political independence of the working class the leadership of the Social-Democratic Party remained essential, and, paradoxical as it may seem, this leadership was exercised precisely in orchestrating a class alliance around the organisation of a revolutionary insurrection and, consequently, in unravelling the strategic confusion represented by the notion of a 'workers' congress' and so on.

As demonstrated in the emergence of the Soviets, the spontaneously social-democratic bent of the working-class struggle was more than receptivity to the political lessons of Marxist class analysis. The workers had not simply put into practice advice supplied by Marxist theory; they had shown themselves capable of political innovation and, in so doing, generated a solution in practice to a key problem on the agenda of Marxist theory. But what they had done in social-democratic fashion was done spontaneously, not consciously. It was Lenin who, by situating their innovation in the context of the politico-strategic logic of the struggle for hegemony, would provide the theory of their practice. Just what had the working class done? Not only had it momentarily disrupted the hegemony of the liberal bourgeoisie and gained for itself some political experience, it had erected a new institutional form through which the diverse revolutionary-democratic forces could mesh together in a coalition of the masses, the worker–peasant alliance, and assume state power. It had thereby demonstrated its own aptitude for hegemony in the bourgeois-democratic revolution.

This hegemonic potential of the Soviet form of organisation could be durably realised only through action in conformity with the politico-strategic logic of the struggle for hegemony. It would require, therefore, the deployment of armed force to meet and defeat the violence of the counter-revolution and the deployment of Marxist analysis to seize the shifting conjunctures of the political struggle and hold the springs of ideological confusion in check. The Soviet could not render the intervention of the Marxist vanguard party superfluous but the Soviet and similar forms of organisation had come to embody an aspect of the struggle for proletarian hegemony that was hardly less requisite. Displacing the conventions that gave politics its shape and texture, they reorganised the space of political life: opening the process of political decision-making to the scrutiny of the popular masses, they encouraged the masses to enter politics; merging the social, economic and cultural demands and grievances of the people in the assault upon the autocratic regime, they palpably expanded the range of the political struggle; dispensing with formalities that barred the path to participation in the struggle, they facilitated the confluence of popular forces in all their contradictory diversity. In all these ways, they restructured the terrain of political struggle along lines that enabled the Marxist vanguard party more effectively to pursue the political project of proletarian hegemony. In thus transforming the terrain of struggle, the institution of the Soviet represented a connection between the idea of proletarian hegemony as the project of a party and the material inscription of proletarian hegemony in the path of the bourgeois-democratic revolution. Theorising the Soviet in this context enabled Lenin to pull together a coherent historical materialist conception of the hegemony of the proletariat.

Some years later, he would have recourse, albeit without specific reference to the Soviets, to a spatial metaphor in order to define the idea of proletarian hegemony:

> He who confines the class to an arena, the bounds, forms and shape of which are determined or permitted by the liberals, does not understand the tasks of the class. Only he understands the tasks of the class who directs its attention (and consciousness, and practical activity, etc.) to the need for so reconstructing this very arena, its entire form, its entire shape, as to extend it beyond the limits allowed by the liberals ... [T]he difference between the two formulations ... [is] that the first *excludes* the idea of 'hegemony' of the working class, whereas the second deliberately defines this very idea. (1963: 422, 423)

The politico-strategic logic of the struggle for hegemony was grounded in the struggle of social classes. It dictated preparedness for armed conflict, readiness to deploy the arts of insurrection. It engaged a battle of ideas, waged with the science of Marxist analysis and the arts of persuasion. But it could not be disengaged from a struggle over the very shape, the contours and dimensions of the battlefield. This struggle might be waged consciously according to the arts of organisation but it would most often unfold spontaneously, the product of impromptu variations upon or challenges to established convention whose bearing is reinforced or transformed in unforeseen ways by the sheer weight of popular involvement. The conventions governing political actors' expectations of each other, deployed in the material environment of politics, shape an arena for political action which, although subject to change at the hands of those implicated in it, both offers various possibilities for action and exerts a kind of structural constraint upon the plans of actors; this arena is encountered by individual actors, like baseball players having to adjust to an idiosyncratic stadium, not exactly as persuasion and not exactly as coercion, but as something like the force of circumstance. Thus, the exercise of hegemony could make itself felt not only in consent to persuasion or fear of coercion but also in adaptation to circumstance. The spontaneous working-class movement, in throwing up the Soviets, had transformed the circumstances of political action in ways that made some constraints more pressing and others less so, some possibilities more real and others less so, some threats more plausible and others less so, some arguments more persuasive and others less so; reconstructing the political arena, it enabled/required actors, not only workers themselves but also peasants, soldiers, sailors, employees, intellectuals (and, of course, landlords and bourgeois), to reorient themselves in relation to the political struggle of the working class for hegemony in the bourgeois-democratic revolution.

Practice and the theory of hegemony

Applying the politico-strategic logic of the struggle for hegemony to the analysis of the spontaneous revolutionary movements of the peasants and the workers, Lenin was able to endow the project of proletarian hegemony with a more concrete orientation. Prior to the revolution, he had characterised the exercise of hegemony by analogy with a tribune of the people, whose function it was to articulate any and all popular grievances against the regime; this universal role is preserved but the emergence of a revolutionary peasant movement required that hegemony take the specific form of an alliance between the working class and the peasantry. Hegemony figured earlier as a kind of generalised proletarian influence, liable to be confused in practice with the mere dissemination of party propaganda; but with the emergence of an institutional form, the Soviet, capable of enacting the proletarian–peasant alliance and exercising revolutionary state power, hegemony could be conceived concretely as embracing the mass action of the working class.

The politico-strategic logic at work in Lenin's political analyses called for receptiveness to conjunctural variations in the class struggle. This endowed his theoretical stance with a certain reflexivity, permitting him to bring the practical experience of the spontaneous mass movements to bear upon the lacunae of Marxist theory. The idea of proletarian self-activity that formed the substance of the Menshevik notion of hegemony was adaptable in quite another sense. Conformable to the limits of any situation, it manifested itself differently in accordance with variations in the circumstances of the class struggle. Whatever form it assumed, however, since the self-activity of the working class was never situated in relation to the strategic logic of the struggle for hegemony, what typified it was that it prefigured the socialist aim, contained it in intention. In this sense there was no distance between theory and reality, no theoretical lacunae but also no possibility of theoretical growth. The form of self-activity appropriate to the given situation would have to develop spontaneously, in an *ad hoc* fashion. The call for proletarian self-activity would be adjusted to an arena of struggle imposed by the defeat of the revolution and, instead of contesting the boundaries of that arena, the Mensheviks would allow the illegal apparatus of the party to fall into disuse and disrepair. Menshevism had long figured, on Lenin's strategic map, as a conduit for the hegemony of the liberal bourgeoisie, but this, he claimed, amounted to an abandonment of the very project of proletarian hegemony in the bourgeois-democratic revolution. The Mensheviks would increasingly abandon the language of hegemony. But they had never held, and so could not have abandoned, the concept of hegemony as Lenin had come to employ it.

The Menshevik discourse of hegemony might be characterised more accurately from Lenin's standpoint as simply another form of subaltern insertion in the deployment of bourgeois hegemony. And in this optic the Menshevik analysis of the Soviets as organs of workers' self-government presents an unlikely homology with contemporary 'post-Marxist' discussion of hegemony and counter-hegemony (Laclau and Mouffe 1985). Where Menshevik self-government signifies, not a struggle to overthrow the autocratic power of the state, but a forum where the workers could educate themselves politically, sheltered hot-house fashion from state power, post-Marxist counter-hegemony signifies, not a project for the reconstruction of the bourgeois social order along new lines and under new leadership, but a critique of any hegemonic project as an overweening claim to foreclose the innovative diversity of the process of individual self-definition and thereby 'suture' the social order. Indeed, the very substitution of 'counter-hegemony' for the Leninist (and Gramscian) term 'proletarian hegemony' suggests that the alternative to bourgeois rule is no social order at all but a universe of autonomously self-defining individuals. Marx's sardonic pronouncement in the 'Critique of the Gotha Programme' that the bourgeois have good reason to attribute 'supernatural creative power' to labour (Marx 1974: 341) suggests, however, that just as one cannot simply produce oneself, neither can one simply define oneself. One always finds oneself already in context and so one is always already defined, even if the terms in which one is understood/understands oneself are contested. In class society, the material available for the arduous work of transforming contexts and redefining political projects, aspirations and identities is supplied by the historical movement of the class struggle and in this context the social, political and ideological relations of capital do not represent a mere static backdrop against which workers and revolutionary intellectuals strive to fashion a socialist project: just as the workers spontaneously innovate in the course of their struggles, the ruling class innovates, through its political and ideological representatives, in response to working-class struggles. The process of working out a socialist project, of elaborating the political self-definition of the working-class movement, is one in which the adversary is inevitably and actively present. To reckon without this presence is to take the contours of the political arena as given and thereby to assume, in the very terms of one's counter-hegemonic struggle, the position of the subaltern. It is to make political leadership, strictly speaking, unthinkable.

Lenin's persistent refusal to equate politics with pedagogy establishes, by contrast, a conceptual field that opens to analysis the nuances of the relation of leadership. Part of leadership is the political education of the led – but only part: vanguard and masses play different, potentially complementary, but sometimes essentially contradictory parts in the class struggle. The very weight of organised numbers in motion, of the masses, can lead to the emergence of unforeseen political forces, possibilities and positions. But a position staked out today can always be invested and transformed tomorrow in accordance with the strategic calculation of an adversary. So the struggle for hegemony presumes the ability to adapt to the changing conjunctures of political struggle, to combine awareness of the underlying forces that shape the logic of struggle with openness to the ways in which different actors, vanguard and masses, adversaries and allies, can innovate in the struggle. Leadership in the class struggle thus demands a conscious vanguard, sensitive to the struggles of the masses yet willing where necessary to counterpose its political analyses to their spontaneous movement. It might be objected that this opposition between leader and led simply provides a sophisticated rationale for minority dictatorship. But this objection would be persuasive only if the concepts and distinctions that inform Lenin's approach to leadership did not afford a superior analysis of the logic of class struggle. The question of the truth of the analysis is, in this sense, unavoidable. And if Lenin's analysis does illuminate the logic and dynamics of mass movements, then the real question is the one posed by Gramsci: 'In the formation of leaders, one premise is fundamental: is it the intention that there should always be rulers and ruled, or is the objective to create the conditions in which this division is no longer necessary?' (Gramsci 1971: 144).

References

Abbott, A. (1997) 'On the concept of turning point', *Comparative Social Research,* 16: 85–105.

Aguiton, C. and Corcuff, P. (1999) 'Mouvements sociaux et politique: entre anciens modèles et enjeux nouveaux', *Mouvements,* 3: 8–18.

Albert, R. (1923) (Victor Serge) 'Les Riches contre la culture', *Clarté,* 48: 459–61.

Allen, P. (1970) *Free Space: A Perspective on the Small Group in Women's Liberation,* Washington, NJ: Times Change Press.

Althusser, L. (1971) *Lenin and Philosophy,* New York: Monthly Review Press.

Anderson, P. (1994) 'Comment: power, politics and the Enlightenment', in David Miliband (ed.), *Reinventing the Left,* Cambridge: Polity Press.

Anweiler, O. (1974) *The Soviets: The Russian Workers, Peasants, and Soldiers Councils, 1905–1921,* New York: Pantheon Books.

Anzulovic, B. (1999) *Heavenly Serbia: From Myth to Genocide,* London: Hurst.

Apter, D. E. and Joll, J. (eds) (1971) *Anarchism Today,* London: Macmillan.

Atkinson, M. (1984) *Our Masters Voices,* London: Methuen.

Atton, C. (1999) 'Green anarchist: a case study of collective action in the radical media', *Anarchist Studies,* 7, 1: 25–49.

Axelrod, P. B. (1976) 'The people's duma and the workers' congress' [1905], in Abraham Ascher (ed.), *The Mensheviks in the Russian Revolution,* Ithaca, NY: Cornell University Press.

Bachrach, P. (1969) *The Theory of Democratic Elitism,* London: University of London Press.

Bakhtin, M. M. (1981) *The Dialogic Imagination: Four Essays,* trans. Caryl Emerson and Michael Holquist, ed. Michael Holquist, Austin: University of Texas Press.

Bakhtin, M. M. (1986) *Speech Genres and Other Late Essays,* trans.

Vern W. McGee, ed. Caryl Emerson and Michael Holquist, Austin: University of Texas Press.

Bakhtin, M. M. (1993) *Toward a Philosophy of the Act*, trans. Vadim Liapunov, ed. Michael Holquist and Vadim Liapunov, Austin: University of Texas Press.

Bakunin, M. (1973) 'God and the state', in A. Lehning (ed.), *Michael Bakunin: Selected Writings*, London: Jonathan Cape.

Bakunin, M. (1983) 'What is authority?', in G. Woodcock (ed.), *The Anarchist Reader*, London: Fontana.

Barker, C. (1986) *Festival of the Oppressed: Solidarity, Reform and Revolution in Poland 1980–81*, London: Bookmarks.

Barker, C. (1987) 'Poland: the self-limiting revolution', in Colin Barker (ed.), *Revolutionary Rehearsals*, London: Bookmarks.

Barker, C. (1996) '"The mass strike" and "the cycle of protest"', paper presented to the Second International Conference on 'Alternative Futures and Popular Protest', Manchester: Manchester Metropolitan University.

Barker, C. (1999) 'Some notes on revolution in the 20th century', *Journal of Area Studies*, 13: 143–83.

Barker, C. (2001) 'Fear, laughter and collective power: the making of Solidarity at the Lenin shipyard in Gdansk, Poland, August 1980', in J. Goodwin, J. M. Jasper and F. Polletta (eds), *Passionate Politics: Emotions and Social Movements*, Chicago: Chicago University Press.

Barker, M. (1980) 'Kant as a problem for Weber', *British Journal of Sociology*, 31: 224–45.

Barker, M. (1989) *Comics: Ideology, Power and the Critics*, Manchester: Manchester University Press.

Barratt-Brown, A. (1938) *Democratic Leadership*, London: George Allen and Unwin.

Barrows, S. (1981) *Distorting Mirrors*, Yale: Yale University Press.

Beetham, D. (1977) 'From socialism to fascism: the relation between theory and practice in the work of Robert Michels', *Political Studies*, 25: 3–22, 161–81.

Beetham, D. (1981) 'Michels and his critics', *European Journal of Sociology*, 22: 81–99.

Bender, C. (1998) 'Bakhtinian perspectives on "everyday life" sociology', in B. Michael Mayerfield and M. Gardiner (eds), *Bakhtin and the Human Sciences: No Last Word*, London: Sage.

Benford, R. D. and Hunt, S. A. (1992) 'Dramaturgy and social movements: the social construction and communication of power', *Sociological Inquiry*, 62, 1: 36–55.

Bennett, R. J. (1978) 'The elite theory as fascist ideology – a reply to Beetham's critique of Robert Michels', *Political Studies*, 26: 474–88.

Bernhard, M. H. (1993) *The Origins of Democratization in Poland: Workers, Intellectuals and Oppositional Politics, 1976–1980*, New York:

Columbia University Press.

Bessel, R. (1993) *Germany After the First World War*, Oxford: Oxford University Press.

Besson, Y. (1990) *Identités et Conflits au Proche-Orient*, Paris: L'Harmattan.

Billig, M. (1996) *Arguing and Thinking: A Rhetorical Approach to Social Psychology*, 2nd edn, Cambridge: Cambridge University Press.

Birchall, I. (1986) *Bailing Out the System: Reformist Socialism in Western Europe 1944–1985*, London: Bookmarks.

Birchall, I. (1998) 'Victor Serge: hero or witness?', *What Next?*, 10: 23–6.

Birchall, I. (1999) 'Ernie Haberkern and Victor Serge', *What Next?*, 12: 40–2.

Birchall, I. (2000) 'The success and failure of the Comintern', in D. Renton and K. Flett (eds), *A Century of Wars and Revolutions: Essays in Twentieth Century History*, London: Rivers Oram.

Bloom, J. (1987) *Class, Race and the Civil Rights Movement*, Bloomington: Indiana University Press.

Bloom, J. M. (1999) 'The Bydgoszcz confrontation in Poland, 1981, as an example of a crucial turning point in a social movement', in Colin Barker and Mike Tyldesley (eds), Proceedings of the Fifth International Conference on 'Alternative Futures and Popular Protest', 29–31 March 1999, Manchester: Manchester Metropolitan University.

Bookchin, M. (1982) *The Ecology of Freedom*, Palo Alto: Cheshire Books.

Bookchin, M. and Foreman, D. (1991) *Defending the Earth: A Dialogue Between Murray Bookchin and Dave Foreman*, ed. Steve Chase, Boston: South End Press.

Bouchet, C. (1992) *L'Aventure Tapie: Enquête sur un citoyen modèle*, Paris: Seuil.

Bouchet, C. (1994) *Tapie, l'homme d'affaires*, Paris: Seuil.

Bourdieu, P. (1984) *Distinction: A Social Critique of the Judgement of Taste*, London: Macmillan.

Bourdieu, P. (1990) *The Logic of Practice*, trans. Richard Nice, Stanford: Stanford University Press.

Branch, T. (1988) *Parting the Waters: Martin Luther King and the Civil Rights Movement 1954–63*, London: Macmillan.

Branch, T. (1998) *Pillar of Fire: America in the King Years, 1963–1965*, New York: Touchstone.

Breiger, R. L. (1974) 'The duality of persons and groups', *Social Forces*, 53: 181–90.

Breines, W. (1980) 'Community and organization: the New Left and Michels's "Iron Law"', *Social Problems*, 27: 419–29.

Breines, W. (1982) *Community and Organization in the New Left 1962–1968: The Great Refusal*, New Brunswick: Rutgers University Press.

Brochier, J.-C. and Delouche, H. (2000) *Les Nouveaux Sans-Culottes:*

Enquête sur l'extrême gauche, Paris: Bernard Grasset.

Broué, P. (1997) *Histoire de l'internationale communiste 1919–1943*, Paris: Fayard.

Brown, R. (1988) *Group Processes*, Oxford: Blackwell.

Buechler, S. M. (2000) *Social Movements in Advanced Capitalism: The Political Economy and Cultural Construction of Social Activism*, New York and Oxford: Oxford University Press.

Buffotot, P. and Hanley, D. (1995) 'Les élections européennes de juin 1994: élection européenne ou élection nationale?', *Modern and Contemporary France,* new series, 3, 1: 1–17.

Bunch, C. (2000) 'Lesbians in revolt', in Barbara Crow (ed.), *Radical Feminism: A Documentary Reader*, New York: University Press.

Calhoun, C. (1995) 'New social movements of the nineteenth century', in M. Traugott (ed.), *Repertoires and Cycles of Collective Action*, London: Duke University Press.

Callinicos, A. (1981) 'The rank and file movement today', *International Socialism*, 17: 1–38.

Callinicos, A. (1995) *Socialists in the Trade Unions*, London: Bookmarks.

Carlyle, T. (1995) *On Great Men,* London: Penguin.

Carson, C. (1993) 'Reconstructing the King legacy: scholars and national myths', in Peter J. Albert and Ronald Hoffman (eds), *We Shall Overcome: Martin Luther King, Jr and the Black Freedom Struggle*, New York: De Capo Press.

Carson, C. (ed.) (1999) *The Autobiography of Martin Luther King, Jr.,* New York: Little, Brown and Company.

Castoriadis, C. (1987) *The Imaginary Constitution of Society*, trans. Kathleen Blamey, Cambridge, MA: MIT Press.

Cliff, T. (1978) *Lenin, Volume 3: Revolution Besieged*, London: Pluto.

Cliff, T. (2000) *A World To Win: Life of a Revolutionary*, London: Bookmarks.

Cliff, T. and Birchall, I. (1968) *France: The Struggle Goes On*, London: International Socialism.

Cliff, T. and Gluckstein, D. (1986) *Marxism and Trade Union Struggle: The General Strike of 1926*, London: Bookmarks.

Cloward, Richard A. and Piven, Frances Fox (1984) 'Disruption and organization: a rejoinder', *Theory and Society*, 13, 4: 587–99.

Cole, A. (1997) *François Mitterrand: A Study in Political Leadership*, 2nd edn, London and New York: Routledge.

Collins, C. (1996) 'To concede or to contest? Language and class struggle', in Colin Barker and Paul Kennedy (eds), *To Make Another World: Studies in Protest and Collective Action*, Aldershot: Avebury.

Collins, C. (1999) *Language, Ideology and Social Consciousness: Developing a sociohistorical Approach*, Aldershot: Ashgate.

Collins, C. (2001) 'Vygotsky on language and social consciousness: underpinning the role of Voloshinov in the study of social protest', *Historical Materialism*, 7.

Coover, V., Esser, C., Deacon, E. and Moore, C. (1978) *Resource Manual for a Living Revolution*, Philadelphia: New Society Press.

Cullen Owens, R. (1984) *Smashing Times: A History of the Irish Suffrage Movement 1889–1922*, Dublin: Attic Press.

Darlington, R. (1994) *The Dynamics of Workplace Unionism*, London: Mansell.

Davis, N. Z. (1978) 'The rites of violence: religious riot in sixteenth century France', *Past and Present*, 59: 51–91.

Degras, J. (1971) *The Communist International 1919–1943: Documents, Volume I*, London: Cass.

Della Porta, D. (1996) 'Social movements and the state: toughts on the policing of protest', in D. McAdam, J. D. McCarthy and M. N. Zald (eds), *Comparative Perspectives on Social Movements: Political Opportunities, Mobilizing Structures and Cultural Framings*, Cambridge: Cambridge University Press.

Della Porta, D. and Diani, M. (1999) *Social Movements: An Introduction*, Oxford: Blackwell.

Desroche, H. (1979) *The Sociology of Hope*, trans. Carol Martin-Sperry, London: Routledge and Kegan Paul.

Deutscher, I. (1963) *The Prophet Outcast: Trotsky, 1929–1940*, London: Oxford University Press.

Diani, M. (1992) 'The concept of social movement', *Sociological Review*, 40, 1: 1–25.

Dix, R. (1999) 'Three meetings and a lobby: discord and motion in strike leadership', in Colin Barker and Mike Tyldesley (eds), Proceedings of the Fifth International Conference on 'Alternative Futures and Popular Protest', 29–31 March 1999, Manchester: Manchester Metropolitan University.

Do or Die (Voices from Earth First!), 2 (1993).

Do or Die (Voices from Earth First!), 7 (n.d.).

Dobbs, F. (1972) *Teamster Rebellion*, New York: Monad Press.

Dolgoff, S. (ed.) (1973) *Bakunin on Anarchy*, London: George Allen and Unwin.

Draper, H. (1977) *Karl Marx's Theory of Revolution, Volume I: State and Bureaucracy*, New York: Monthly Review Press.

Draper, H. (1990) *Karl Marx's Theory of Revolution, Volume IV: Critique of Other Socialisms*, New York: Monthly Review Press.

Draper, H. (1992a) 'In defence of the new radicals', in *Socialism From Below*, New Jersey: Humanities Press.

Draper, H. (1992b) 'The principle of self-emancipation in Marx and Engels', in *Socialism From Below*, New Jersey: Humanities Press.

Draper, H. (1992c) 'The two souls of socialism', in *Socialism From Below*,

New Jersey: Humanities Press.

Dray, J. (1987) *SOS Génération: Histoire de l'intérieur du mouvement des jeunes de novembre–décembre 1986*, Paris: Ramsay.

Drury, J. (1996) 'Collective action and psychological change', Ph.D. thesis, University of Exeter.

Drury, J. and Reicher, S. (1999) 'The intergroup dynamics of collective empowerment: substantiating the social identity model of crowd behaviour', *Group Processes and Intergroup Relations*, 2: 381–402.

Drury, J. and Reicher, S. (2000) 'Collective action and psychological change: the emergence of new social identities', *British Journal of Social Psychology*, 39, 4: 579–604.

Dunayevskaya, R. (1991) *Rosa Luxemburg, Women's Liberation, and Marx's Philosophy of Revolution*, 2nd edn, Urbana and Chicago: University of Illinois Press.

Duyvendak, J. W. (1994) *Le Poids du politique: Nouveaux mouvements sociaux en France*, trans. C. Lambrechts, Paris: L'Harmattan.

Earth First! (1992) *Action Update*, 3, Spring.

Earth First! (1993) *What is Earth First!*, briefing pack for activists.

Eckersley, R. (1992) *Environmentalism and Political Theory*, London: UCL Press.

Edinger, L. J. (1967) 'Introduction', in L. J. Edinger (ed.), *Political Leadership and Industrialised Societies: Studies in Comparative Analysis*, New York: John Wiley and Sons.

Edwards, B., and McCarthy, J. D. (1992) 'Social movement schools', *Sociological Forum*, 7, 3: 541–50.

Ehrlich, H. J., Ehrlich, C., De Leon, D. and Morris, G. (eds) (1979) *Reinventing Anarchy*, London: Routledge and Kegan Paul.

Ellingson, S. (1995) 'Understanding the dialectic of discourse and collective action: public debate and rioting in antebellum Cincinnati', *American Journal of Sociology*, 101, 1: 100–44.

Emirbayer, M. and Mische, A. (1998) 'What is agency?', *American Journal of Sociology*, 103: 962–1023.

Epstein, B. (1991) *Political Protest and Cultural Revolution: Nonviolent Direct Action in the 1970s and 1980s*, Berkeley: University of California Press.

Eyerman, R. and Jamison, A. (1991) *Social Movements: A Cognitive Approach*, Cambridge: Polity Press.

Fairclough, A. (1983) 'Was Martin Luther King a Marxist?', *History Workshop Journal*, 15: 117–125.

Fairclough, A. (1987) To *Redeem the Soul of America: The Southern Christian Leadership Conference and Martin Luther King Jnr*, Athens: University of Georgia Press.

Fairclough, A. (1990) *Martin Luther King Jr*, Athens: University of Georgia Press.

Fantasia, R. (1988) *Cultures of Solidarity: Consciousness, Action and Contemporary American Workers*, Berkeley: University of California Press.

Fernandez, R. and McAdam, D. (1988) 'Social networks and social movements: multiorganizational fields and recruitment to Freedom Summer', *Sociological Forum*, 3: 257–382.

Fielding, K. and Hogg, M. (1997) 'Social identity, self-categorization and leadership: a field study of small interactive groups', *Group Dynamics*, 1: 39–51.

Firestone, S. (1968) 'The Jeanette Rankin Brigade: woman power', *Notes from the First Year*, a mimeographed journal published by New York Radical Women, June 1968.

Foreman, D. (1992) 'What is happening to our movement?', *Earth First! Journal*, 12, 5: 32–3.

Foucault, M. (1982) 'Afterword on the subject and power', in H. Dreyfus and P. Rabinow (eds), *Michel Foucault: From Structuralism to Hermeneutics*, Brighton: Harvester Press.

Fox, R. (1938) *Louie Bennett: Her Life and Times,* Dublin: Talbot Press.

Freeman, J. (1972–73) 'The tyranny of structurelessness', *Berkeley Journal of Sociology*, 17: 151–64.

Freeman, J. (1984) 'The tyranny of structurelessness', *Untying the Knot: Feminism, Anarchism and Organisation*, London: Dark Star/Rebel Press.

Friedman, S. R. (1984–85) 'Mass organizations and sects in the American student movement and its aftermath', *Humboldt Journal of Social Relations*, 12, 1: 1–23.

Friedman, S. R. (1985) 'Worker opposition movements', in L. Kriesberg (ed.), *Research on Social Movements, Conflict and Change*, 8: 133–70.

Gamson, W. A. and Schmeidler, E. (1984) 'Organizing the poor: an argument with Frances Fox Piven and Richard A. Cloward', *Theory and Society*, 13, 4: 567–85.

Ganz, M. (1997) 'What is organizing', mimeo, Kennedy School, Harvard University.

Ganz, M. (2000) 'Resources and resourcefulness: strategic capacity in the unionization of California agriculture, 1959–1966', *American Journal of Sociology*, 105: 1003–62.

Gardiner, M. (1992) *The Dialogics of Critique: M. M. Bakhtin and the Theory of Ideology*, London: Routledge.

Garrow, D. J. (1978) *Protest at Selma: Martin Luther King, Jr., and the Voting Rights Act of 1965*, New York: W. W. Norton.

Garrow, D. J. (1988) *Bearing the Cross: Martin Luther King, Jr. and the Southern Christian Leadership Conference*, London: Vintage.

Garrow, D. J. (1993) 'Martin Luther King, Jr., and the spirit of leadership', in Peter J. Albert and Ronald Hoffman (eds), *We Shall Overcome: Martin Luther King, Jr and the Black Freedom Struggle*, New York: De Capo Press.

Geras, N. (1986) 'Marxism and proletarian self-emancipation', in *Literature of Revolution: Essays on Marxism*, London: Verso.

Gerlach, L. P. and Hine, V. H. (1970) *People, Power, Change: Movements of Social Transformation*, Indianapolis: Bobbs-Merrill.

Giner, S. (1976) *Mass Society*, London: Martin Robertson.

Gluckstein, D. (1984) 'The missing party', *International Socialism*, 22: 3–43.

Gluckstein, D. (1985) *The Western Soviets: Workers' Councils versus Parliament 1915–1920*, London: Bookmarks.

Goodwin, J. and Jasper, J. M. (1999) 'Caught in a winding, snarling vine: the structural bias of political process theory', *Sociological Forum*, 14, 1: 27–54.

Goodwyn, L. (1991) *Breaking the Barrier: The Rise of Solidarity in Poland*, New York: Oxford University Press.

Gouldner, A. (1955) 'Metaphysical pathos and the theory of bureaucracy', *American Political Science Review*, 49: 496–507.

Gramsci, A. (1971) *Selections from the Prison Notebooks*, London: Lawrence and Wishart.

Gras, C. (1971) *Alfred Rosmer (1877–1964) et le mouvement révolutionnaire international*, Paris: Maspéro.

Grunberg, G. (1995) 'Les élections européennes en France', in *SOFRES: L'état de l'opinion, 1995*, Paris: Seuil.

Gubbay, J. (1997) 'A Marxist critique of Weberian class analysis', *Sociology*, 31: 73–89.

Haberkern, E. (1998a) 'Victor Serge and "libertarianism"', *What Next?*, 9: 40–6.

Haberkern, E. (1998b) 'Ian Birchall and Victor Serge', *What Next?*, 11: 27–8.

Haberkern, E. (1999) 'Two notes', *What Next?*, 13: 23.

Hains, S., Hogg, M. and Duck, J. (1997) 'Self-categorization and leadership: effects of group prototypicality and leader stereotypicality', *Personality and Social Psychology Bulletin*, 23: 1087–99.

Hall, J. K. (1995) '(Re)creating our worlds with words: a sociohistorical perspective of face-to-face interaction', *Applied Linguistics*, 16, 2: 206–32.

Hallas, D. (1970) 'Towards a revolutionary socialist party', in Tony Cliff, Duncan Hallas, Chris Harman and Leon Trotsky, *Party and Class*, London: Pluto Press.

Hampton, H. and Fayer, S. (1995) *Voices of Freedom: An Oral History of the Civil Rights Movement from the 1950s through the 1980s*, London: Vintage.

Hands, G. (1971) 'Roberto Michels and the study of political parties', *British Journal of Political Science*, 1, 2: 157–172.

Hanisch, C. (2000a) 'A critique of the Miss America Protest', in Barbara Crow (ed.), *Radical Feminism: A Documentary Reader*, New York: University Press. First published in Shulamith Firestone and Anne Koedt (eds), *Notes from the Second Year: Women's Liberation*, New York, 1970.

Hanisch, C. (2000b) 'The personal is political', in Barbara Crow (ed.), *Radical Feminism: A Documentary Reader*, New York: University Press. First published in Shulamith Firestone and Anne Koedt (eds), *Notes from the Second Year: Women's Liberation*, New York, 1970.

Hanley, D. (1993) 'Socialism routed? The French legislative elections of 1993', *Modern and Contemporary France*, new series, 1, 4: 417–27.

Harcave, S. (1965) *First Blood: The Russian Revolution of 1905*, London: Bodley Head.

Harlan, L. R. (1993) 'Thoughts on the leadership of Martin Luther King, Jr.', in Peter J. Albert and Ronald Hoffman (eds), *We Shall Overcome: Martin Luther King, Jr and the Black Freedom Struggle*, New York: De Capo Press.

Harman, C. (1968–69) 'Party and class', *International Socialism*, 35: 24–32.

Harman, C. (1982) *The Lost Revolution: Germany 1918 to 1923*, London: Bookmarks.

Harman, C. (1988) *The Fire Last Time: 1968 and After*, London: Bookmarks.

Harré, R. (1984) *Personal Being*, Cambridge, MA: Harvard University Press.

Harrington, M. (1972) *Fragments of the Century: A Social Autobiography*, New York: Saturday Review Press.

Hart, L. (1997) 'In defence of radical direct action: reflections on civil disobedience, sabotage and violence', in J. Purkis and J. Bowen (eds), *Twenty-First Century Anarchism*, London: Cassell.

Haslam, A. (2001) *Psychology in Organizations: The Social Identity Approach*, London: Sage.

Hazelkorn, E. (1988) 'The social and political views of Louie Bennett', *Saothar*, 13: 32–44.

Hiro, D. (1992) *Desert Shield to Desert Storm*, London: Paladin.

Hitler, A. (1980) *Mein Kampf*, London: Hutchinson.

Hogg, M. (1996) 'Intragroup processes, group structure and social identity', in W. Robinson (ed.), *Social Groups and Identities: Developing the Legacy of Henri Tajfel*, London: Butterworth.

Holy, L. (1996) *The Little Czech and the Great Czech Nation: National Identity and the Post-Communist Transformation of Society*, Cambridge: Cambridge University Press.

Hopkins, N. and Reicher, S. (1997a) 'Constructing the nation and collective mobilisation: a case study of politicians' arguments about the meaning of Scottishness', in C. C. Barfoot (ed.), *Beyond Pug's Tour: National and Ethnic Stereotyping in Theory and Literary Practice*, DQR Studies in Literature 20, Amsterdam/Atlanta: Rodopi.

Hopkins, N. and Reicher, S. (1997b) 'The construction of social categories and processes of social change', in G. Breakwell and E. Lyons (eds), *Changing European Identities*, London: Butterworth.

Huggins, N. I. (1993) 'Commentary', in Peter J. Albert and Ronald Hoffman (eds), *We Shall Overcome: Martin Luther King, Jr and the Black Freedom Struggle,* New York: De Capo Press.

Hunter, R. (1980) *The Greenpeace Chronicle*, London: Picador.

IM'média/REFLEX (1997) *Sans-papiers: Chroniques d'un mouvement*, Paris: Éditions REFLEX/IM'média.

Jasper, J. M. and Poulsen, J. (1993) 'Fighting back: vulnerabilities, blunders and countermobilization by the targets in three animal rights campaigns', *Sociological Forum*, 8, 4: 639–57.

Joffrin, L. (1987) *Un coup de jeune: Portrait d'une génération morale*, Paris: Éditions Arléa.

Johnson, A. (1996) '"It's good to talk": the focus group and the sociological imagination', *Sociological Review*, 44, 3: 517–38.

Johnson, A. (1997) '"New track may have to be laid": the "special class" and the social movement in the Marxism of Hal Draper', paper presented to the Third International Conference on 'Alternative Futures and Popular Protest', Manchester: Manchester Metropolitan University.

Johnson, A. (2000a) 'Democratic Marxism: the legacy of Hal Draper', in M. Cowling and P. Reynolds (eds), *Marxism, the Millennium and Beyond*, London: Macmillan.

Johnson, A. (2000b) 'The making of a poor people's movement: a study of the political leadership of Poplarism, 1919–1925', in Michael Lavalette and Gerry Mooney (eds), *Class Struggle and Social Welfare*, London: Routledge.

Kautsky, K. (1910) *The Road to Power*, Chicago: Charles Kerr.

Kean, H. (1994) 'Searching for the past in present defeat: the construction of historical and political identity in British feminism in the 1920s and 1930s', *Women's History Review*, 3, 1: 57–80.

Kean, H. (1998) 'Some problems of constructing and reconstructing a suffragette's life', *Women's History Review*, 7, 4: 475–93.

Keegan, J. (1987) *The Mask of Command*, London: Jonathan Cape.

Kimeldorf, H. (1988) *Reds or Rackets? The Making of Radical and Conservative Unions on the Waterfront*, Berkeley: University of California Press.

King, C. S. (1993) 'Thoughts and reflections', in Peter J. Albert and Ronald Hoffman (eds), *We Shall Overcome: Martin Luther King, Jr and the Black Freedom Struggle*, New York: De Capo Press.

King, M. L. (1964) *Why We Can't Wait*, New York: Mentor.

King, R. H. (1993) 'Martin Luther King, Jr. and the meaning of freedom: a political interpretation', in Peter J. Albert and Ronald Hoffman (eds), *We Shall Overcome: Martin Luther King, Jr and the Black Freedom Struggle*,

New York: De Capo Press.

King, R. H. (1996) *Civil Rights and the Idea of Freedom*, Georgia: University of Georgia Press.

Klandermans, B. (1992) 'The social construction of protest and multiorganizational fields', in Aldon D. Morris and Carol McClurg Mueller (eds), *Frontiers in Social Movement Theory*, New Haven: Yale University Press.

Klandermans, B. (1997) *The Social Psychology of Protest*, Oxford: Blackwell.

Kovel, J. (1998) 'Negating Bookchin', in A. Light (ed.), *Social Ecology After Bookchin*, New York: Guilford Press.

Kriesi, H. (1995) 'The political opportunity structure of new social movements: its impact on their mobilisation', in J. C. Jenkins and B. Klandermans (eds), *The Politics of Social Protest: Comparative Perspectives on States and Social Movements*, London: UCL Press.

Kriesi, H., Koopmans, R., Duyvendak, J. W. and Giugni, M. (1995) *New Social Movements in Western Europe*, London: UCL Press.

Kropotkin, P. A. (1939) *Mutual Aid: A Factor of Evolution*, London: Penguin.

Kurzman, C. (1994) 'A dynamic view of resources: evidence from the Iranian Revolution', *Research on Social Movements, Conflict and Change,* 17: 53–84.

Laba, R. (1991) *The Roots of Solidarity: A Political Sociology of Poland's Working-Class Democratization*, Princeton: Princeton University Press.

Labour Party (1984) *Report of the Annual Conference of the Labour Party 1984*, London: Labour Party.

Laclau, E. and Mouffe, C. (1985) *Hegemony and Socialist Strategy: Towards a Radical Democratic Politics*, London and New York: Verso.

Lane, T. (1974) *The Union Makes Us Strong*, London: Arrow.

Le Bon, G. (1947) *The Crowd: A Study of the Popular Mind* [1895], London: Ernest Benn.

Le Gendre, B. (1990) 'A quoi sert SOS-Racisme?', *Le Monde*, 9 January: 1 and 10.

Lenin, V. I. (1961a) 'A talk with defenders of economism' [1901], in *Collected Works*, Volume V, Moscow: Progress Publishers.

Lenin, V. I. (1961b) 'What is to be done?' [1902], in *Collected Works*, Volume V, Moscow: Progress Publishers.

Lenin, V. I. (1962a) 'A new revolutionary workers' association' [1905], in *Collected Works*, Volume VIII, Moscow: Progress Publishers.

Lenin, V. I. (1962b) 'Two tactics of Social-Democracy in the democratic revolution' [1905], in *Collected Works*, Volume IX, Moscow: Foreign Languages Publishing House.

Lenin, V. I. (1962c) 'A most lucid exposition of a most confused plan' [1905] in *Collected Works*, Volume IX, Moscow: Foreign Languages Publishing

House.

Lenin, V. I. (1962d) 'The first victory of the revolution' [1905], in *Collected Works*, Volume IX, Moscow: Foreign Languages Publishing House.

Lenin, V. I. (1962e) 'Our tasks and the Soviet of Workers' Deputies: a letter to the editor' [1905], in *Collected Works*, Volume X, Moscow: Progress Publishers.

Lenin, V. I. (1962f) 'The reorganisation of the party' [1905], in *Collected Works*, Volume X, Moscow: Progress Publishers.

Lenin, V. I. (1962g) 'Learn from the enemy' [1905], in *Collected Works*, Volume X, Moscow: Progress Publishers.

Lenin, V. I. (1962h) 'Socialism and anarchism' [1905], in *Collected Works*, Volume X, Moscow: Progress Publishers.

Lenin, V. I. (1962i) 'The socialist party and non-party revolutionism' [1905], in *Collected Works*, Volume X, Moscow: Progress Publishers.

Lenin, V. I. (1962j) 'A tactical platform for the unity congress of the RSDLP: draft resolutions' [1906], in *Collected Works*, Volume X, Moscow: Progress Publishers.

Lenin, V. I. (1962k) 'The victory of the Cadets and the tasks of the workers' party' [1906], in *Collected Works*, Volume X, Moscow: Progress Publishers.

Lenin, V. I. (1962l) 'Guerrilla warfare' [1906], in *Collected Works*, Volume XI, Moscow: Progress Publishers.

Lenin, V. I. (1963) 'Fundamental problems of the election campaign' [1911–12], in *Collected Works*, Volume XVII, Moscow: Progress Publishers.

Lenin, V. I. (1966) 'Five years of the Russian Revolution and the prospects of the world revolution' [1922], in *Collected Works*, Volume XXX, Moscow: Progress Publishers.

Leon, B. (1972) 'Let the quiet women speak', *Woman's World*, July–September.

Leon, B. (1975) 'Consequences of the conditioning line', in Redstockings (ed.), *Feminist Revolution*, New Paltz, NY: Redstockings. Also published by Random House, 1978.

Levenson, L. and Natterstad, J. (1986) *Hanna Sheehy Skeffington: Irish Feminist*, New York: Syracuse University Press.

Levine, C. (1984) 'The tyranny of tyranny', in *Untying the Knot: Feminism, Anarchism and Organisation*, London: Dark Star/Rebel Press.

Lewis, D. (1982) 'Martin Luther King and the promise of nonviolent populism', in John Hope Franklin and August Meir (eds), *Black Leaders of the Twentieth Century*, Urbana: University of Illinois Press.

Liebman, M. (1970) 'Lenin in 1905: a revolution that shook a doctrine', *Monthly Review*, April: 57–75.

Liebman, M. (1975) *Leninism Under Lenin*, London: Jonathan Cape.

Light, A. (ed.) (1998) *Social Ecology After Bookchin*, New York: Guilford Press.

Lipset, S. M., Trow, M. and Coleman, J. (1956) *Union Democracy*, New York: Doubleday–Anchor.

Lockwood, D. (1992) *Solidarity and Schism: 'The Problem of Disorder' in Durkheimian and Marxist Sociology*, Oxford: Clarendon Press.

Luddy, M. (1995) *Hanna Sheehy Skeffington,* Dublin: Historical Association of Ireland.

Lukács, G. (1971) *History and Class Consciousness*, London: Merlin.

Luxemburg, R. (1964) *The Mass Strike, The Political Party and the Trade Unions* [1906], Ceylon: Young Socialist.

Luxemburg, R. (1966) *Social Reform or Revolution* [1899], Ceylon: Young Socialist.

McAdam, D. (1982) *Political Process and the Development of Black Insurgency, 1930–1970*, Chicago: University of Chicago Press.

McAdam, D. (1996) 'The framing functions of movement tactics: strategic dramaturgy in the American civil rights movement', in D. McAdam, J. D. McCarthy and M. N. Zald (eds), *Comparative Perspectives on Social Movements: Political Opportunities, Mobilizing Structures and Cultural Framings*, Cambridge: Cambridge University Press.

McAdam, D., McCarthy, J. D. and Zald, M. N. (eds) (1996) *Comparative Perspectives on Social Movements: Political Opportunities, Mobilizing Structures and Cultural Framings*, Cambridge: Cambridge University Press.

McCann, E. (1974) *War and and Irish Town*, Harmondsworth: Penguin Special.

McCarthy, J. D. (1996) 'Constraints and opportunities in adopting, adapting and inventing', in D. McAdam, J. D. McCarthy and M. N. Zald (eds), *Comparative Perspectives on Social Movements: Political Opportunities, Mobilizing Structures and Cultural Framings*, Cambridge: Cambridge University Press.

McCarthy, J. D., Britt, D. and Wolfson, M. (1991) 'The institutional channeling of social movements by the state', *Research in Social Movements, Conflict and Change*, 13: 45–76.

McClelland, J. S. (1989) *The Crowd and the Mob: From Plato to Canetti*, London: Unwin Hyman.

MacIntyre, A. (1985) *After Virtue: A Study in Moral Theory*, London: Duckworth.

McKay, G. (1996) *Senseless Acts of Beauty: Cultures of Resistance since the Sixties*, London: Verso.

McKnight, G. D. (1997) *The Last Crusade: Martin Luther King Jr., the FBI, and the Poor People's Campaign*, Boulder, CO: Westview Press.

McPhail, C. (1991) *The Myth of the Madding Crowd,* New York: Aldine de Gruyter.

Machin, H. (1993) 'How the socialists lost the 1993 election to the French parliament', *West European Politics*, 16, 4: 595–606.

Maitron, J. (1964) 'De Kibaltchiche à Victor Serge: Le Rétif (1909–1919)', *Le Mouvement social*, 47: 45–78.

Maitron, J. (1975) *Le Mouvement anarchiste en France des origines à 1914*, Paris: Gallimard.

Mandel, E. (1986) 'The role of the individual in history: the case of World War Two', *New Left Review*, 157: 61–77.

Marable, M. (1992) *Crisis of Color and Democracy: Essays on Race, Class and Power*, Monroe, MN: Common Courage Press.

Marable, M. (1998) *Black Leadership*, New York: Columbia University Press.

Marshall, P. (1988) *Revolution and Counter-Revolution in Iran*, London: Bookmarks.

Martel, F. (1999) *The Pink and the Black: Homosexuals in France since 1968*, trans. J. M. Todd, Stanford: California University Press.

Marx, K. (1974) 'Critique of the Gotha Programme' [1875], in *The First International and After*, Harmondsworth: Penguin.

Marx, K. (1975) 'Concerning Feuerbach' [1845], in *Early Writings*, London: Pelican.

Mayhall, L. N. (1995) 'Creating the suffragette spirit: British feminism and the historical imagination', *Women's History Review*, 4, 3: 319–44.

Meier, A. (1965) 'On the role of Martin Luther King', *New Politics*, 4, 1: 52–9.

Mellor, C. and Miller, J. (1969) *Women: A Journal of Liberation*, Winter.

Melucci, A. (1980) 'The New Social Movements: a theoretical approach', *Social Science Information*, 19: 199–226.

Melucci, A. (1985) 'The symbolic challenge of contemporary movements', *Social Research*, 52: 789–816.

Melucci, A. (1989) *Nomads of the Present: Social Movements and Individual Needs in Contemporary Society*, ed. John Keane and Paul Mier, London: Hutchinson Radius.

Melucci, A. (1995a) 'The New Social Movements revisited', in L. Maheu (ed.), *Social Movements and Social Classes*, London: Sage.

Melucci, A. (1995b) 'The process of collective identity', in Hank Johnston and Bert Klandermans (eds), *Social Movements and Culture*, London: UCL Press.

Melucci, A. (1996) *Challenging Codes: Collective Action in the Information Age*, Cambridge: Cambridge University Press.

Meyer, D. S. and Tarrow, S. (1998) 'A movement society: contentious politics for a new century', in David S. Meyer and Sidney Tarrow (eds), *The Social Movement Society: Contentious Politics for a New Century*, Lanham, MD: Rowman and Littlefield.

Michels, R. (1959) *Political Parties: A Sociological Study of the Oligarchical Tendencies of Modern Democracy*, New York: Dover.

Milgram, S. and Toch, H. (1969) 'Collective behaviour: crowds and social movements', in G. Lindzey and E. Aronson (eds), *Handbook of Social Psychology*, Volume 4, Reading, MA: Addison Wesley.

Miliband, R. (1962) *Parliamentary Socialism*, London: Merlin.

Miliband, R. (1991) *Divided Societies: Class Struggle in Contemporary Capitalism*, Oxford: Oxford University Press.

Mills, C. W. (1948) *The New Men of Power*, New York: Harcourt Brace.

Molyneux, J. (1987) *Arguments for Revolutionary Socialism*, London: Bookmarks.

Mommsen, W. J. (1981) 'Max Weber and Roberto Michels: an asymmetrical partnership', *European Journal of Sociology*, 22: 100–16.

Moore, J. (1997) 'Anarchism and post-structuralism', *Anarchist Studies*, 5, 2: 157–61.

Morland, D. (1997) 'Anarchism, human nature and history: lessons for the future', in J. Purkis and J. Bowen (eds), *Twenty-First Century Anarchism*, London: Cassell.

Morris, A. D. (1984) *The Origins of the Civil Rights Movement: Black Communities Organizing for Change*, New York: Free Press.

Morris, A. D. (1993) 'A man prepared for the times: a sociological analysis of the leadership of Martin Luther King, Jr.', in Peter J. Albert and Ronald Hoffman (eds), *We Shall Overcome: Martin Luther King, Jr and the Black Freedom Struggle*, New York: De Capo Press.

Moscovici, S. (1981) *L'Age des Foules*, Paris: Fayard.

Moses, G. (1997) *Revolution of Conscience: Martin Luther King Jr. and the Philosophy of Nonviolence*, New York: Guilford Press.

Moses, R. P. (1993) 'Commentary', in Peter J. Albert and Ronald Hoffman (eds), *We Shall Overcome: Martin Luther King, Jr and the Black Freedom Struggle*, New York: De Capo Press.

Mosse, G. (1991) *The Nationalization of the Masses*, Ithaca, NY: Cornell University Press.

Most, Elizabeth (1975) 'The double standard of organization', in Redstockings (ed.), *Feminist Revolution*, New Paltz, NY: Redstockings. Also published by Random House, 1978.

Mouriaux, R. and Subileau, F. (1996) 'Les grèves françaises de l'automne 1995: défense des acquis ou mouvement social?', *Modern and Contemporary France*, new series, 4, 3: 299–306.

Mueller, C. (1994) 'Conflict networks and the organisation of women's liberation', in Enrique Larana, Hank Johnston and Joseph R. Crusfield (eds), *New Social Movements: From Ideology to Identity*, Philadelphia: Temple University Press.

Mulgan, G. (1994) *Politics in an Anti-political Age*, Cambridge: Polity Press.

Naples, Nancy A. (ed.) (1998) *Community Activism and Feminist Politics*, London: Routledge.

Nye, R. (1975) *The Origins of Crowd Psychology*, London: Sage.

O'Connor, L. E. (1971) 'Instructions from the Woman's Page on method, organization and program', *The Woman's Page*, 5, April–May: n.p.

Oates, S. B. (1982) *Let the Trumpet Sound: A Life of Martin Luther King, Jr.*, Edinburgh: Payback Press.

Offe, C. (1985) 'New Social Movements: challenging the boundaries of institutional politics', *Social Research*, 52: 817–68.

Offe, C. and Wiesenthal, H. (1985) 'Two logics of collective action', in Claus Offe, *Disorganized Capitalism: Contemporary Transformations of Work and Politics*, ed. John Keane, Cambridge: Polity Press.

Offen, K. (1992) 'Defining feminism: a comparative historical approach', in G. Bock and S. James (eds), *Beyond Equality and Difference*, New York: Routledge.

Pataud, E. and Pouget, E. (1990) *How We Shall Bring About the Revolution?* [1909], London: Pluto.

Pateman, C. (1971) *Participation and Democratic Theory*, Cambridge: Cambridge University Press.

Perrie, M. (1976) *The Agrarian Policy of the Russian Socialist-Revolutionary Party*, Cambridge: Cambridge University Press.

Peukert, D. J. K. (1987) *Inside Nazi Germany: Conformity, Opposition and Racism in Everyday Life*, New Haven: Yale University Press.

Piven, F. Fox and Cloward, R. A. (1977) *Poor People's Movements: Why They Succeed, How They Fail*, New York: Pantheon.

Plekhanov, G. V. (1940) *The Role of the Individual in History*, London: Lawrence and Wishart.

Preis, A. (1972) *Labor's Giant Step: Twenty Years of the CIO*, New York: Pathfinder Press.

Purkis, J. (1996a) 'The city as a site of ethical consumption and resistance', in D. Wynne and J. O'Connor (eds), *From the Margins to the Centre*, Aldershot: Arena.

Purkis, J. (1996b) 'Daring to dream: idealism in the philosophy, organization and campaigning strategies of Earth First!', in C. Barker and P. Kennedy (eds), *To Make Another World*, Aldershot: Avebury.

Purvis, J. (1996) 'A pair of infernal queens? A reassessment of the dominant representations of Emmeline and Christabel Pankhurst, First Wave Feminism in Edwardian Britain', *Women's History Review*, 5, 2: 259–80.

Quin, M. (1979) *The Big Strike*, New York: International Publishers.

Ratcliff, R. E. (1984) 'Introduction', *Research in Social Movements, Conflict and Change*, 6: ix–xvi

Ray, L. (1993) *Rethinking Critical Theory: Emancipation in the Age of Global Social Movements*, London: Sage.

Reddy, W. (1977) 'The textile trade and the language of the crowd at Rouen, 1752–1871', *Past and Present*, 74: 62–89.

Rees, J. (1998) *The Algebra of Revolution: The Dialectic and the Classical Marxist Tradition*, London: Routledge.

Reicher, S. (1982) 'The determination of collective behaviour', in H. Tajfel (ed.), *Social Identity and Intergroup Relations*, Cambridge: Cambridge University Press, and Paris: Maison des Sciences de l'Homme.

Reicher, S. (1984) 'The St Paul's "riot": an explanation of the limits of crowd action in terms of a social identity model', *European Journal of Social Psychology*, 14: 1–21.

Reicher, S. (1987) 'Crowd behaviour as social action', in J. Turner, M. Hogg, P. Oakes, S. Reicher and M. Wetherell, *Rediscovering the Social Group: A Self-categorization Theory*, Oxford: Blackwell.

Reicher, S. (1991) 'Mad dogs and Englishmen: telling tales from the Gulf', paper presented to the British Association 'Science '91' meeting, Plymouth.

Reicher, S. (1996a) 'The crowd century: reconciling theoretical failure with practical success', *British Journal of Social Psychology*, 35: 535–53.

Reicher, S. (1996b) 'The Battle of Westminster: developing the social identity model of crowd behaviour in order to deal with the initiation and development of collective conflict', *European Journal of Social Psychology*, 26: 115–34.

Reicher, S. (1996c) 'Social identity and social change: rethinking the context of social psychology', in P. Robinson (ed.), *Social Groups and Identities: Developing the Legacy of Henri Tajfel*, London: Butterworth.

Reicher, S. (1996d) 'Collective psychology and the psychology of the self', *BPS Social Psychology Section Newsletter*, 36: 3–15.

Reicher, S. and Hopkins, N. (1996a) 'Constructing categories and mobilising masses: an analysis of Thatcher's and Kinnock's speeches on the British miner's strike 1984–5', *European Journal of Social Psychology*, 26: 353–71.

Reicher, S. and Hopkins, N. (1996b) 'Seeking influence through characterising self-categories: an analysis of anti-abortionist rhetoric', *British Journal of Social Psychology*, 35: 297–312.

Reicher, S. and Hopkins, N. (2001) *Self and Nation*, London: Sage.

Reicher, S. and Potter, J. (1985) 'Psychological theory as intergroup perspective: a comparative analysis of "scientific" and "lay" accounts of crowd events', *Human Relations*, 38: 167–89.

Reicher, S., Hopkins, N. and Condor, S. (1997a) 'Stereotype construction as a strategy of influence', in R. Spears, P. Oakes, A. Haslam and N. Ellemers (eds), *Stereotyping and Social Identity*, Oxford: Blackwell.

Reicher, S., Hopkins, N. and Condor, S. (1997b) 'The lost nation of psychology', in C. C. Barfoot (ed.), *Beyond Pug's Tour: National and Ethnic Stereotyping in Theory and Literary Practice*, DQR Studies in Literature 20, Amsterdam/Atlanta: Rodopi.

Reicher, S., Spears, R. and Postmes, T. (1995) 'A social identity model of deindividuation phenomena', *European Review of Social Psychology*, 6: 161–98.

Reynaud, E. (1980) 'Le militantisme moral', in H. Mendras (ed.), *La sagesse et le désordre: France 1980*, Paris: Gallimard.

Riewald, P. (1949) *De L'Esprit des Masses*, Neuchatel: Delachaux and Niestle.

Robnett, B. (1996) 'African-American women in the civil rights movement, 1954–1965: gender, leadership, and micromobilisation', *American Journal of Sociology*, 101, 6: 1661–93.

Robnett, B. (1997) *How Long? How Long? African-American Women in the Struggle for Civil Rights*, New York: Oxford University Press.

Rosenthal, N. and Schwartz, M. (1989) 'Spontaneity and democracy in social movements', *International Social Movement Research*, 2: 33–59.

Rosenthal, N., Fingrutd, M., Ethier, M., Karant, R. and McDonald, D. (1985) 'Social movements and network analysis: a case study of nineteenth-century women's reform in New York State', *American Journal of Sociology* 90: 1023–54.

Rosmer, A. (1926) 'La Liquidation du "Putschisme"', *La Révolution prolétarienne*, 14: 1–4.

Rosmer, A. (1936) *Le Mouvement ouvrier pendant la guerre*, Paris: Librairie du travail.

Rosmer, A. (1951) 'Il y a quarante ans', *La Révolution prolétarienne*, January: 1–3.

Rosmer, A. (1987) *Lenin's Moscow* [1953], London: Bookmarks.

Rosmer, A. (2000) 'Speech to the Congress of the Red International of Labour Unions in July 1921', *Revolutionary History*, 7, 4: 67–80.

Royall, F. (1998) 'Le mouvement des chômeurs en France de l'hiver 1997–1998', *Modern and Contemporary France*, 6, 3: 351–65.

Rucht, D. (1999) 'Linking organization and mobilization: Michels's iron law of oligarchy reconsidered', *Mobilization*, 4, 2: 151–69.

Ryan, L. (1992) 'The *Irish Citizen* newspaper 1912–1920: a document study', *Saothar*, 17: 105–11.

Ryan, L. (1994a) 'Publicising the private: the campaign of the constitutional Irish suffrage movement', *Women's History Notebook*, 1: 26–52.

Ryan, L. (1994b) 'Women without votes: the political strategies of the Irish suffrage movement', *Irish Political Studies*, 9: 119–39.

Ryan, L. (1995) 'Traditions and double moral standards: the Irish suffragists' critique of nationalism', *Women's History Review* 4, 4: 487–503.

Ryan, L. (1996) *Irish Feminism and the Vote*, Dublin: Folens Publishers.

Ryan, L. (1997) 'A question of loyalty: war, nation and feminism in early twentieth-century Ireland', *Women's Studies International Forum*, 20, 1: 21–32.

Sarachild, K. (1975) 'The politics of history', in Redstockings (ed.), *Feminist Revolution*, New Paltz, NY: Redstockings. Also published by Random House, 1978.

Scaff, L. A. (1981) 'Max Weber and Robert Michels', *American Journal of*

Sociology, 86: 1269–86.

Scarce, R. (1990) *Eco-Warriors: Understanding the Radical Environmental Movement*, Chicago: Noble Press.

Schumpeter, J. A. (1965) *Capitalism, Socialism, Democracy*, London: Allen and Unwin.

Schutz, A. (1967) *The Phenomenology of the Social World*, trans. George Walsh and Frederick Lehnert, Evanston, IL: Northwestern University Press.

Schwartz, M., Rosenthal, N. and Schwartz, L. (1981) 'Leader-member conflict in protest organizations: the case of the Southern Farmers' Alliance', *Social Problems*, 29: 22–36.

Schwarz, S. (1967) *The Russian Revolution of 1905*, Chicago: University of Chicago Press.

Sedgwick, P. (1984) 'The unhappy elitist: Victor Serge's early Bolshevism', *History Workshop*, 17: 150–6.

Sefton Defence Campaign (1994) *Solidarity Means Victory*, Liverpool: Sefton Defence Campaign.

Serge, V. (1940) *Portrait de Staline*, Paris: Grasset.

Serge, V. (1961) *Vie des révolutionnaires* [1930], Paris: UCI.

Serge, V. (1967) *Memoirs of a Revolutionary 1901–1941* [1951], London: Oxford University Press.

Serge, V. (1970) *Birth of Our Power* [1931], Harmondsworth: Penguin.

Serge, V. (1979) *What Everyone should Know about Repression* [1925], London: New Park.

Serge, V. (1989) *Le Rétif: articles parus dans 'l'anarchie' 1909–1912*, Paris: Librairie Monnier.

Serge, V. (1990) *Notes d'Allemagne* [1923], Paris: La Brèche.

Serge, V. (1992) *Year One of the Russian Revolution* [1930], London: Bookmarks/Pluto.

Serge, V. (1994) 'Lenin in 1917' [1925], *Revolutionary History 5*, 3: 3–53.

Serge, V. (1997a) *Revolution in Danger*, London: Redwords.

Serge, V. (1997b) 'Thirty years after the Russian Revolution', in S. Weissman (ed.), *The Ideas of Victor Serge*, Glasgow: Critique Books.

Shandro, A. (1995) '"Consciousness from without": Marxism, Lenin and the proletariat', *Science and Society*, 59, 3: 268–97.

Shanin, T. (1986) *Revolution as a Moment of Truth*, London: Macmillan.

Shotter, J. and Billig, M. (1998) 'A Bakhtinian psychology: from out of the heads of individuals and into the dialogics between them', in Michael Mayerfield Bell and Michael Gardiner (eds), *Bakhtin and the Human Sciences: No Last Word*, London: Sage.

Smith, K. L. (1989) 'The radicalisation of Martin Luther King Jr.: the last three years', *Journal of Ecumenical Studies*, 26, Spring: 270–88.

Snow, D. A. and Benford, R. D. (1988) 'Ideology, frame resonance, and participant mobilization', *International Social Movement Research* 1:

197–217.

Snow, D. A. and Benford, R. D (1992) 'Master frames and cycles of protest', in A. D. Morris and C. M. Mueller (eds), *Frontiers in Social Movement Theory*, New Haven: Yale University Press.

Snow, D. A., Rochford, E. B. Jr., Worden, S. K. and Benford, R. D. (1986) 'Frame alignment processes, micromobilization, and movement participation', *American Sociological Review*, 51: 464–81.

Somers, M. (1992) 'Narrativity, narrative identity, and social action: rethinking English working-class formation', *Social Science History*, 16, 4: 591–630.

Spencer, P. (1997) 'On the Leninist tradition', in S. Weissman (ed.), *The Ideas of Victor Serge*, Glasgow: Critique Books.

Staniszkis, J. (1984) *Poland's Self-Limiting Revolution*, ed. Jan T. Gross, Princeton: Princeton University Press.

Stanley, J. P. (1975) 'Notes on the Edge', *Win Magazine*, 26 June.

Ste Croix, G. E. M. de (1981) *The Class Struggle in the Ancient Greek World*, London: Duckworth.

Steinberg, M. W. (1998) 'Tilting the frame: considerations on collective action framing from a discursive turn', *Theory and Society*, 27: 845–72.

Steinberg, M. W. (1999a) 'The talk and back talk of collective action: a dialogic analysis of repertoires of discourse among nineteenth-century English cotton spinners', *American Journal of Sociology*, 105, 3: 736–80.

Steinberg, M. W. (1999b) *Fighting Words: Working-Class Formation, Collective Action, and Discourse in Early Nineteenth Century England*, Ithaca, NY: Cornell University Press.

Steinberg, S. (1994) 'The liberal retreat from race', *New Politics*, 17: 30–51.

Stern, J. (1984) *Hitler: The Führer and the People*, London: Flamingo.

Stott, C. J. and Drury, J. (1999) 'The intergroup dynamics of empowerment: a social identity model', in P. Bagguley and J. Hearn (eds), *Transforming Politics: Power and Resistance*, London: Macmillan.

Stott, C. J. and Drury, J. (2000) 'Crowds, context and identity: dynamic categorisation processes in the "poll tax riot"', *Human Relations*, 53: 247–73.

Stott, C. J. and Reicher, S. (1998) 'Crowd action as intergroup process: introducing the police perspective', *European Journal of Social Psychology*, 26: 509–29.

Stott, C. J., Hutchison, P. and Drury, J. (2001) '"Hooligans" abroad? Intergroup dynamics, social identity and participation in collective "disorder" at the 1998 World Cup Finals', *British Journal of Social Psychology*.

Tajfel, H. (1978) *Differentiation Between Social Groups*, London: Academic Press.

Tajfel, H. (1982) *Social Identity and Intergroup Relations*, Cambridge: Cambridge University Press and Paris: Maison des Sciences de l'Homme.

Tajfel, H. and Turner, J. (1986) 'The social identity theory of intergroup behaviour', in S. Worchel and W. G. Austin (eds), *Psychology of Intergroup Relations*, Chicago: Nelson-Hall.

Tarrow, S. (1988) 'National politics and collective action: recent theory and research in Western Europe and the United States', *Annual Review of Sociology*, 14: 421–40.

Tarrow, S. (1991) '"Aiming at a moving target": social science and the recent rebellions in Eastern Europe', *PS: Political Science and Politics*, 24, 1: 12–20.

Tarrow, S. (1996) 'States and opportunities: the political structuring of social movements', in D. McAdam, J. D. McCarthy and M. N. Zald (eds), *Comparative Perspectives on Social Movements: Political Opportunities, Mobilizing Structures and Cultural Framings*, Cambridge: Cambridge University Press.

Tarrow, S. (1998) *Power in Movement: Social Movements, Collective Action and Politics*, 2nd edn, Cambridge: Cambridge University Press.

Taylor, B. (1991) 'The religion and politics of Earth First!', *The Ecologist*, 21, 6: 258–66.

Taylor, V. (1999) 'Gender and social movements', *Gender and Society*, 13, 1: 8–33.

The Feminists (1970) 'The Feminists: a political organization to annihilate sex roles', in Shulamith Firestone and Anne Koedt (eds), *Notes from the Second Year: Women's Liberation*, New York: Firestone/Koedt.

Thompson, E. P. (1963) *The Making of the English Working Class*, London: Gollancz.

Thompson, E. P. (1965) 'The peculiarities of the English', in Ralph Miliband and John Saville (eds), *The Socialist Register 1965*, London: Merlin.

Tilly, C. (1995) *Popular Contention in Great Britain 1758–1834*, Cambridge, MA: Harvard University Press.

Touraine, A. (1985) 'An introduction to the study of social movements', *Social Research*, 52: 749–88.

Trotsky, L. (1965) *A History of the Russian Revolution*, London: Gollancz.

Trotsky, L. (1969) *Fascism, Stalinism and the United Front, 1930–34*, London: International Socialism.

Trotsky, L. (1973) *1905*, Harmondsworth: Penguin.

Turner, J., Hogg, M., Oakes, P., Reicher, S. and Wetherell, M. (1987) *Rediscovering the Social Group: A Self-categorization Theory*, Oxford: Blackwell.

Turner, J., Oakes, P., Haslam, A. and McGarty, C. (1994) 'Self and collective: cognition and social context', *Personality and Social Psychology Bulletin*, 20: 454–63.

Turner, V. (1974) 'Social dramas and ritual metaphors', in *Dramas, Fields and Metaphors: Symbolic Action in Human Society*, Ithaca, NY: Cornell University Press.

Volosinov, V. N. (1976) *Freudianism: A Marxist Critique*, trans. I. R.

Titunik, New York: Academic Press.

Volosinov, V. N. (1986) *Marxism and the Philosophy of Language*, trans. Ladislav Matejka and I. R. Titunik, Cambridge, MA: Harvard University Press.

Voss, K. (1996) 'The collapse of a social movement: the interplay of mobilizing structures, framing, and political opportunities in the Knights of Labor', in D. McAdam, J. D. McCarthy and M. N. Zald (eds), *Comparative Perspectives on Social Movements: Political Opportunities, Mobilizing Structures, and Cultural Meanings*, Cambridge: Cambridge University Press.

Vygotsky, L. (1986) *Thought and Language*, trans. and ed. Alex Kozulin, Cambridge, MA: MIT Press.

Wall, D. (1999) *Earth First and the UK Anti-Roads Movement*, London: Routledge.

Ward, M. (1982) 'Votes first above all else: an account of the Irish suffrage movement', *Feminist Review*, 10: 21–36.

Ward, M. (1995) 'Conflicting interests: the British and Irish suffrage movements', *Feminist Review*, 50: 127–47.

Ward, M. (1997a) *Hanna Sheehy Skeffington: A Life*, Cork: Cork University Press.

Ward, M. (1997b) 'Nationalism, pacifism, internationalism: Louie Bennett, Hanna Sheehy Skeffington and the problems of defining feminism', in A. Bradley and M. Valiulis (eds,) *Gender and Sexuality in Modern Ireland*, Boston: University of Massachusetts Press.

Weber, M. (1978) *Economy and Society*, 2 vols, Berkeley: University of California Press.

Welsh, I. and McLeish, P. (1996) 'The European road to nowhere: anarchism and direct action against the UK roads programme', *Anarchist Studies*, 4, 1: 27–44.

West, C. (1993) 'The religious foundations of the thought of Martin Luther King, Jr.', in Peter J. Albert and Ronald Hoffman (eds), *We Shall Overcome: Martin Luther King, Jr and the Black Freedom Struggle*, New York: De Capo Press.

Wheen, F. (1999) *Karl Marx*, London: Fourth Estate.

Wickham, J. (1979) 'Social fascism and the division of the working-class movement: workers and political parties in the Frankfurt area 1929/1930', *Capital and Class*, 7: 1–34.

Wills, G. (1994) *Certain Trumpets: The Nature of Leadership*, New York: Simon and Schuster.

Wolfreys, J. (1999) 'Class struggles in France', *International Socialism*, 84: 31–68.

Zald, M. N. and Garner, R. A. (1966) ' Social movement organisations: growth, decay and change', *Social Forces*, 44: 327–41.

Zald, M. N. and McCarthy, J. D. (1987) *Social Movements in a Organiza-*

tional Society: Collected essays, New Brunswick: Transaction Books.

Zirakzadeh, C. E. (1997) *Social Movements in Politics: A Comparative Study*, Harlow: Longman.

Index